Praise for 5-Gen Le

"There are so many nuances that take place within a school that we need to understand, and Mark White focuses on one of the most important. *5-Gen Leadership* engages educators into understanding how different generations teaching within our school approach our greatest issues and provides the tools to begin those conversations."

Peter DeWitt, EdD
Leadership Coach
Author, *Collective Leader Efficacy* and *Instructional Leadership*

"Here is a publication that celebrates the different generations that schools now have teaching in and attending them. It offers practical tips to include the skills of all the generations to offer the best teaching and learning for everyone."

Joy Rose, Retired High School Principal
Westerville City Schools
Worthington, OH

"Where you stand depends sometimes on where you sit. And where you sit is often influenced by how and when you grew up. Mark's analysis and unique understanding of the impact and needs necessary for today's leaders to work with different generations is timely, relevant, and revealing. One size rarely fits all."

Jim Mahoney, Former CEO
Battelle for Kids

"How do we prepare today's students for the rapidly changing workplace and society in which they will live, work, and interact in an education system designed for a century that has passed us by? In *5-Gen Leadership: Leading 5 Generations in Schools in the 2020s*, Mark White clearly provides a well-lit path to assist educators to successfully make the necessary cultural, structural and instructional changes that are needed."

Bill Daggett, Founder
International Center for Leadership in Education (ICLE)

5-Gen Leadership

For my family and staffs, without whom this work would not have happened.

5-Gen Leadership

Leading 5 Generations in Schools in the 2020s

Mark White
Foreword by Eric Sheninger

FOR INFORMATION:

Corwin
A SAGE Companyy
2455 Teller Road
Thousand Oaks, California 91320
(800) 233-9936
www.corwin.com

SAGE Publications Ltd.
1 Oliver's Yard
55 City Road
London EC1Y 1SP
United Kingdom

SAGE Publications India Pvt. Ltd.
B 1/I 1 Mohan Cooperative Industrial Area
Mathura Road, New Delhi 110 044
India

SAGE Publications Asia-Pacific Pte. Ltd.
18 Cross Street #10-10/11/12
China Square Central
Singapore 048423

President: Mike Soules
Associate Vice President and Editorial Director:
    Monica Eckman
Senior Acquisitions Editor: Ariel Curry
Senior Editorial Assistant: Caroline Timmings
Senior Content Development Editor: Desirüe Bartlett
Production Editor: Astha Jaiwal
Copy Editor: Amy Hanquist Harris
Typesetter: Hurix Digital
Proofreader: Jeff Bryant
Cover Designer: Candice Harman
Marketing Manager: Katie Stoddard

Printed in the United States of America

ISBN: 978-1-0718-3702-3

This book is printed on acid-free paper.

21 22 23 24 25 10 9 8 7 6 5 4 3 2 1

Table of Contents

FOREWORD   ix

PUBLISHER'S ACKNOWLEDGMENTS   xi

ABOUT THE AUTHOR   xiii

INTRODUCTION   1

  CHAPTER 1: FROM BOOMERS TO ALPHAS   5
    Understanding the Four Generations in Staffs Today   8
    Two Groups Are Trying to Lead, and Two Groups Are
        Trying to Fit In. Sort of . . .   11
    Millennial Teachers Are Walking Away   13
    Making Generational Adjustments   16
    Trouble in the Gen Z Teaching Pipeline   19
    Recruiting Gen Z Teachers   20
    Take Steps Now to Become a 5-Gen Leader   23
    And After We Recruit and Retain Them . . .   25

  CHAPTER 2: THE IMPACT OF THE SILENT GENERATION
  AND GEN ALPHA   27
    Lessons From the Silent Generation   28
    Gen Alpha, the New Generation   34
    Gen Alpha's Impact on Education   37
    The Transcendent Power of Relationships   41

  CHAPTER 3: MOVING FROM MANAGING TO COACHING   45
    The Challenge of Transitioning to a New Model   47
    Millennials, Gen Zers, and Gen Alphas: Handle With Care   49
    Coaching Into Grit and Professionalism   52
    Rethinking Evaluations   56
    New Channels for Communication   59

CHAPTER 4: TEACHING DISTRACTED GENERATIONS   63

  Our Evolving Brains   64

  Distracted Students, Distracted Teachers   65

  Clues in the News   70

CHAPTER 5: TACTICS FOR CREATING
MULTIGENERATIONAL PD   75

  Acknowledging the PD Problem   76

  A Global Leadership Question: "How Do We Train These
    Different Generations?"   78

  Relevancy in PD   80

  Finding the Generations in the Staff   84

  Mind the Gap!   85

  Presentation Methods for Teacher Z   92

CHAPTER 6 GENERATIONAL LESSONS OF COVID-19   97

  Gen Z and Gen Alpha: The New Lost Generations?   101

  The New Digital Divide   103

  A Flipping of the Paradigm   105

  Adjusting Mindsets   107

  Advice for Changing Mindsets   109

  The Digital Gap in Administrators   110

CHAPTER 7: UPAGERS AND POLITICAL ACTIVISM   113

  Gen Z Survivors Leading the Way on Gun Reform   115

  Gen Z Leading the Way in the Pursuit of Racial Justice   117

  Lessons From a University Protest   118

  The Coming of the Minority Majority   120

CHAPTER 8: MILLENNIALS AND GEN Z ASCENDING
IN THE 2020s   125

  Four Key Points and Questions for the 2020s   128

  The University Model Could Affect the PreK–12 Model 129

  New Paths to Leadership   131

  The Future: Millennial Teachers, Gen Z Teachers, and AI Teachers?   132

  Being Human in the 2020s   137

50 TIPS FOR TRANSITIONING TO 5-GEN LEADERSHIP   147

REFERENCES   151

INDEX   163

Foreword

Growing up as a kid in the late 1970s and throughout the 1980s brought about immense benefits in my opinion. Through my lens, I experienced rapid technological change, where some of the greatest inventions ever created made their way into my life. I vividly remember the first computer that I laid my hands on: the Commodore 64. It was a beast of a device with limited functionality, but I didn't care. Just being able to have access to a computer was awesome because up until this point I had only either seen them on commercials or read about them in encyclopedias.

It wasn't long before the beloved Commodore 64 was replaced with the more impressive Apple IIe in my house. My brothers and I were able to play a variety of games using different floppy disks. There was this baseball game I played all the time that allowed us to pick from a variety of historically great teams. I was mostly privy to selecting the all-star roster that included the likes of Hank Aaron, Willie Mays, Babe Ruth, Lou Gehrig, and others. Even though there was no real skill involved, every canned home run that was hit by one of these icons felt magical.

Computer use became secondary when the most incredible gaming system ever invented made its way into our house. Now, I say this because of the impact it had at the time and the fact that this invention revolutionized video games while laying the foundation for all that we have today. Those of you who grew up during the same time that I did know that I am talking about Atari. Even though the graphics were horrible, iconic games such as Pac Man, Donkey Kong, and Space Invaders filled my life with so much joy. My brothers and friends and I engaged for countless hours in friendly and, at times, unfriendly competition. Collaboration and communication fueled each experience. To this day, I still have the original Atari system that I had as a kid. Even though it doesn't work, it provides fond memories as well as a reminder of the early years of my generation.

I am a proud member of Generation X and was taught by baby boomers. Exponential change has pretty much been a staple in my life. There was no internet or cell phones when I was growing up, but I experienced firsthand the evolution of both as a student and teacher. While Atari influenced me the most as a child, the World Wide Web was utterly transformative in my mind. From dial-up internet to AOL instant messaging, technology constantly impacted my life.

While everything seemed to change at a rapid pace, one particular aspect was stuck in time: how I was taught.

Now, this isn't to say that I had a poor educational experience. On the contrary, it served me well at the time. I had caring teachers and administrators who did what they thought was best, and that almost always aligned with the way things have always been done. Each class was pretty much a carbon copy of another and was delivered in a mass-model format. Even though I was a child growing up mostly during the Third Industrial Revolution, the methodologies squarely resided in those most appropriate for the first Industrial Revolution preparedness. There was little connection to the world that I was currently growing up in or what might be needed as I headed into the great unknown. This lesson is something that many leaders are still grappling with today.

So much has changed since the internet began to rapidly evolve in the 2000s. Exponential change has created numerous generations of staff that are now teaching in our schools. These include baby boomers, Gen Xers, millennials, Gen Zers, and Gen Alphas. Don't worry if you have never heard of or know the defining characteristics of each group, as this book will thoroughly explain each. I myself had never heard of Gen Alpha. The important takeaway as a leader is understanding that the premise of "business as usual" needs to be disrupted. Each group has been influenced by radically different experiences, and as such, the way in which they are led has to be dynamic as opposed to static.

Leadership is not about telling people what to do, but instead taking them where they need to be. Understanding the unique characteristics, qualities, and attributes each group possesses will become indispensable as you work to create a culture primed for success. As you will learn in this book, discounting what each generation provides can result in challenges to move important initiatives forward, inhibiting your district's progress. It can also result in issues with retaining and attracting the best staff possible. Knowledge is power only if it is used to develop and support the various personalities you are tasked with leading.

Leaders need to think, act, and learn differently not only to help different generations gel together but also to respond to a myriad of nonstop forces that are disruptive in nature. It's not just technological change that has and continues to influence educators and students alike; it's also the COVID-19 pandemic. As schools pivoted to remote and hybrid learning, we saw firsthand how the experiences of each generation coalesced, resulting in scalable change the likes that have never been seen before in education. It is important to not forget these powerful lessons and continue to leverage the most dynamic resource available—your people—to lead forward. This book will pave the way. It's up to you to initially follow and then create your own path.

Eric Sheninger, Author
Disruptive Thinking and Digital Leadership, 2nd Edition

Publisher's Acknowledgments

Corwin gratefully acknowledges the contributions of the following reviewers:

Margaret Bartlett, Teacher-in-Training
Azusa Pacific University
San Dimas, CA

Sean Beggin, Associate Principal
Anoka-Hennepin Secondary Technical Education Program
Anoka, MN

David Cash, Professor of Education
Governance Chair
University of Southern California
Long Beach, CA

Delsia Malone, Former Principal
Gadsden, AL

Joy Rose, Retired High School Principal
Westerville City Schools
Worthington, OH

About the Author

Mark White is a school leadership and training consultant. Previously, he was the director of education and outreach at Mindset Digital and academic principal in the International Department of the Beijing National Day School in Beijing, China. As the superintendent of the Gahanna-Jefferson Public Schools in Gahanna, Ohio, he played a key role in the design of Clark Hall and the implementation of global skills and technology into its curriculum. During his tenure as superintendent, the district earned the state's highest academic ranking, opened Clark Hall, and achieved financial stability. Mr. White has been a consultant to both the College Board and the ACT and has served on two national education reform committees. He has frequently been a guest speaker at schools and universities and at local, state, and national conferences. Prior to being a superintendent, Mr. White was a band director, high school English teacher and department head, high school assistant principal, principal, and assistant superintendent. He may be reached at suptmarkwhite@gmail.com.

Introduction

In March of 2021, as the final edits of this book were being completed, I was sitting in an elementary school conference room with some school administrators. I was there to coach teachers, and we were discussing what we had just observed in a classroom. Someone knocked softly on the conference room door, and when the principal opened it, she found a young student standing there with a teacher. The student wanted to have a conversation with the principal.

"I want to go back to remote learning," the student said to her. This student, like many others, had just recently returned to in-person learning, and he was still adjusting to school—or in this case, *not* adjusting.

"Why?" the principal asked. "Don't you want to give school a longer try? We like you and want you here. We think you should be here."

"I have a really good camera on my computer," the student said firmly. "I think I learn better at home."

Then the assistant principal said, "But we're only here tomorrow, and then we're out for the Easter holidays. Next week only has four school days. You can be here that long, can't you?"

"Yeah," the student responded hesitantly, and then he added more confidently, "but I still want to go back to remote learning."

An administrator sitting beside me turned to me and laughingly whispered, "He's *negotiating* with his principal!"

The principal pleaded with the student to give in-person school another chance, and the teacher was eventually able to lead the student back to the classroom. When the conference room door closed again, I asked which grade the student was in.

"Second grade," said the principal. "We have kids coming to us every day wanting to go back to remote learning. Maybe they miss the freedom of being at home. Maybe they're still adjusting to the structure of school."

"Perhaps," I said. "But he's also a member of Gen Alpha. He's part of a generation that's going to demand more choices in how it's educated than previous generations." Then I added, "But just think about this: That little second grader was brave enough to walk down here to confront the principal and demand another way of learning. As a baby boomer at his age, I would never have done that. He's part of a new generation with new ways of looking at the world."

Which brings us to the topic of this book: If we're going to make the most of reforming our schools in the 2020s, we must understand today's students and the four disparate generations in our staffs.

It used to not be this complicated. When I began teaching in the early 1980s, the generation gaps were not as deep. But the world is shifting more quickly now. Knowledge is doubling at faster rates, and new generations are being created every 15 years. In our staffs, we have the baby boomers, Gen Xers, millennials, and Gen Zers. Yes, members of Gen Z, those tech-minded youngsters, are now in our teaching ranks. And more of them are coming.

Two of today's generations, the boomers and Gen Xers, grew up before the advent of the internet, while the other two generations, the millennials and Gen Zers, grew up with the internet. The two older groups grew up in an analog world, and the two younger groups grew up in a digital world. This has led to wider generation gaps than at any time in history. Each group has a different learning style with varying views of the world and education.

Business leaders who are attempting to bridge these gaps in the private sector are 4-Gen leaders, but school leaders also lead a fifth generation: Gen Alpha, the students born since 2011—including the second grader who wanted to negotiate his return to remote learning. School leaders must develop a new sort of lens, a multigenerational lens, through which to view their staffs and the challenges they will face in this decade. Those administrators who understand and meet the challenges of the tumultuous 2020s, many of which will be rooted in generational dissonance, will be 5-Gen leaders.

To develop this multigenerational lens, this book will help school leaders

- Understand the four distinct generations in the teaching staffs

- Understand our youngest students, Gen Alpha

- Recognize how much of our work today was introduced by the Silent Generation

- Move from a management model to a coaching model to help our younger teachers

- Understand why today's students and adults are so distracted

- Provide tips for transforming professional development (PD) to meet the learning needs of a new type of adult learner called Teacher Z

- Close the digital generation gaps that emerged during the COVID-19 school closures

- Realize Gen Z has a global view formed through the internet and is the most socially/politically active generation yet to pass through our schools

- Look ahead to the end of the decade to see a future in which millennial and Gen Z educators ascend into leadership roles and bring their global, tech-oriented perspectives into school reform

As this book is going to press, the world is emerging from the worst pandemic in a century. Trying to predict the future of schools in the massive reset of education that is now upon us is like looking through a shifting fog to see what awaits at the far end of the highway. We can see where we are now and see glimpses of what is in front of us; however, we can be sure that our success in dealing with the generational disparities will play a role in how well we navigate the fog and where we reach the other side in the 2020s.

I've written this book as a baby boomer, and I've tried to develop my own multi-generational lens. As I say over and over again in this book, when I write about the characteristics of teachers and administrators in certain generations, I am writing of broad characteristics. I am the first to say I don't possess all of the characteristics of a boomer, and I will be the first to acknowledge that readers might not possess all of the characteristics of their generations. However, I find I own many boomer traits, and in my many interactions with teachers and administrators, I see their generational characteristics coming through again and again.

I'd like to thank all of the educators with whom I've conversed in the past five years as I've consulted in schools from New York City to Southern California and many spots in between. I've been lucky enough to train and coach thousands of teachers and principals. I've been in over a thousand PreK–12 classrooms, and during the pandemic, I viewed hundreds of online lessons that were either live or taped. I've seen leadership and teaching from a lot of angles, and I've been blessed to have great conversations with many teachers. Those insights are included in this book.

I have a great deal of respect for Eric Sheninger, and I'm grateful to him for taking time out of his incredibly hectic schedule to write the foreword. I appreciate the opportunities given to me through my work with the International Center for Leadership in Education, and I'd also like to thank Ariel Curry and Corwin Press for their help in making this project a reality. Last but not least, I'd like to thank the many educators who contributed their insights and words to this book.

The 2020s will be an era of massive change accelerated by the pandemic. I hope this look at educators through this new sort lens helps school leaders, teachers, and students of all generations to be more successful.

Mark White
April 2021
St. Petersburg, Florida

CHAPTER 1

From Boomers to Alphas

Key Points of This Chapter

- Four distinct generations are now in our teaching staffs.

- Generation gaps are more pronounced than ever because the rapid growth of technology has resulted in very different growth experiences.

- Millennial teachers are leaving the profession in record numbers, and fewer Gen Zers are choosing to become teachers.

- School leaders need to adjust their recruiting and leadership tactics to successfully recruit and retain young teachers.

"OK, boomer . . ."

In November of 2019, this phrase became a generational battle cry when 25-year-old Chloe Swarbrick, a member of the New Zealand Parliament, addressed her fellow parliament members about the dangers of climate change—or more precisely, about their lack of action in preventing it. "In the year 2050, I will be 56 years old. Yet right now, the average age of this 52nd Parliament is 49 years old," she said, hoping to spur her colleagues into action (Thebault, 2019). As Swarbrick spoke, an older parliament member sitting in the audience began to heckle her. Without pausing, Swarbrick deftly, calmly interjected, "OK, boomer," into the middle of a sentence and continued her speech, silencing the heckler—and becoming a viral sensation (Thebault, 2019). Within hours, her response was being shown on news stations around the world. Today, it has been viewed millions of times (New Zealand Parliament, 2019).

While Swarbrick didn't invent the catchphrase "OK, boomer," she became its heroic face for millennials and Gen Zers everywhere who have grown increasingly frustrated with the societal and political structures put into place by baby boomers. What was accepted in the past will not be readily accepted by today's younger

■ Chloe Swarbrick addressing the New Zealand Parliament.

generations, and Swarbrick's "OK, boomer" moment sums up the angst of young people around the world as they interact with older family members, business executives, and politicians.

And by of some our younger teachers who deal with structure imposed upon them by older generations of educators.

I am a baby boomer, and in November of 2019, as Swarbrick sparred with her colleague in the New Zealand Parliament, I had my own "OK, boomer" moment—one not nearly as dramatic as Swarbrick's, but one that was deeply prophetic.

I was a consultant, leading a professional development (PD) session for 40 elementary teachers. One of the goals was to understand how today's students have evolved into a new type of learner that is different from previous generations. To help make this point, I wanted the teachers to briefly explore the characteristics of the four generations in their teaching staff: the baby boomers (also known as boomers), Gen Xers, Gen Yers (also known as millennials), and Gen Zers.

Yes, take a deep breath—the Gen Z kids are now old enough to join our teaching staffs. And they're here. That first-year teacher who is 22 or 23 years old? He or she is a Gen Zer.

Three Gen Z teachers were in the group I was training, and at the end of the exercise, I asked them a question: "If you could change PD, what would you change?" The question put them on the spot. They were surrounded by their older, more experienced peers. They were all in their first, second, or third year of teaching, and they didn't want to be seen as experts or rebels when answering. They smiled, and they blushed, and then one teacher bravely said, "Sometimes, I just wish they [the presenters] would just leave us alone. Tell us what they want done and let us go figure it out."

This brought a lot of laughter from the group. I laughed, too, but that young teacher had plunged a Gen Z dagger into my boomer heart. I'll never forget the

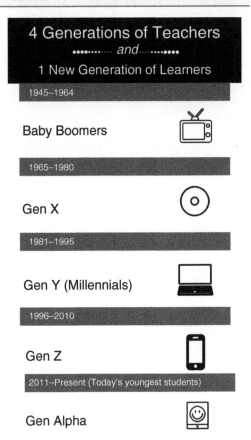

FIGURE 1.1   Generations of Teachers

4 Generations of Teachers
·········· *and* ··········
1 New Generation of Learners

1945–1964

Baby Boomers

1965–1980

Gen X

1981–1995

Gen Y (Millennials)

1996–2010

Gen Z

2011–Present (Today's youngest students)

Gen Alpha

feeling. I had trained teachers all over America, and I had felt a shift taking place in the younger teachers. I had spent over three decades leading teachers, but I had sensed they needed a new type of PD and a new type of leadership. Her words clarified it for me: For better or worse, Gen Z teachers have grown up as independent learners, finding their way through new smartphones, apps, video games, and websites. While Gen Z teachers still need our guidance, they and their older millennial siblings want more room than any previous generation to "figure it out" in their PD sessions and in other things they do in school. They are the "figure-it-out" generations.

As I stood in front of that group, a jumble of thoughts raced through my head about the four generations in our staffs. Boomers and Xers, millennials and Zers, are all mixed together in a school staff stew. Most of today's school leaders are Gen Xers and baby boomers, who grew up in eras that were more conformist. They don't "figure it out" like the younger generations. They do what they're told and tend to expect the same of their peers. How does this mindset work when leading millennials and Gen Zers? And to make school leadership even more challenging, our youngest students, the ones born since 2010? They're our newest generation of student: Gen Alpha. New generations are now rolling in every 15 years, which means in 2025 Gen Beta will begin and be in our schools by the end of the decade.

It has always been hard to lead schools, but this generational disparity just laid a new layer of complexity into everything we do. Because of the steady and accelerating advance of personal technology, the four generations all grew up with different life experiences. They all tend to see the world through the lens of their age group, and they are all constantly adjusting to each other (Jenkins, 2019).

Two new terms have emerged for business leaders managing these four generations: "generational leadership" and "4-Gen leadership." These terms can be applied to school leaders, but when we consider that school leaders are also leading their Gen Alpha students (discussed in Chapter 2), it can be said that today's school administrators are some of the first 5-Gen leaders in the history of the world. So, from this point forward I'll use the term "5-Gen leaders" to describe 21st century school leadership.

Understanding the Four Generations in Staffs Today

Exactly who are these four generations of teachers we are leading in schools today, and how are they similar and different? Before I dive into the perilous process of generational stereotyping, I want to make a few quick points about teachers in all of the generations.

- They are all individuals, and it's possible some of them don't fit many of the stereotypes.

- Some people might feel the generational characteristics don't fit them at all, and they could be right.

- Some people see themselves as a mixture of all the generations.

We should *never* make a blanket assumption that all people of a certain age have certain characteristics, but I've done enough research, spoken to enough teachers, and looked at how people in my training sessions respond to certain tactics and how teachers in the classrooms teach to propose that school leaders should at least consider generational characteristics to understand their staffs. In other words, birth years often matter (see Figure 1.1). When we recognize each teacher's formative decades, then we are more likely to help them bridge the generation gaps and understand each other.

BOOMERS

My fellow baby boomers (birth years 1945–1964) were shaped by the civil rights movement, the Vietnam War, and the Watergate scandal. They had Silent Generation parents who had survived the Great Depression and World War II, so they were raised to be loyal, committed, and to have a sense of duty. Their parents also taught them that you need to pay your dues to get ahead; success comes to those who work hard and play the game right. They grew up in an age when households had one phone that hung on a wall; they still believe in the power of phone calls and face-to-face communication (Purdue Global, 2021). Boomers grew up using paper and had to make late transitions to digital products. However, 90 percent of boomers have Facebook pages, and they have adapted to other technology, mainly to stay in touch with younger family members and friends (Kasasa, 2019).

In schools today, boomers have become the senior citizens of our teaching staffs. Sometimes, they see themselves as the sages, the wise ones, the teachers who remember teaching before it became a series of tests and labels. Over the last three decades, they've seen education become busier and more complex. I've noticed the boomers who are still teaching often fall into one of two categories: those who have adapted to the current best practices in education—and those who spend their days pining for a forgone era and are dragged reluctantly through each iteration of change.

While some boomers are working long into their senior years, many boomers have reached retirement age and are rapidly fading out of our staffs. As their fellow boomers leave the profession, they are replaced by Gen Zers with whom they have less in common than previous generations.

GEN X

Then we have Gen Xers (birth years 1965–1980), the latchkey, MTV generation who first began to reap the benefits of cable and digital devices like the Sony Walkman that made entertainment personal and mobile. They came of age during the AIDS epidemic and the dot-com boom. They like to balance work with their personal life; they are just as concerned about their personal interests as they are about the company's interests. They can resist change if it affects their personal lives (Purdue Global, 2021). They are thought of as the forgotten generation, wedged between the boomers and the millennials.

In our teaching staffs, Gen Xers are in their 40s and 50s. Like the boomers, they, too, have become the formal and informal leaders of our schools. The reforms of the last two decades have been perhaps the toughest on this generation. When I speak with Xers, I hear the frustration in their voices about the state of education today. Boomers are close to retirement, but Gen Xers feel trapped between standardized testing and the years they still have to work to reach their pensions. "How long do you have before you can retire?" I ask, and I inevitably hear a deep sigh before they answer. It might be eight years, 10 years, 15 years.

By 2028, Gen Xers will outnumber the baby boomers (Purdue Global, 2021). Some of them have become principals and superintendents, and more of them will move into senior leadership positions in the next few years. They are the last pre-internet generation of leaders in our schools. After the Gen Xers, all of the leaders will have grown up with the internet.

After the Gen Xers, all of the leaders will have grown up with the internet.

MILLENNIALS

The millennials (birth years 1981–1995), also known as Gen Y), have been shaped by Columbine, 9/11, and the internet. They grew up as the internet entered society on a broad scale, and it gave them an outlook and expectations noticeably different than their predecessors. They are the first set of digital natives. They like to use new types of devices. They use social media and are connected. Because of their financial insecurities, they've been less likely to buy houses, and they have waited longer to get married. Millennials embrace Uber and other services they can share with society; for them, it's not about ownership, but instead, it's about access. They believe in wellness. They exercise more, eat smarter, and drink less than previous generations—and they like to keep track of their progress on apps (*The Washington Post*, 2015).

Millennials are viewed as the sheltered kids who always got trophies whether they won or lost their soccer game. and they became the helicopter parents of Gen Z. They like to communicate via texts, personal messaging, and email (Purdue Global, 2021). Some have referred to them as the new "Lost Generation" because they started entering the workforce during the recession that began in 2008 with record amounts of debt and fewer opportunities for high-paying jobs. Outside of teaching, they make up the majority of America's bartenders, half the restaurant workers, and a large share of its retail workers. Millennials were especially harmed financially during the COVID-19 pandemic in the spring of 2020: A staggering 52 percent of people under the age of 45 were laid off, put on leave, or had their hours reduced, compared with 26 percent of people over the age of 45 (Lowrey, 2020).

Millennials in our school staffs have several distinctions. They are the first generation to grow up in high-stakes testing. They entered the teaching force from preparation programs that gave them "best practices" and "here's-how-to-understand-your-data" methods. They are the first group of teachers to have grown up with the internet. Today, millennials are the largest group in the American workforce, and they are the largest group in the American teaching force.

GEN Z

The Gen Zers (birth years 1996–2010) are entering our teaching force. They can be characterized as the most technologically savvy, socially challenged, and distracted group we've ever led. Think of them as millennials on steroids. Their mindset has been formed since birth by the internet, social media, Starbucks, and artificial intelligence in a post-9/11 world. They tend to be more independent, and they value their devices more than any previous generation. The Girl Scouts of America recently redesigned their uniforms, and the number-one request from the girls was a pocket for their iPhones (Testa, 2020). They prefer to work with millennial managers because they have more in common with them than with boomers and Gen Xers. They love new technologies (Purdue Global, 2021); most of them got their first smartphone when they were 10.3 years old (Kasasa, 2019). America has been at war during their entire lives. They tend to be more fiscally conservative than millennials because they've seen how millennials are burdened with college debt (Kasasa, 2019).

Gen Z also is shaping up to be our most diversified, highest-educated generation (Fry & Parker, 2020). They want to chase their dreams because they've seen some of their peers achieving great things on the internet. For example, who are some of the most well-known anti-gun leaders today? David Hogg and Emma Gonzalez, survivors of the Parkland High School shootings, who became famous as high school students. And who is perhaps the world's most famous advocate for stopping climate change? Greta Thunberg, a teenager from Sweden. Gen Zers have admired them as they have achieved fame and followers around the world through news outlets and their social media platforms. Gen Zers have seen other young people start their own online companies, become wealthy e-gamers, and create apps, but they are also seeing that 5 percent of today's college graduates can't find a job. One study found that 41 percent of them plan to be entrepreneurs, and half of them believe they can change the world (Entrepreneur Staff, 2019).

In our schools, they are the students in the upper-elementary grades, middle schools, and high schools. They tend to be more deeply engaged when using technology, and they need both guidance from the teacher and the freedom to work with peers and to be creative and unique. As students, they tend to be more driven than millennials, and their drug abuse, smoking, drinking, and teen pregnancies are lower than in previous generations (Preville, 2019).

Two Groups Are Trying to Lead, and Two Groups Are Trying to Fit In. Sort of . . .

As we begin to look at how all of these groups mesh together, let's start with this realization: The crux of most 5-Gen leadership issues comes down to helping older and younger educators work together. Older educators, especially leaders, want to lead the way, and the young educators, who are often still teachers, want to be led but have a different idea of how that might look (see Figure 1.2).

The crux of most 5-Gen leadership issues comes down to helping older and younger educators work together.

Leading schools and teaching used to not be this complicated.

As a teacher beginning his career in the 1980s, I was happy *not* to figure it out. As a baby boomer, I was happy to have someone *please* tell me step by step how to do something. When I started leading teachers as a high school department head a few years later, I didn't have to worry about generational differences because back then we were all pretty much the same. Some of the teachers were baby boomers, and our older peers were members of the Silent Generation— they had lived through the Great Depression and World War II. Most of them would do what they were asked to do without asking too many questions (Purdue Global, 2021).

FIGURE 1.2 Generational Challenges

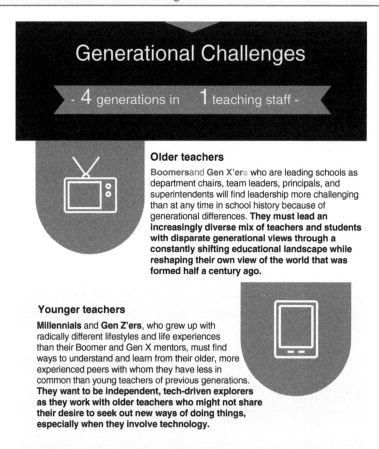

The rate of change was slower. Technology was advancing, but it was a slower acceleration. In the second edition of my previous book, *Leading Schools in Disruptive Times: How to Survive Hyper-Change* (written with Dwight Carter and first published by Corwin Press in 2018), I wrote about how Moore's Law, which explained that processing speeds had doubled every 18 to 24 months for decades, had led to an explosion of knowledge as chronicled in Buckminster Fuller's (1981) book *Critical Path*. All of this helps explain the amazing technology advancements we've seen since the 1970s. Each decade brought incredible advances—and new devices, new mobility, new individualism, and new, broader views of the world for young people growing up in those decades. This means boomers, Xers, millennials and Gen Zers all grew up with different life experiences and with increasingly different views. These experiences shaped who they are today (Jenkins, 2019).

We've always had generation gaps throughout history when the younger generation doesn't buy in to the beliefs and actions of the older generations. But the rise of the internet society has deepened these gaps and accelerated their numbers. We now have digital generation gaps between all four generations, as shown in Figure 1.3.

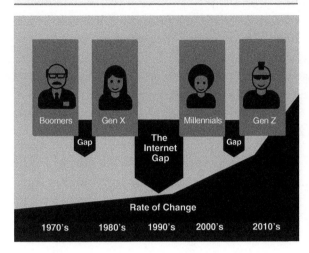

FIGURE 1.3   The Internet Gap

Boomers · Gen X · Millennials · Gen Z

Gap · The Internet Gap · Gap

Rate of Change

1970's · 1980's · 1990's · 2000's · 2010's

Think of the gaps between the boomers and Gen X as one crack in the ground, and think of the gap between the millennials and Gen Z as another crack. But the gap between the boomers/Gen X and the millennials/Gen Z is deeper because it's the internet gap; actually, it's more of a valley. The internet lifestyle that emerged in the 1990s drove a wedge between the older and younger generations: The boomers and Gen Xers are emailing each other and wondering why the young teachers aren't responding to their emails, and the millennials and Gen Zers are direct messaging each other via social media and wondering why the older teachers aren't answering their messages.

And the technology did more than create digital generation gaps: It reshaped brains (Horvath, 2015). Each successive generation has a brain that has developed differently than its predecessors. This means our younger teachers, our Gen Zers and millennials who grew up with the internet, have brains and views that are more similar to their students than to the brains and views of their boomer and Gen X colleagues (Zachos, 2019). The biggest generation gap in school history is now occurring in elementary schools between boomer teachers and their Gen Alpha students.

There are multiple challenges for 5-Gen leaders to solve today, but two of the challenges are existential threats that are endangering the teaching profession: Too many teachers are leaving the profession, and too few people are choosing to become teachers.

Both threats have their roots in the digital generation gaps.

Millennial Teachers Are Walking Away

We know the teaching profession has been in trouble. We've heard the political attacks, watched teacher pay stagnate, felt the budget cuts, and observed (or participated in) the walkouts in recent years that rocked Oklahoma, Arizona, Colorado, West Virginia, Kentucky, and Los Angeles. If it were a patient, we would have been panicked by its declining health in the past two decades. Today, the teaching profession as a patient would be in intensive care.

The result? Teachers are leaving the profession in record numbers. Overall, it's estimated that 8 percent of teachers leave the profession each year and another 8 percent leave the classroom to take another job in education. The situation has gotten worse in past 20 years; in the 1990s, only 5 percent of teachers left the workforce (Carver-Thomas & Darling-Hammond, 2017). The numbers are higher in "poor districts and among teachers of color, who are more likely to have students of color" (Varathan, 2018). A record number of teachers quit in 2018 (Fulwood, 2018). In that year, there was a national teacher shortage of 110,000 teachers. That number is expected to grow to 200,000 by 2025 (Boyce, 2019).

Millennials are leading the way out of the school parking lot. While teachers of all generations continue to leave the classroom, most of the teachers who now leave are millennials, and they're leaving in record numbers. The majority of them depart when they are between the ages of 25 and 34 (Varathan, 2018). Think of where these teachers are in their development at these ages. They have completed their first years in the classroom and have a clear understanding of what is expected of them—and they decide they don't want to be teachers. They experience the long hours, lack of respect, and diminished funding and choose other ways to spend their lives (Akhtar, 2019).

One study found that 44 percent of American teachers leave the profession in the first five years (Will, 2018), which means Gen Z teachers have joined the group of millennial teachers who can't find the door fast enough. And who do districts often hire as their replacements? Young, inexperienced Gen Z and millennial teachers who often get thrown into tough environments and are quickly overwhelmed and leave the profession. And the cycle continues.

This is an American problem. Two countries that are considered to have highly effective education systems, Finland and Singapore, usually have attrition rates of 3 percent or 4 percent (Carver-Thomas & Darling-Hammond, 2017), half of that found in the United States. Our teachers are leaving because of problems in the American education system. According to one study from 2017,

> The most frequently cited reasons in 2012–13 were dissatisfactions with testing and accountability pressures (listed by 25% of those who left the profession); lack of administrative support; dissatisfactions with the teaching career, including lack of opportunities for advancement; and dissatisfaction with working conditions. These kinds of dissatisfactions were noted by 55% of those who left the profession and 66% of those who left their school to go to another school. (Carver-Thomas & Darling-Hammond, 2017, p. v)

To expand on these ideas, the centralization of American education, especially with its increasingly lockstep curricula and heavy accountability measures, means a lot of the choice and individualization have been removed from teaching. Teachers of all generations inherently don't buy into scripted programs. This is especially true and problematic when it comes to Gen Z and millennial teachers, who more than previous generations were raised to value individual freedom and to walk independent paths. Put another way, we have raised the most independent young people in history and put them into a teaching box and told them what to do and how to think. Another difference as they were raised is that they had more input into family decisions; in schools, they are troubled by the constant administrative turnover and a lack of input into organizational operations, including selecting textbooks and other classroom materials (Boyce, 2019).

And of course there's the pay issue—or more precisely, the diminished pay. The average weekly pay for teachers has dropped over the past 20 years; when compared with similarly educated adults, it had dropped by 21.4 percent in 2018 (Gould, 2019). Almost half of American teachers work a second job to supplement their income (Wade, 2019). Throw in the fear of being killed in a school shooting, and we can see why young teachers (and teachers of older generations) are dissatisfied with their jobs. One recent poll shows half of all teachers are actively searching for other jobs (Mulvahill, 2019).

> *We have raised the most independent young people in history and put them into a teaching box and told them what to do and how to think.*

The vacancies created by teachers who choose to leave make up 90 percent of all teacher vacancies (Carver-Thomas & Darling-Hammond, 2017). In other words, nine out of ten teachers hired each year are replacements for teachers who left the classroom. If America could cut its attrition rate by half, it would almost eliminate the nation's teacher shortages (Carver-Thomas & Darling-Hammond, 2017). Think of all the time and energy that could be saved in screening and interviewing teacher candidates each year. And think of the money saved. Those trips to job fairs, mentor stipends, inservice days, and other services for new teachers? Their costs add up to over $20,000 per year per teacher in urban districts (Carver-Thomas & Darling Hammond, 2017) and a total of $7.3 billion per year across the United States (Mulvahill, 2019). Just think if we could cut that cost by half. That would pump another $3.6 billion back into districts.

Where do a lot of these teachers go? Many of them take jobs in health care and social work. On average, these jobs pay less, but they offer more security and better benefits (Varathan, 2018). These are people who became teachers because they wanted to help people. They wanted to make a difference in the world. But the teaching profession couldn't offer them enough to stay in it, so they jumped into other fields where they can use their skills and assist individuals and families.

In an attempt to produce more teaching candidates, states have implemented alternative certification programs that offer less content preparation and fewer student teaching opportunities. The retention data for these teachers is even more abysmal: Teachers who come from these programs are 25 percent more likely to leave the profession (Carver-Thomas & Darling-Hammond, 2017).

Making Generational Adjustments

As we look at ways to retain young teachers, let's remember one of the frustrating conditions of school leadership: There's only so much we can do to improve our profession. Some factors are beyond the control of school administrators, like teacher pay, class sizes, violence in schools, state testing, and some of the other national, state, and societal pressures that stress school leaders and teachers today.

However, there's lots of room for improvement. A 2020 Gallup poll shows only 6 percent of superintendents think their districts understand what millennials need in the workplace (Hodges, 2020). Again, in which age groups are most superintendents today? Boomers and Gen Xers. And if they don't understand millennials, then they certainly don't understand Gen Z. Many school leaders might not even understand that Gen Z teachers are in their teaching staffs. This is not meant to criticize the administrators; they are working harder than ever, and these generation gaps are new leadership issues. But it shows these generation gaps are real.

It's time to start making personnel adjustments built around generational knowledge. As they transition in to 5-Gen leadership, boomer and Gen X school leaders need to acknowledge that young teachers respond differently and are looking for different sorts of experiences than the leaders were seeking when they joined the profession—which means they are looking for different things in the workplace.

According to Staffbase (Lockley, 2017), a company that helps corporations merge multiple generations of employees who work remotely, there are five characteristics that Gen Z and millennials are seeking in their work environment—*and these things are often missing in our schools today.*

1. **High wages and career advancement.** While we know there's a problem with teacher salaries, let's look at this issue from a generational viewpoint. Gen Z and millennials are entering the workforce with more college debt than previous generations. *They need more money.* Collectively, they have over $500 billion in outstanding loans (Friedman, 2020). They could spend decades crawling out of debt; thus, salaries are critically important for them, even more important than they were to previous generations. When Gen Z and millennials choose their majors, they know they will be in debt when they leave college, and they are looking ahead to the types of salaries they will draw. The low teacher salaries make the positions less attractive than in the past. And it's hard to advance through the hierarchy. When advancing in a school system to serve on committees or move into

administrative or other positions, they often are expected to wait their turn behind older, more experienced teachers, regardless of ability.

2. **The latest technology.** Young people live with technology in their personal lives; they want to be in environments that embrace it. While schools have made progress in implementing more devices and digital tools, they are not on the cutting edge of digital change. They are still well behind the curve. Schools are not seen as cool places where workers can have access to the latest apps, devices, and digital practices.

3. **Leadership training.** Millennials are now old enough and experienced enough to begin moving into leadership positions in their organizations, yet they feel they lack the "soft skills" to lead older generations of workers (Lockley, 2017). They feel they need more help than aspiring leaders of the past and want hands-on, mentor-guided programs to help them become leaders. And Gen Z leaders are not far behind. Instead, how do school leaders traditionally acquire leadership skills? Mainly through a bruising period of trial and error and by studying leadership skills in university graduate courses that hopefully translate into authentic leadership practices.

4. **Feedback and engagement.** Gen Z workers and millennials want more conversations with their leaders, more feedback, and more engagement than previous generations, yet only 55 percent of employees worldwide think there are enough collaboration and communication with leaders and across departments (Lockley, 2017). Many school leaders are Gen Xers and baby boomers. They are less likely to value this concept, and the demands placed on school leaders today mean they are working at faster paces than previous leaders, which makes it harder to find time to communicate and converse with young teachers. Young people today know school environments are not seen as collaborative, creative spaces where teachers have constant interaction with administrators and play active roles in decision-making.

5. **Help in managing stress.** In one study, workers were asked to rate their stress level on a scale of 1 to 10. The average score was 4.9, but the average score for Gen Z and millennial workers was 5.4, meaning they are feeling more stressed than other generations (Lockley, 2017). When we combine this number with the idea that teachers continually cite stress levels as one of the contributing factors of burnout, we can see younger teachers are especially likely to feel stressed. High school students see what their teachers endure on a daily basis; they hear the complaints from their teachers and hear the reports in the news about low morale levels among educators. Thus, they view a life as a teacher as a life filled with high stress and little reward (Lockley, 2017).

Notice a commonality of these five characteristics: They all have their roots in 21st century societal changes. Young people are more in debt than previous generations, they value technology more than previous generations, they are less confident than previous generations, they need more encouragement and feedback than previous generations, and they are more stressed than previous generations.

School leaders can be better in these five areas. When forming a strategy to retain millennial and Gen Z teachers, boomer and Gen X leaders can begin by breaking down how to help young teachers advance in different ways through the school culture and hierarchy, use abundant education technology, learn to lead, receive feedback and be engaged, and manage their stress.

Let's compare the traditional leadership model with the 5-Gen leadership model in how they would address these areas (see Figure 1.4).

FIGURE 1.4   Retaining Millennial Teachers

Traditional Leadership	Versus	5-Gen Leadership
Teachers have to "pay their dues" before they are placed on committees or are considered for prominent committees or positions. There is little chance for early advancement.	Wages and advancement	Young teachers are purposely placed on school or district committees to get their input and to keep them engaged. They are given chances to apply for positions that might increase salary.
Teachers might have interactive whiteboards and students might have Chromebooks. Training is haphazard, and young teachers might be able to offer their opinions. All teachers tend to use the same digital tools.	Technology	Technology training is systemized, and young teachers are encouraged to be innovative in using new digital tools. The school constantly updates its devices and gives young teachers chances to model their tactics for their peers.
There is little or no leadership training for teachers. They are expected to learn as they go if they happen to be placed in a position where they formally or informally influence others.	Leadership training	Teachers are paired with leader mentors (either with teachers or administrators) who take a systemized, proactive approach to helping the teacher learn how to lead in a school.
Administrators meet with teachers periodically. It might be part of the evaluation process or as issues arise. Administrators often want to engage more with teachers but their busy schedules prevent it.	Feedback and engagement	Administrators seek new ways to give feedback. They connect via social media. Teacher leaders are asked to engage more with young teachers. Systems are in place for teachers to give each other feedback.
Some school leaders recognize the importance of stress management and have begun to put programs in place. Others don't have the resources or have not prioritized it.	Managing stress	School leaders give stress management a high priority and partner with outside parties, fund initiatives, provide space, and promote it as a necessary part of leading schools today.

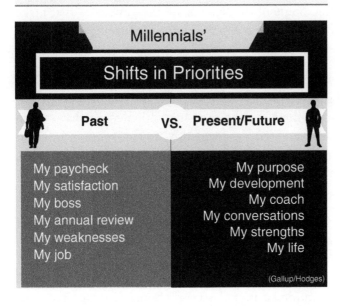

FIGURE 1.5 Millennials' Shifts in Priorities

Millennials'

Shifts in Priorities

Past   VS.   Present/Future

My paycheck   My purpose
My satisfaction   My development
My boss   My coach
My annual review   My conversations
My weaknesses   My strengths
My job   My life

(Gallup/Hodges)

The Gallup organization summed up changes in job perspectives for millennials (see Figure 1.5). For this generation, developing the company is no longer the priority. Instead, the priority is developing the individual.

For school leaders, this also means millennials still care about school and being professionals, but the leaders should approach them with the concept of coaching them (not just supervising them), focusing on their strengths as teachers (not just their weaknesses), and understanding that millennials will place a priority on living a high-quality life (and will not place the highest priority on a career). These ideas can also be applied to most Gen Z teachers.

This sums up the challenge of 5-Gen leadership: understanding what motivates each generation, respecting the desires of each generation, understanding how each generation learns, and using tactics to help all generations understand and assist each other (which will be explored in Chapter 2 when we look at what happens when the four generations are working together in one group).

Trouble in the Gen Z Teaching Pipeline

We know a cohesive staff is a challenged, happy staff, but what happens when we can't find enough young teachers to join our staffs?

To compound the problems in the generational teaching ranks, we're seeing fewer Gen Zers who want to even want to become teachers. Millennials are leaving in record numbers, and Gen Zers don't even want to start.

According to one study, since 2010 national enrollment in teacher preparation programs has dropped by one-third. In 2016 to 2017, almost 350,000 *fewer* students were enrolled in the programs than were enrolled in 2008 to 2009 (Partelow, 2019). In some states, it's even worse. Oklahoma, Illinois, and Michigan have seen enrollment in their teacher preparation programs drop by 50 percent since 2010 (Akhtar, 2019). More teachers are leaving; fewer teachers are coming in. The teacher pipeline is drying up.

Why is this happening? A number of factors are discouraging Gen Z students from entering the profession. Some of the reasons are the same ones that make millennials want to leave. But they've also experienced new generational problems in schools.

They've grown up in the age of No Child Left Behind and the Common Core. They are the "most tested generation." The standardized tests and the bevy of formative assessments preparing them for the tests mean they might have taken extensive formative assessments and tests "as frequently as twice per month and an average of once per month" (Boyce, 2019). Today's high school graduates are less likely to see K–12 public schools as a place of free thinking and intellectual growth than as a place where the goal is to prepare for and take standardized tests.

Also, while millennials and older teachers have had to adjust to the possibility of experiencing a school shooting, Gen Zers are the first generation of students to spend their *entire school lives* fearing school shootings. From their first year of school in early 2000s, they have gone through lockdown drills and have lived with the incessant fear of being murdered in a classroom. Some of them, like their teachers, have written their last will and testaments (DeGuerin, 2019). And some of them have gone online to buy bulletproof backpacks (Reagan, 2019).

They are already heavily stressed. One study found Gen Z high school students are more worried about their grades than they are about unplanned pregnancies and binge drinking (*The Economist*, 2019). When we add worries about testing and safety to what social media is doing to them psychologically in their teenage years, we can see that schools for them are not bastions of intellectual freedom and prosperity. Instead, they are stressful, accountability-driven, potentially deadly places. It's not surprising fewer Gen Z students are choosing *not* to spend their professional lives in this system when they choose their college majors. Become a teacher today? For many of them, the answer is, "No way!"

Recruiting Gen Z Teachers

We, as school leaders, cannot solve all of the societal ills that are keeping Gen Zers from joining our profession, but if we adjust some of our organizational practices (as listed earlier for the millennials) and adjust our Gen Z recruiting tactics, we'll make school environments that will be more likely to attract and retain more young people. Plus, if there are fewer Gen Z teachers from whom to choose to fill teaching vacancies, it makes it *even more imperative* that school leaders understand Gen Z's professional preferences in order to successfully recruit the best candidates into their staffs.

School leaders work with Gen Z students every day, but information is now emerging about how Gen Z is meshing into the workforce. An article on LinkedIn

(McLaren, 2019) for corporate recruiters had these nuggets of information to help them understand Gen Z workers:

- Gen Zers make up 24 percent of the overall workforce.

- They are seeking stability: paid time off, good health care, and high wages.

- They'd rather ask Google than ask for advice.

- They are independent, but risk-averse.

- They seek constant interaction with their supervisors.

- They want to be recognized for their efforts.

- They are seeking a diverse a workforce, and 75 percent of them say it will affect where they choose to work.

- They want to work for ethical companies, and the top qualities they are seeking in a leader are integrity and transparency.

- They are competitive.

- They want to use the latest social media platforms.

- They want to use technology in their jobs; 91 percent of them say how they get to use technology will affect their job choice.

Now think of what this information means for school administrators recruiting Gen Z teachers. When they speak with Gen Z teaching candidates over the phone, at job fairs, in one-on-one interviews at their schools, or when the candidate is interviewing with teams of teachers, the administrators need to be sure to focus on the things about which Gen Zers are most concerned. Figure 1.6 shows some essential points to work into the conversation.

Here's another tip: Since Gen Zers prefer having millennial managers (but the millennials might not be administrators yet in some schools), administrators should try to include a Gen Z or millennial teacher from the staff in the interview process. Pull the teacher into the office to help out. Take the teacher to job fairs. And let *the teacher* do a lot of the talking. Maybe the teacher could cover the points listed in Figure 1.6. If possible, give them time to talk alone. Let the young teacher give the tour of the building or create some other opportunity in which the recruit can connect with the other young professional.

FIGURE 1.6 Tips to Recruit Gen Z

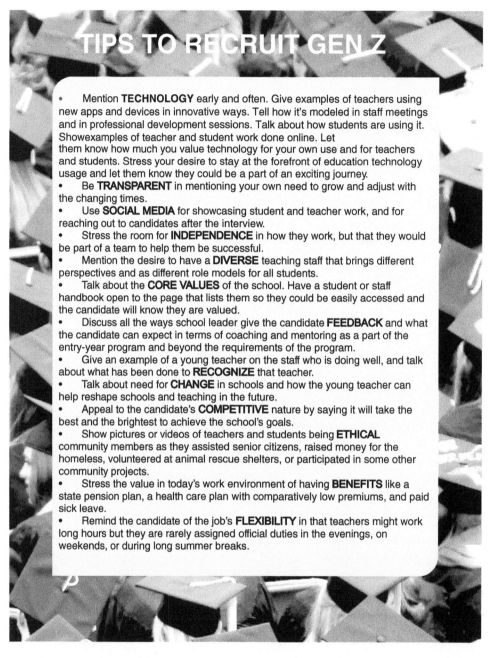

TIPS TO RECRUIT GEN Z

• Mention **TECHNOLOGY** early and often. Give examples of teachers using new apps and devices in innovative ways. Tell how it's modeled in staff meetings and in professional development sessions. Talk about how students are using it. Showexamples of teacher and student work done online. Let them know how much you value technology for your own use and for teachers and students. Stress your desire to stay at the forefront of education technology usage and let them know they could be a part of an exciting journey.

• Be **TRANSPARENT** in mentioning your own need to grow and adjust with the changing times.

• Use **SOCIAL MEDIA** for showcasing student and teacher work, and for reaching out to candidates after the interview.

• Stress the room for **INDEPENDENCE** in how they work, but that they would be part of a team to help them be successful.

• Mention the desire to have a **DIVERSE** teaching staff that brings different perspectives and as different role models for all students.

• Talk about the **CORE VALUES** of the school. Have a student or staff handbook open to the page that lists them so they could be easily accessed and the candidate will know they are valued.

• Discuss all the ways school leader give the candidate **FEEDBACK** and what the candidate can expect in terms of coaching and mentoring as a part of the entry-year program and beyond the requirements of the program.

• Give an example of a young teacher on the staff who is doing well, and talk about what has been done to **RECOGNIZE** that teacher.

• Talk about need for **CHANGE** in schools and how the young teacher can help reshape schools and teaching in the future.

• Appeal to the candidate's **COMPETITIVE** nature by saying it will take the best and the brightest to achieve the school's goals.

• Show pictures or videos of teachers and students being **ETHICAL** community members as they assisted senior citizens, raised money for the homeless, volunteered at animal rescue shelters, or participated in some other community projects.

• Stress the value in today's work environment of having **BENEFITS** like a state pension plan, a health care plan with comparatively low premiums, and paid sick leave.

• Remind the candidate of the job's **FLEXIBILITY** in that teachers might work long hours but they are rarely assigned official duties in the evenings, on weekends, or during long summer breaks.

Many principals today are justifiably driven by test scores, so they often spend a lot of time in interviews recounting percentages, accountability labels, and what the administration and teachers are doing to raise scores. Young candidates need to know this, but it probably won't be exciting for them. Actually, if the candidates think they will be walking into an environment driven by test scores, it could discourage them. The administrators should balance the accountability piece with the motivation of having an exciting job.

It's important to note that boomers and Gen X leaders don't need to change who they are as people in order to work with young teachers; they just need to adjust some of their tactics and leadership philosophies. They don't need to act like Gen Zers to be accepted. As one Gen Zer has written, "Just because you're trying to appeal to us doesn't mean you have to try to be like us. . . . If you're authentic, you will stand apart from your competition because authenticity resonates with Gen Z" (McLaren, 2019).

Of course, some of these points appeal to multiple generations and can be used when interviewing all generations of teachers. While there are some differences between Gen Z and millennial candidates, many of these tactics can be used to recruit millennials as well. For example, they also value mentoring, purpose, social media, and ethical actions. A few of these concepts could be highly valued by Gen X and baby boomer candidates. They often value diversity and advancement; however, they tend to be less interested in mentoring, social media, and having the latest technology. This means today's 5-Gen school leaders need to know the workplace characteristics valued by different generations, and they must be able to pivot between each one as they address different types of candidates.

Take Steps Now to Become a 5-Gen Leader

In my conversations with school leaders, I often hear them say they understand today's young people are different. They know millennial and Gen Z teachers have grown up in a different world and are plugged into technology and social media, and they understand these teachers have a different way of looking at life. They understand how hard it is to hold on to millennials, and they've heard through the professional grapevine that fewer Gen Zers are heading their way as teachers. But when I ask these school leaders *exactly what they are doing to specifically attract and retain young teachers*, they often don't have clear answers. I don't write this to be critical. They have crazy hectic lives, and as I mentioned, this is a new problem that has only recently been identified. Still, they need to do more than say they know the issue is there; they need to commit to action.

Businesses have begun to use formal retention plans to recruit and hold on to younger employees, and schools should do the same. A plan can be done in four steps:

1. Analyze retention data.

2. Choose strategies.

3. Form a plan of action.

4. Create the document. (Perucci, 2020)

School district personnel could analyze their millennial and Gen Z teacher data, brainstorm tactics to use to recruit and retain young teachers, pull the ideas together in a loose format, and then create the written document. They could call it the Teacher Recruiting and Retention Plan (TRRP) and have action steps and dates for implementation. These don't have to be complex, lengthy documents. A good rule would be to write them as if they are being written for millennials and Gen Zers: They should be concise and easily understood. School districts and individual schools have one-year and multiyear strategic plans that outline their goals; they could add the TRRP to these documents. Figure 1.7 shows an example of how one might look.

FIGURE 1.7   Teacher Recruiting and Retention Plan

Teacher Recruiting and Retention Plan

OBJECTIVE: Study and use the recruiting and retention data.
KEY QUESTIONS: Are we successfully hiring the teachers we want? Are we retaining them?

Person in charge of analyzing the data: _____
How the results will be disseminated: _____
Date by which it will be done: _____

OBJECTIVE: Retain more young teachers.
KEY QUESTION: Which 5-Gen leadership ideas are we using?

Person in charge of gathering the ideas: _____
How the leaders will be trained: _____
Date by which it will be done: _____

OBJECTIVE: Be more successful in hiring young teachers.
KEY QUESTIONS: Which Gen Z recruiting tips are we using?
How are we appealing to Millennial teachers as we recruit them?

Person in charge of gathering the information: _____
How the recruiters will be trained: _____
Date by which it will be done: _____

And After We Recruit and Retain Them . . .

There are other issues to resolve in 5-Gen leadership. Teachers in different generations respond differently to various types of leadership. They need different tactics in professional development, and they respond differently to societal changes. We need to understand Gen Alpha and prepare for the end of the decade when Gen Beta enters our schools. Millennials are now joining the administrative ranks. How will they mesh with older leaders? And what will be the impact on schools at the end of the decade as Gen Z teachers start to become administrators and link up with their millennial siblings? The world is changing rapidly, and so are our leadership ranks, teaching force, and student populations. Helping to lead education into this environment begins with transitioning to 5-Gen leadership.

OK, boomer?

FIGURE 1.8   Tips for Transitioning to 5-Gen Leadership

Tips for Transitioning to 5-Gen Leadership

1. Know four distinct generations are in our teaching staffs, including Gen Z.
2. Understand the differences in the four teaching generations.
3. Recognize the digital generation gaps between each generation.
4. Realize the biggest digital generation gap is the one between the boomers/Gen Xers and the millennials/Gen Zers.
5. Know millennials are leaving the profession in record numbers and fewer Gen Zers are joining the teaching profession.
6. Study the characteristics millennials and Gen Zers are looking for in a workplace and adjust practices.
7. Adjust recruiting strategies to find the best Gen Z teaching candidates.
8. Study the district's recruiting and retention data, brainstorm solutions, create a loose format, and then create a written Teacher Recruiting and Retention Plan.

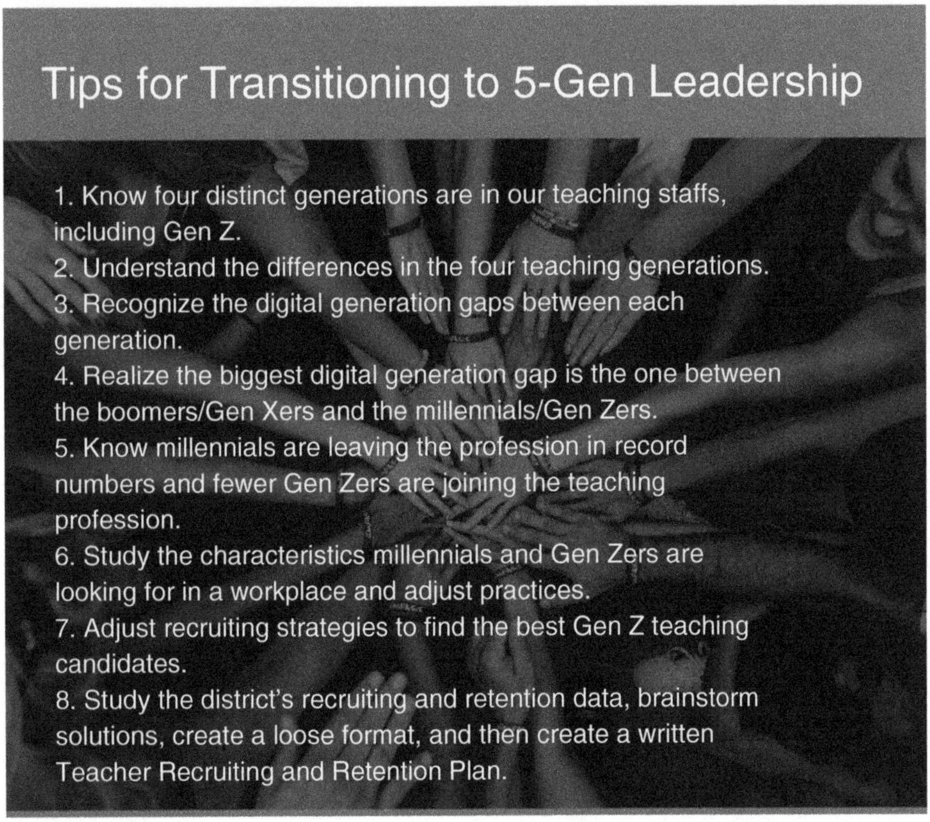

CHAPTER 2

The Impact of the Silent Generation and Gen Alpha

Key Points of This Chapter

- The Silent Generation shaped a significant part of the culture of our current schools.

- Gen Alpha will be the most tech savvy and advanced generation in history.

- We need to repurpose our schools to meet the needs of Gen Z and Gen Alpha students.

- Some ideas, like the power of professional mentorships and positive relationships with students, transcend the generations.

Allow me to tell you a tale of two Theodores, a tale of two generations at separate ends of our education history.

One Theodore is Theodore "Ted" Smith, and the other Theodore is his great-grandson, who is named after Ted and goes by the name of "Theo." Ted was born in 1933 and is a member of the Silent Generation (T. Smith, personal communication, July 12, 2020). Theo was born in 2014 and is a member of Gen Alpha. Ted is 88 years old, and Theo is five years old; Ted is a retired school administrator, and Theo has just started kindergarten. They are separated by four generations—83 years of technology accelerations, dramatic societal shifts, a globalized economy, and vastly varied life experiences.

If we understand these two Theodores, it can help us make more sense of where we are and where we need to go as 5-Gen leaders. Think of these two groups as the bookends of 5-Gen leadership. Their generations represent our education past and our education future.

Lessons From the Silent Generation

First, let's look at the impact of Ted's generation on American schools. When we look at the history of generational leadership in schools, we would be remiss not to mention the generation that did so much to create the school systems we have today: the Silent Generation, whose members were born between 1925 and 1945. They are the parents of the boomers, and they led our schools through the 1960s, 1970s, and 1980s.

They had a tough start. This generation grew up in some of the most frightening times in American history. In their formative years, they experienced the uncertainty of the Great Depression in the 1930s, the existential fear brought about by World War II in the 1940s, and the global tensions created by the Atomic Age that lasted through the 1950s and 1960s.

Imagine the nightmares coming out of *that* trifecta of American angst.

The Silent Generation was given its name by *Time* magazine in 1951 because its members didn't complain about their lives or the state of the world; they kept their heads down and remained silent (Howe, 2014). They were taught to survive. To them, work was a privilege, and they took whatever job they could find. They didn't believe in fads or quick success stories. They believed the way to success was through hard work, and there were no shortcuts. Members of the Silent Generation were known as being persistent. They couldn't survive a Depression and a world war unless they knew how to dig deep and see the job through to the end. They were able to ride the growing post–World War II American economy for most of their adult lives. Money was to be saved, so their thriftiness allowed them to become our wealthiest generation. The remaining members of the Silent Generation today still tend to be civic-minded and patriotic, and they vote in high numbers. Conformity is still valued, and they are known as team players (Kane, 2019).

The Silent Generation school leaders didn't have to deal with social media, school shootings, and the challenges of preparing students to enter a global economy, but they led schools through a radically changing American society: the civil rights movement and the integration of schools, the counterculture and hippie movement, the introduction of illegal drugs on a broad scale into American life, and the Vietnam War protests. Those could not have been easy times to lead schools for many Silent Generation leaders.

I think of my superintendents and principals, who were members of the Silent Generation, I knew when I was a student in the 1960s and 1970s. Most of the school leaders in my hometown were white men who wore white shirts and bland ties with silver tie clips. I would guess their leadership abilities ranged from average to good. Maybe one or two were great, and perhaps one or two weren't competent. I wouldn't know about that. The public was often shielded from what happened behind the principal's door—it was a different time when leadership foibles were less public and weak administrators could be more easily hidden.

I sometimes wonder what I would say to my former principals if I could go back in time and sit across their desk from them, a school leader from the future talking to a school leader from the past, which brings us to a bigger question: "What can we learn today from the Silent Generation school leaders?"

I interviewed our first Theodore, Ted Smith, to find out (T. Smith, personal communication, July 12, 2020). He spent most of his education career as a school administrator, and he epitomizes the Silent Generation (see Figure 2.1).

Ted was born in 1933 in Huntsville, Ohio, and like many other members of the Silent Generation, he grew up in a small town. By 1920, more Americans lived in cities and small towns than lived on farms (Recchiuti, n.d.). Technology took a huge step in the 1920s and early 1930s when radios were introduced on a broad scale into American households (Scott, n.d.). Ted remembers his family's radio, which was large. He estimates it was over 30 inches tall, about half as large as the

FIGURE 2.1   Equity Through the Generations

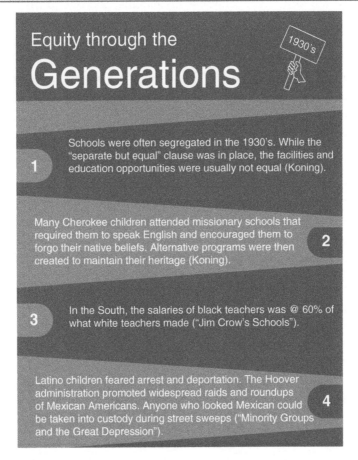

television he watches today. "We had electricity," he said, "but my grandparents both had battery-operated radios. . . . They had kerosene lights in their house."

When asked what kind of toys he had as a child, Ted dug back into his memory and said, "I had a wooden truck, and I had a wind-up car." He laughed and added, "That was high tech for those days!" Games were an important part of childhood fun for the Silent Generation, and they were usually played with others, not alone. *Checkers* was a popular game, he said, "and card games like euchre. My cousins always came to my grandparents' house on Sundays. We would play 'Red Rover, Come Over.'"

I can't help but compare Ted's childhood to my childhood as a boomer. I see some similarities, but technology was already changing toys. The technology transition had begun. Some of my toys in the 1960s were wind-up, but we had a lot of toys powered by batteries. The batteries didn't last nearly as long as they do today. I remember a lot of batteries being dead by Christmas night. I played "Red Rover, Come Over" on my elementary school playground in the 1960s. Perhaps it was taught to us by one of our Silent Generation teachers who, like Ted, had played it in her youth? All of my elementary teachers were women. It was one of the few professional avenues open to Silent Generation females. I visit a lot of elementary schools today, but I don't see "Red Rover, Come Over" played at recess anymore.

Ted attended the same high school as his parents, and one of his teachers had taught his parents, which means *that* teacher had probably begun teaching in the early part of the previous century. Ted played varsity basketball for all four years—there were only 11 boys in the entire school, so being on the basketball team was *mandatory* in order for the school to field a team. He was the valedictorian of his graduating class. And here's something wonderful Ted shared about his school: "It was such a small school that if a new family moved in and new students came into the school, we all went down to talk to them, to say, 'Hi.'"

Ted's childhood occurred during the Great Depression and during the food-rationing days of World War II, but Ted's family was lucky: Both sets of his grandparents were farmers. "Farmers always had plenty of food," he said. "Even though we didn't live on a farm, we'd go to my grandparents' and bring back food we'd cook later." It helped that his father had a steady paycheck. "My father was lucky," said Ted. "He had a teaching job. . . . For those times, we were fairly well off."

Now let's compare Ted's youth to his Gen Alpha great-grandson, five-year-old Theo, a member of Gen Alpha in today's schools. While Ted grew up with wooden toys and a big box radio, Theo is growing up with an iPad, apps, and YouTube videos. For Ted, playing card games with his cousins was an interactive, social event. Theo likes to play a few card games, but most of his games are found on his iPad—and he plays them alone. One of Theo's favorite activities is to FaceTime his grandmother, who lives over a thousand miles away. He can take his mother's phone (he figured out the password to open the phone by watching her), open the app, and tap on his grandmother's name to initiate the call. As a child, Ted's view of the world came from what he heard on the radio and what he saw in his small town, but Theo's boundaries will stretch as far as his YouTube videos and FaceTime conversations will take him. As an adult in his 20s, Ted's life changed when he got a television. Try to imagine the technology Theo will have in his life when he is 25 years old in 2040. Then think about what he'll experience in 2050, 2060, and beyond.

Like the Silent Generation, Gen Alpha will have to overcome its own childhood existential challenges. The Silent Generation grew up with outbreaks of polio and whooping cough. Theo, in the fall of 2020, began his first official year of his schooling (kindergarten) at home because of the COVID-19 pandemic. As a five-year-old, he learned to look forward to a future when the virus would be less of a threat. "When the virus is over . . ." he would say, and then he would talk about how much fun it would be to take a vacation and swim in a pool again.

Ted began his career as a junior high school science and history teacher. "Junior high" was the term used at the time, and the schools usually had seventh, eighth, and ninth graders in them. Today's middle school concept of forming an environment to help young adolescents didn't exist; junior high schools were designed to leave the elementary culture behind and to systematically prepare students for the perceived rigors of high school. After all, think of their names: junior high schools. They were mini high schools for the younger students (Davis, 2008). The members of the Silent Generation attended junior high schools, and then some of them helped reshape junior high schools into middle schools. It was a bold move: School leaders of the Silent Generation pushed back against a deeply ingrained education philosophy that had been around for almost a hundred years.

The idea of forming junior highs came out of a reform effort launched in 1888 by the president of Harvard University, Charles Eliot. At that time, American education often had two levels: elementary schools, which were Grades 1–8, and high schools, which were Grades 9–12. Eliot and his peers, who formed the powerful National Education Association's Committee of Ten on Secondary School Studies, wanted to increase the rigor of the upper-elementary grades to better prepare them for high school, so they decided to shift the seventh and eighth grades into more of a secondary setting: They kept six grades (Grades 1–6) in the elementary schools and moved Grades 7 and 8 into the secondary level. Thus, we had six grades in the lower level and six grades in the upper levels of American education. Secondary schools across America began to form into intermediary schools (Grades 7–8), junior high schools (Grades 7–9), and junior–senior high schools (Grades 7–12). By the 1940s, over half of America's young adolescents were in junior high schools. By 1960, that number had climbed to 80 percent (Middle Schools, 2021).

It wasn't just middle school educators that began to form a new philosophy of teaching and learning in the last two decades of the 20th century; during the Silent Generation's tenure as leaders, the overall American K–12 system began to recognize the fundamental importance of emotional well-being in the formation of academically successful students. This philosophy continues in American schools today.

Sort of.

The shift to the middle school concept is also symbolic of a strange paradox in American schools, one we have to resolve if we are going to transition into schools that fit the needs of Gen Z and Gen Alpha: At the time we began to focus on developing each individual, we also began to give them standardized tests and accountability labels. Educators said to their students, "Be who you are! Let us help you develop as an individual!" while the system was saying, "But take this test now regardless of where you are in in your individual growth or abilities! You are this age, so you take this test, and this is how we will rank you, your teacher, your school, and your district!" Educators were gravitating to more student-centered views at the same time government leaders were moving toward mass accountability. This conflict survives in schools today. It is at the heart of the tension in school reform movements. Educators want to treat students as individuals, yet most of them in the public schools are forced to throw their students into the meat grinder of standardized testing (more of this topic will be covered in Chapter 3).

Ted later became a high school principal and an assistant superintendent in various spots in Ohio. When asked about his biggest challenge as a principal in the 1950s and 1960s, he says it was having to discipline students—but it wasn't quite like the discipline challenges school leaders face to today. "The kids were much different then," he said. The transgressions were simpler. Corporal punishment was an accepted form of discipline in American schools. "If you got a paddling at school," he said, "you got one at home. It was a rural area, and the kids were usually honest. I didn't have to call the parents when they got a paddling; the kids would tell them, and then they got one at home. They would come back and tell me."

While it was a tumultuous time in American society, Ted was somewhat shielded from it in his schools. "In the country schools, there weren't a lot of social issues," he said. Even when Ted became an assistant superintendent in a suburban community in the late 1960s and 1970s, he didn't have to deal with the student unrest that was roiling university campuses at that time. Social media and viral videos were still four decades away, and while some middle school and high school students were politically active, many of them had views of the world that were more confined to their own city blocks and schools.

Ted is most proud of impact on the quality of teachers he was able to bring into the school. "I hired good teachers. They made me as a principal," he said. A significant number of his hires would have been boomers. Times were already changing, and teacher preparation programs were beginning to transform. "I thought the younger teachers might have been better prepared than the older teachers," Ted added.

While Ted's generation is generally thought of as being risk averse, some of its school leaders were extreme risk takers: They led the way into one of the most daring concepts ever tried in American schools, the open classroom experiment of the 1970s (Cuban, 2011). This generation grew up conforming, yet it tore down the classroom walls. In that decade, they also presided over a period of increased opportunities for African American students, for immigrant students, and for students with learning and physical disabilities. Women began to take on more prominent roles in school leadership (Encyclopedia.com, 2020); some of the Silent Generation leaders opened the leadership doors for them—and some of the boomer women had to kick in the leadership doors to get into those offices. From 1988 to 1998, the percentage of female school principals increased from 20 percent to 48 percent (Helterbran & Rieg, 2004). Today, 54 percent of American principals are women (Ramaswamy, 2020), which means they have achieved a slight majority in building leadership positions.

One of these early pioneers was Dr. Mena Leo, a former superintendent in the Rio Grande Valley of Texas. Dr. Leo is a boomer who was born shortly after World War II, and she led through the transition as more opportunities opened for women. When asked about her challenges, she points to challenges many professional women today experience: the balancing of a career with motherhood. "My greatest challenge was that of being a mother to five children as I was being expected to be available to staff and parents and community."

Dr. Leo offers these insights from her leadership days.

It's clear Dr. Leo, like other female trailblazers, had to be resilient, especially to move all the way up the leadership ladder to the superintendent's office. That resiliency is still needed today. Even in 2021, female administrators are brushing up

When I assumed my first administrative jobs, the trend was beginning to change regarding female administrators. The greatest challenge was probably that of men who had been in administrative positions for some time. They did not readily accept that women were now leading building staff. They had been accustomed to doing minimal job requirements and to keep their verbal responses to a minimum. As more women entered into leadership positions, there was a silent resentment from males to females "doing more than was necessary to get the job done."

I remember sitting in a meeting with 20 other principals, participating in a lively discussion about our guiding staff to change our philosophy about the teaching/learning process. I was sitting next to my former boss, a male middle school principal who never offered any of his thoughts. He had been a principal for over 10 years. I had been somewhat verbal, thinking how exciting it was to learn from one another. At the end of the session, I asked him why he had not participated in the discussion. His answer was, "Why? The more you talk, the more they call on you and the longer we have to be in there!" Needless to say, that was not enough to keep me quiet, ever.

(M. Leo, personal communication, September 14, 2020)

against the glass ceiling when it comes to being a superintendent. Three-fourths of American educators are females, but only 24 percent of American superintendents are women (Ramaswamy, 2020). If the majority of the building-level leaders are female, why don't we have more female superintendents? There could be a number of reasons. Like Dr. Leo, many female leaders today still balance the roles of being an administrator and a mother. Moving up the administrative ladder often requires a series of moves from one district to another, and if the administrator is the primary parent, this could be hard on kids, which makes it hard for the administrator to change districts. One study found 81 percent of superintendents came from middle schools and high schools, and men have 67 percent of the high school principal positions and 60 percent of the middle school principal positions, while women fill 68 percent of the elementary positions (Ramaswamy, 2020). Men appear to have the inside track to superintendent's office.

Other reasons are also in play. Some women won't apply because they might view their qualifications differently than men. A study by Hewlett-Packard in 2013 showed that men are more likely to apply for a job if they have some of the qualifications, but women often won't apply unless they have the majority or all of the qualifications. This was backed up by a LinkedIn study of what it had observed through its site in 2019 (Youn, 2019). A Pew Research Center (2015) study found that most people believe it's easier for men to achieve key leadership positions than it is for women.

It's fair to say many female educators and educators of color must still fight harder to get into leadership positions. But it's also fair to say we've never had as great of a need for diverse leadership as we have today—because Gen Z and Gen Alpha are the most diverse generations in history (Fry & Parker, 2020). They need to see role models who look like them in leadership roles.

Gen Alpha, the New Generation

Before we take a close look at the generation at the other end of our leadership lens, Gen Alpha, let's first consider some commonly asked questions: "How did we get the name Gen Alpha? How did we jump from Z to A, from Gen Z to Gen Alpha? Who's making up these names?"

To get the answers, we have to jump across the Pacific, all the way to Australia, and study the work of Mark McCrindle. He's also a demographer, futurist, and social commentator—and he and his company are credited with creating the Gen A moniker (Bologna, 2019). According to McCrindle, a movement was already underway to follow the name of Generation Z with the name of Generation A, but he felt a more appropriate moniker was needed, so he suggested Alpha, which translates more into a beginning or the "start of something new" (Bologna, 2019).

It's appropriate to think of Gen Alpha as the beginning; we are entering a new phase in global history. In *Leading Schools in Disruptive Times* (2021, 2nd ed.), I wrote with Dwight Carter about three essential points to know if we are going to understand technology accelerations: Processing speeds keep getting faster, which leads to more information, which has brought the world to a point that knowledge is doubling every year and will be doubling every 12 hours in the future (see Figure 2.2). This is the world in which Theo and his Gen Alpha peers will live: The information learned this morning will be supplanted by twice as much information this evening, and it will be doubled twice tomorrow, the next day, and the next day.

Gen Alpha is already showing trends that separate it from previous generations. Its members can be called "upagers" because it is expected they will physically mature faster and adolescence will arrive earlier in their lives. They are also expected to be more sophisticated socially, psychologically, educationally, and commercially at an earlier age than their millennial and Gen Z predecessors (McCrindle Staff, n.d.a). Much of this is because of what they are seeing and experiencing on the internet.

A study by Common Sense Media in 2017 found 98 percent of Gen Alpha students under the age of eight in America are growing up in a household with mobile

FIGURE 2.2 Three Things to Know About the Rate of Change in the World

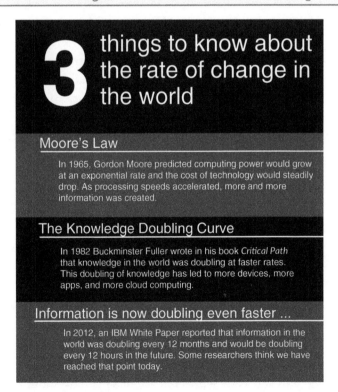

SOURCES: Moore's Law ("Over 50 Years of Moore's Law"; Knowledge Doubling Curve (Rosenberg); Information is now doubling. . .(Rosenberg)

devices like tablets and cell phones. That number is up dramatically: Six years ago, the percentage was 52 percent. The number of minutes of usage has grown from five minutes per day in 2011 to 15 minutes per day in 2013 to 48 minutes per day in 2017 (Kamenetz, 2017). Another study by Common Sense Media in 2019 found Gen Alpha and Gen Z students between the ages of 8 and 12 spend almost five hours each day online, and Gen Z teenagers spend seven-and-a-half hours online. That doesn't count the number of minutes spent online in school—and this was before the school closures of 2020 when kids were home all day doing school online and had more free time for online gaming (Rideout & Robb, 2019).

According to researcher Mark McCrindle, Gen Alpha come from families that move more often, increasingly live in urban environments, and have parents who change careers more frequently (Bolonga, 2019). Elwood Carlson, a demographer and professor at Florida State University, says that Gen Alpha has a higher number of kids who are not growing up with two biological parents in the household. In the United States, this generation will have more young people who have immigrant parents or are immigrants themselves (Bologna, 2019).

If we thought Gen Z was the technology generation, consider the life of Gen Alpha: When Gen Alpha was "born" in 2010, the iPad was introduced, and the American Dialect Society's word of the year was "app." McCrindle says Gen Alpha is being born into "the great screen age" (McCrindle Staff, n.d.a). Another name given to Gen Alpha is "Generation Glass" because of the way they will constantly interact with their computer screens, the pop-up screens they will have on their vehicle dashboards, and the interactive desks at which they will sit in the future (Bologna, 2019). They will be the most tech-savvy generation ever, even more than Gen Z (McCrindle Staff, n.d.b): "Not since Gutenberg transformed the utility of paper with his printing press in the 15th century has a medium been so transformed for learning and communication purposes as glass—and it has happened in the lifetime of Gen Alpha" (McCrindle Staff, n.d.a, para. 13).

Take a moment and think about that comment: The 2020s will be a decade of the most dramatic teaching and learning transformation since the 1400s.

The 2020s will be a decade of the most dramatic teaching and learning transformation since the 1400s.

Natalie Franke, the head of community at the business management firm HoneyBook, believes Gen Alpha will merge with technology more completely as increasingly powerful technology enters its daily life. She says they might "prefer a virtual world over their real world." They will live with autonomous cars, stronger AI, and have more apps that do things for them. "I predict this will lead to an unprecedented rise in creativity, education and self-care, with Gen Alpha spending more time exploring their passion, prioritizing mental wellness and seeking education for the simple joy of learning," notes Franke (Bologna, 2019, para. 23). Furthermore, Franke believes "technological advancements, combined with the rising cost of college, will allow Generation Alpha to reject traditional education and pursue learning through other avenues. That attitude promotes 'the passion economy' as younger generations may continue the growing trend of freelancing and starting their own businesses" (Bologna, 2019, para. 24).

In 2030, Theo will be a teenager, and he will have devices, apps, and artificial intelligence that we can barely imagine. He already loves his iPad; his journey on the Gen Alpha moving sidewalk of change has begun.

Gen Alpha's Impact on Education

Now, what can we do as 5-Gen leaders today to help Theo and his Gen Alpha and Gen Z peers stay ahead of the massive societal/economic shifts that will shape their lives?

Assuming Franke is right and Gen Alpha rejects traditional education, it means they will be searching for a new model. Today's school leaders have the expertise, research, and experience to create new types of schools for Gen Alpha.

To begin to understand how to transform our schools, let's look at the legacy handed to us by the Silent Generation and see how parts of it can help us to educate Gen Alpha and which parts must be overcome as we move into this new model.

Our schools are meant to be mirrors of American democracy, and the Silent Generation built the pillars that still support today's school cultures. Think of this: Which character values are most rigorously promoted in schools today? Here are some of them: hard work, tenacity, a respect for authority, efficiency, safety, security, consistency, teamwork, fairness, and friendliness. In many ways, these quintessential American school values given to us by the Silent Generation form the "American Way" of doing things. These are the ideals most often associated with the Silent Generation (Kane, 2019). These traits are still considered great values, and they can still be a part of a roadmap to success in the 21st century for Gen Z and Gen Alpha.

Yet when we look at Gen Alpha's screen-dominated, independent lifestyle, we have to ask: *Can today's schools add to or adjust their cultural pillars to make room for students whose learning styles, interests, and goals are more varied and more independent than ever before?* Remember how Ted told us part of the reason he was successful was that he "worked hard"? Besides being a part of the Puritan work ethic that has been passed down through generations since the colonialization of America, the characteristic of hard work is an integral part of the Silent Generation. It was an era of conformity; Ted was expected to play basketball for the good of the school and the team. And he did. While there are still some small schools where students would make this sacrifice, most Gen Alpha and Gen Z students are being raised differently from the Silent Generation; students have become more independent, and their voices are heard today. They usually are not expected to participate in an extracurricular team activity unless they *want* to do so.

Schools in the 2020s must balance the need to teach collaboration with the need to promote entrepreneurial thinking. The students will have *to want to come to school*. As one researcher has written,

> Existing evidence suggests that our schools will have to establish their presence in more than content and skill. Generation Alpha students will look for reasons to go to school that are beyond learning to read and master numeracy skills. These expectations start in kindergarten and are expected to continue. They will love their teachers and enjoy their friends but question why they have to spend six hours (or more), five days a week inside of a school. They will look at software programs that are used (often with fidelity) to develop literacy and numeracy skills and wonder why they are using programs at school (instead of being in the comfortable confines of their home or public library). For this generation it is the experience and action that leads to learning; not just instruction and content-based inquiry. (Britten, 2019, para. 20)

Our graduates will need to have an entrepreneurial mindset, which means we have to build an education model for Gen Alpha and Gen Z centered on creativity, not standardized test scores. In a world in which people explore their passions, learn for the sake of learning, and have increasingly powerful virtual worlds into which to escape, students and parents simply will not tolerate an education model centered on high-stakes testing. Gen Alpha's constant exposure to screens is resulting in shorter attention spans, higher levels of digital literacy, lower levels of social competency, and a greater need for schools to employ digital gamification to engage them (McCrindle Staff, n.d.b). Their biggest requests are for more devices and screen time (Pasquarelli & Schultz, 2019). The teaching and learning must have a strong technology component. Artificial intelligence can't be shunned in the classroom; it must be embraced (see Figure 2.3).

Let's think of the type of school five-year-old Theo will need in this decade. As he matures and reaches a point where he wants to learn in his own way, will the system allow him to do so? What if he wants a different schedule, a different end and start time to his school day, a mix of synchronous and asynchronous learning, and his own way of showing he has learned something? These are the traits of Gen Alpha, not the traits of today's schools.

Consider this: Theo will graduate from high school in 2033. We need to imagine the world of 2033, 2043, and 2053. But we can't stop there. Because of advances in medicine, procedures, and gene modification, the average Gen Alpha child will

FIGURE 2.3   Five Steps to Lead Gen Alpha

Steps

5

to Lead Gen Alpha

01 Hold on to the values of the past but allow for more entrepreneurial thinking in teaching and learning.

02 Embrace artificial intelligence. It will be a central part of Gen Alpha's life and should be an integral part of teaching and learning.

03 Redesign school days around the needs, lifestyles, and learning preferences of Gen Alpha and Gen Z.

04 Curricula should have some traditional elements but should be more focused on 21st century skills.

05 Have a transformative mindset to quickly adjust practices for each new generation and wave of technology.

FIGURE 2.4   New Pillars for Gen Alpha

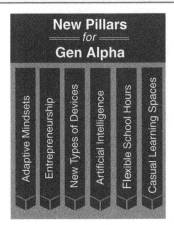

probably live to be over 100 years of age (Malito, 2019), which means Theo could be alive in 2120. Gen Alpha will be the first generation of this century to survive in record numbers to see dawn of the 22nd century (McCrindle Staff, n.d.c). That's a long life built upon the skills we help them acquire today.

So 5-Gen leaders must retain pillars given to us by the Silent Generation, but 5-Gen leaders must add six new pillars to serve Gen Alpha (see Figure 2.4).

Adaptive mindset: A part of the new education model is to understand that the teaching profession will have to adapt at constantly faster speeds to keep up with accelerating increases in artificial intelligence. One of my favorite sayings for teachers in my trainings is "We must be comfortable being uncomfortable."

Entrepreneurship: As we reconfigure schools today, we also need to push our imaginations out into a *Star Trek* world and think of Theo's life in 2080 and 2090. Can we see what that future will be? No. But we know we need to give our students a head start in developing their own entrepreneurial mindsets so they can more effectively sort through options and create new paths and new lifestyles.

New types of devices: Hopefully, we've reached a point in our progression where we will readily adapt and use new technology as it appears in our classrooms, from artificial intelligence to robots to holograms. But this means we must be willing to let go of some of our old technology. When I was in junior high, I was taught to use a slide rule (a slide rule is a ruler-like, hand-operated computer used to figure mathematical equations). Besides learning of the novelty of the device, it was pretty much a waste of teaching and learning time: I've never used a slide rule in my life other than in 8th-grade science class. I don't fault the teacher or the district; electronic calculators were just being introduced, and slide rules were still used in industry. But the slide rule can be a metaphor of technology that was once a mainstay in classrooms and has been relegated to the history pile. As education technology in the future morphs into something incomprehensible today, will laptops or handheld calculators become the slide rules of the 21st century? Old devices must be abandoned more quickly than ever to keep up with accelerating change.

Artificial intelligence (AI): Consider how AI will affect schools in this decade. In 2020, a company called OpenAI launched a new software called GPT-3, which was "the most powerful 'language model' ever created" (Manjoo, 2020). In other words, it could write letters, reports, scripts, and short stories in a more convincing manner than any previous software. We already have speech-to-text apps on our phones, and they are becoming more popular. In 2018, 20 percent of Google searches were done with voice commands; that number was expected to jump to 50 percent by 2020 (Romero, 2018). The day is coming when Gen Alpha students will ask, "Why do I have to write this paper when my AI does all of my writing at home?" Or "Why do I have to solve this math or science problem when I can quickly ask Alexa to do it for me?" And what does this mean for standardized testing as we know it? We are already using an obsolete testing model; will we also be testing obsolete skills? By the end of the decade, 5-Gen leaders will have to lead their staffs through a complicated, torturous, thrilling process of determining what it means for Gen Alpha to be educated.

Flexible hours: The rise of artificial intelligence, the demands of Gen Z and Gen Alpha, and the COVID closures of 2020 will force schools to do what other businesses are doing: take a hard look at the set hours and schedules for schools, especially in the upper levels of high school for students who are more independent and mature. We are in the last iteration of huge brick-and-mortar high schools. The Gen Z and Gen Alpha upagers will be looking for new options. School will be where they use their AI; it will not always be the desk where they sit in the classroom.

Casual learning spaces: Have you been in a new school lately? Almost every school built today has some form of common, flexible learning space where students can spread out, sit in alternative types of furniture, make presentations, and work together. We will still need schools in the 2030s and beyond, but the increase in education apps that link learning, the lifestyles of students, and the demands for collaboration, creativity, critical thinking, and communication will mean the schools will continue to morph into new floor plans and functionalities.

To build these pillars, school leaders must create staffs that function as strong collaborative teams while allowing individual teachers to take new, entrepreneurial approaches to teaching. As we saw in Chapter 1, our younger teachers— our millennials and Gen Z teachers—sometimes feel they are in too restrictive of a teaching environment. This problem is only going to deepen with each passing year as more Gen Alphas rise through our schools in the 2020s and begin to join the millennials and Gen Zers in our teaching ranks in the early 2030s. As 5-Gen leaders create new types of schools, they must create new types of staffs. They must hold on to the values provided by the Silent Generation, look at Gen Alpha's needs, and then translate these ideas into new types of teaching and learning.

The Transcendent Power of Relationships

Finally, two of Ted Smith's recollections provide insight into how leaders of the Silent Generation are similar to today's generations of educators. More precisely, they remind us that, as we take steps to repurpose our schools, we must remember the importance of using our kindness and wisdom to help others.

First, Ted was effusive in his praise of his mentor, Jim Diley. Diley had been Ted's coach in high school, and he later became an administrator who hired Ted. Then Ted followed him through several school districts, working his way up under Diley's tutorage from teacher to principal to assistant superintendent. "Mentors did a lot for me. They determined my career," Ted said. "What Jim Diley did for me allowed me to take all those steps. I'm grateful for what he did for me and my family. He was really influential on my career. And I tried hard."

Can't most educators today, especially school administrators, point to mentors who helped them at key points in their careers? As Ted points out, mentors can be heavily influential. It's a reminder that the mentorship chain though the generations of educators is vital and powerful. When we mentor young educators today and then they mentor younger educators during their careers, it means we are doing more than just helping our younger associates—we are shaping education far into the future. The leadership chain continues. Think of it this way: Part of our mission now is to mentor the next group of leaders so we can assist the Gen Z, Gen Alpha, and Gen Beta leaders we will never know. And with the changes coming to the world and to education in the next decade, mentorship is more essential than ever.

Here's a second powerful point to consider that transcends generations: the satisfaction to be found in positive relationships with students and other educators. Ted said helping young people was the best part of his job:

> *I particularly liked the students. I knew all the students' names and knew basically their abilities, and we had really outstanding students. I guess the best part was just knowing the students and knowing their families and where they came from and knowing about their lives. It was a school district where we knew the parents. Many of them were from farm families or worked locally for other farmers. Just being able to know the students and their parents [was the best part].*

Dr. Leo (personal communication, September 14, 2020) also mentioned helping students and educators:

> *For myself, the most enjoyable part of being an administrator was that of being able to help other educators grow in their personal beliefs about how they, too, could influence others around them to make the educational experience for children more relevant. I valued the skills and abilities of others and wanted to help them develop to their fullest capacity.*

We shouldn't be surprised by this, should we? That message resonates with me as a boomer. As I consult in schools, I spend around 170 days on the road each school year. I usually take 45 to 50 flights per year, and I'm in a lot of airports, shuttle buses, rental cars, and hotels. It's a hard, exhausting trek, but luckily, I get to spend my days in schools. When I become weary, I often remind myself, "It's about the students. What you are doing to help principals and teachers will help their students."

When I speak with teachers and school leaders of younger generations, they, too, get the most excited when they discuss their students. This is the magic thread of purpose and fulfillment that runs through generations of educators: It's an innate, altruistic desire to help young people to live better lives, to help them grow and to be happy. It will always be dominant. If five-year-old Theo, as a member of Gen Alpha, dedicates his life to education and is a teacher in the middle of the 21st century, then he probably will say the same thing. Regardless of what technology can do at that time, students will still need human interaction. Educators will play a vital, somewhat new role in the 2020s and beyond: *In a world increasingly shaped by artificial intelligence, teachers will show students the beauty of being human.*

> *This is the magic thread of purpose and fulfillment that runs through generations of educators: It's an innate, altruistic desire to help young people to live better lives, to help them grow and to be happy.*

FIGURE 2.5   Tips for Transitioning to 5-Gen Leadership

Tips for Transitioning to 5-Gen Leadership

9. Honor and build upon the work of previous generations of educators.

10. Recognize the themes that link the generations of school leaders: the love of working with students, the power of teachers, and the need to mentor the next generation of leaders.

11. Continue the work done before us to equalize opportunities for all ethnicities, genders, and lifestyles.

12. Understand the speed with which technology is reshaping our lives and education.

13. Know the characteristics of Gen Alpha and consider how to adjust teaching and learning to fit its needs.

14. Examine school culture to ensure it has the pillars needed to support Gen Alpha.

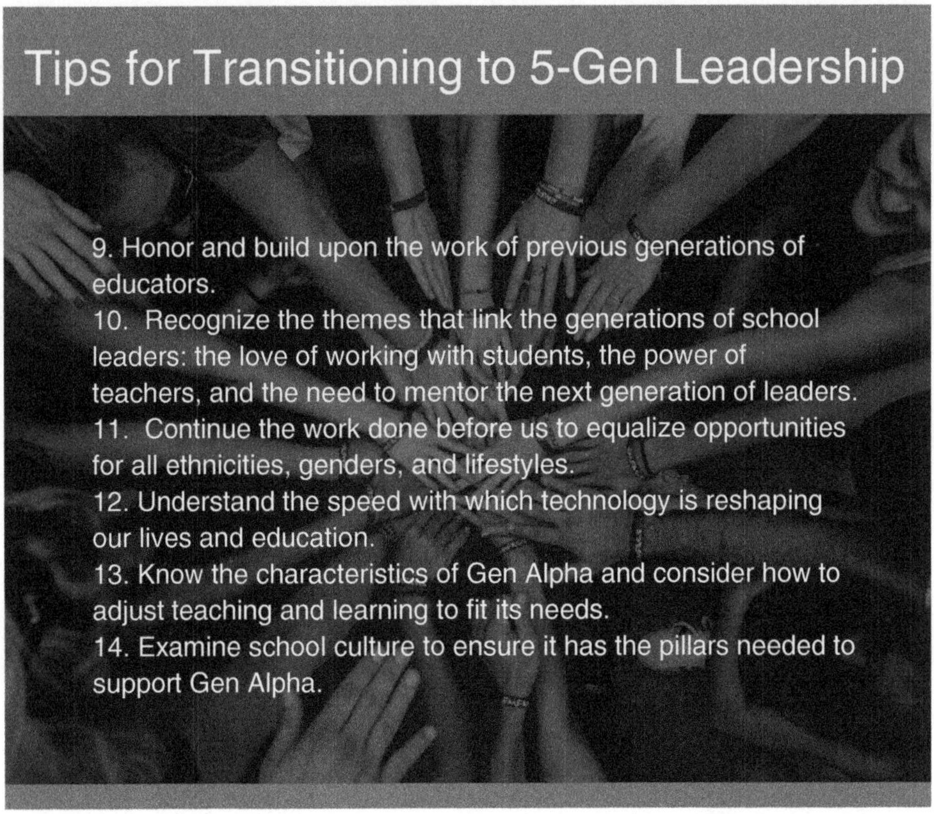

CHAPTER 3

Moving From Managing to Coaching

Key Points of This Chapter

- 5-Gen leaders must be coaches, not managers.

- Millennials and Gen Z teachers tend to be more stressed about their evaluations than boomers and Gen Xers.

- Millennials and Gen Z teachers want constant feedback.

- 5-Gen leaders must know and use the communication methods that work best for the different generations.

A few years ago, I made a decision that had far-reaching consequences on my daily life: I switched from using a PC to using a MacBook. In today's world, switching platforms is a big event. My laptop is a huge part of my life. I write, prepare my keynotes, make slides, and type all of my coaching notes on my computer. It's more than a computer—it's my digital doorway into my work and into much of my entertainment. If I don't have a good computer, I feel like our Gen Z and Gen Alpha students do when their phones are offline.

When I was in the Apple Store talking with the sales rep—a tech ninja millennial—I noticed he was called a "specialist," not a sales rep. Most, not all, of the specialists I saw were Gen Zers and millennials. The store manager happened to be walking by, and he introduced himself as the "team leader." The team leader, who was probably a Gen Xer, led the team of "specialists." I wondered what other terminology and phrases Apple used, so when I got home, I checked its website.

And I found an introduction taken from the millennial and Gen Z playbook.

> Do you love music? Photography? Fitness? Games? Video? Whatever your passion, bring it. Because sharing what you love through Apple products sparks others to pursue their own passions. And that's why

we're continuously reinventing the retail experience: to open up all kinds of potential for our customers—and you. . . . Whether you work up front or backstage, every day you'll have the chance to make a big difference—for your customers, your team, and yourself. (Apple, 2020, para. 1)

Music, fitness, games, and video. Helping others pursue passions. Reinventing the system. Helping "you" reinvent yourself. Making a big difference. Apple has realized something most businesses and school systems don't yet comprehend: The Gen Z and millennial employee needs to feel that they matter, that they are organic individuals and not just cogs in the corporate machine.

I wondered what the job description would have said 20 years ago for boomer and Gen X applicants. Perhaps something like this:

Wanted: Someone who knows how to help others use new technology. Good pay and benefits. Apply in the store between the hours of 9:00 and 5:00 on weekdays. Ask for the store manager.

As 5-Gen leaders create productive staffs, they need to make sure the millennial and Gen Z teachers feel almost as important as the customer. It's a good philosophy to have for the boomers and Gen Xers too; everyone wants to feel they matter.

It also made me think about the titles we use in schools in the 2020s. A "teacher" is a highly evolved specialist. The title of "teacher" is still a revered title in our society; there's no need to ponder a new moniker. But what about the leader, the "school administrator"? The word "administrator" conjures forth images of men sitting at a desk administrating: signing papers, issuing edicts, and being in control of all situations. In the 20th century, Silent Generation and boomer administrators administrated, but in the 21st century, the changing workforce is forcing them to evolve. Like the Apple Store manager, they must become team leaders. Being a collaborative school leader isn't a new concept; researchers have constantly stressed this idea (Anrig, 2015). However, when viewed through a multigenerational lens, the need to be a coach instead of a manager becomes even more imperative. Perhaps we should do away with the term "school principal" and replace it with "school leader."

> When viewed through a multigenerational lens, the need to be a coach instead of a manager becomes even more imperative.

I looked up the description Apple was using on its website to attract leaders:

As an Apple leader, you'll do more than manage employees. You'll help build diverse, highly collaborative teams that deliver the amazing customer experiences people expect from Apple. You'll lead through inspiration, using our culture of open, honest feedback to actively develop each team member's talent and skills. You'll also build relationships with the local community and its businesses, creating an atmosphere where all are welcome. (Apple, 2020, para. 5)

What if we rewrote this job description to make it fit school leadership?

As one of our school leaders, you'll do more than manage teachers. You'll help build diverse, highly collaborative teams that deliver the amazing educational experiences people expect from our district. You'll lead through inspiration, using our culture of open, honest feedback to actively develop each team member's talent and skills. You'll also build relationships with teachers, students, parents, and community members, creating an atmosphere where all stakeholders are welcome.

Isn't this what we're trying to do? But note that this job description uses the pronoun "you," as in "You'll help build . . ." and "You'll lead . . ."

Now consider the wording of job descriptions posted in the job vacancy section of school websites. The descriptions often begin with, "The administrator will . . ." do this and do that. It's all written in "legalese," that cold, boring, impersonal language that keeps people from being sued. I've written like that too. Like other school administrators, I can flip a switch in my brain and suddenly become a technical writer and use the language of the school machine. It's the language of "educationese," and it's meant to be professional, but it's so much less personal than "you'll." We are taught in ELA classes not to use "you" and to write in the third person in our formal writing, but it's a less formal world now, which brings us to the crux of the problem in switching leadership styles from managing to coaching: A struggle has begun between the professional and personal sides of who we are. It used to be clear what was expected of us as professionals, but as the line blurs, it becomes harder to know how to appeal to the different generations. Writing formal job descriptions would be fine for boomers and Gen Xers, but millennials and Gen Zers are looking for more passion. They're looking for "you'll."

This shift to a less formal leadership and writing style will benefit the majority of our teachers. The torch has been passed from the older generations to the younger ones; by 2017, millennials had become the largest part of the American workforce (Fry, 2020), and they and the Gen Zers make up the majority of the new hires in the American teaching force (Hodges, 2020).

The Challenge of Transitioning to a New Model

As 5-Gen leaders shift their leadership philosophy from management to leadership, boomers and Gen X leaders who were trained in the last century could find this shift challenging because it conflicts with the leadership model we were trained to use, the one most revered, in which the tough leader stands up and leads the masses through sheer force of will and tenacity. We grew up watching John Wayne movies where he led people by shouting and punching people (he was like an Avenger in a cowboy hat).

In my first teaching job in the 1980s, a boomer school leader told me, "Mark, all I care is that I have 51 percent of the people who support me. If the other 49 percent don't support me, then that's their problem." He was a successful leader, and he was revered by 51 percent of the community—but despised by the other 49 percent. He had such a strong personality that he could successfully command his supporters while ignoring his detractors; the slight majority empowered him while almost half the town detested him.

But that was in the 1980s before smartphones gave every detractor a camera and before social media gave every detractor a microphone. If 49 percent of the people are constantly posting and attacking a dictatorial, high-profile school leader today, it's extremely hard for that leader to be effective. Or to survive. The acrimonious complaints are just too loud and heard by too many people. A contemporary scenario would be to look at the leadership style of our last president, Donald Trump, who thought he could bend all people to his will. Look at the anger and hostility unleashed on both sides through social media. Can we imagine a school leader this controversial surviving today? It's interesting to note Trump was born in 1946, which is the first birth year of the boomer generation. He represents the oldest boomers. He, too, grew up watching John Wayne movies.

This doesn't mean team leadership is naturally easier for millennials and Gen Zers. I recently spoke with a fine principal I've known for many years. The principal is a Gen Xer, and she was having a conflict with a millennial assistant superintendent. When I dug a little deeper, I heard stories of how the assistant superintendent, who had been rapidly promoted without a deep reservoir of experience or leadership skills, would retreat to the ancient, "I am your boss, and you will do what I say!" mentality when challenged. In other words, when she became frightened by a subordinate or couldn't summon a good rejoinder when put into an uncomfortable situation, she would retreat to the administrative cave that bosses have used for centuries: the one where collaboration is abruptly cast to the side in favor of authoritarian rule. Leadership is hard for everyone; being young and in tune with apps and collaborative peers doesn't always translate into leadership success.

All 5-Gen leaders, from boomers to millennials, must understand how to move from being administrators to being team leaders. In other words, we must move from behind the principal's desk to sit in the chair beside the teachers. Now more than ever we must be their guide on the side. We must focus more on the "you."

Millennials, Gen Zers, and Gen Alphas: Handle With Care

How did "you" become the center of the 21st century leadership model? I found an answer when talking with a teacher.

During the COVID-19 closures, as I sat at home and watched the world grind to a halt, I tried to focus on completing positive daily tasks, such as reaching out to a few great teachers and leaders from my past to see how they were doing. When I asked a Gen X high school teacher who has spent over 20 years teaching what it was like teaching today's Gen Z students, he said this: "It used to be I could criticize my students, but these kids today are *so fragile*. They're like glass."

This is the second time we've come across the glass metaphor to describe today's students. We saw in Chapter 2 that Gen Alpha can be referred to as "Generation Glass" because its members will be interacting with so many screens in their lives, but this teacher has given us another reason to call them that: They're easily breakable. Before I proceed, I want to make a quick, perhaps redundant disclaimer: I am discussing characteristics that fit generations, but it *doesn't mean all of today's young people* have these characteristics. Not all young people are fragile; some are incredibly resilient. When I write about millennials and Gen Z, I know there are exceptions to the broad brush I am using to make my points.

But I've seen and heard enough in my coaching, and studied enough data, to realize today's younger people need a different, slightly softer leadership style than was used in the past. If we understand how our millennials, Gen Zers, and Gen Alphas became easily breakable as kids, we can understand more about how to lead them as adults. And millennial leaders can learn more of what they can do to reach across the generation gaps to lead boomers and Gen Xers.

This fragility begins with parenting.

My Silent Generation parents raised me in the 1960s and 1970s with a different mindset from the one used today. It's not that one style is necessarily better or worse; the styles are just different. All parents of all generations have loved their kids, but the relationships and expectations have shifted through the decades.

In my workshops, I tell the story of an adage my mother used to say to me, a quote that was not uncommon and is now associated with a different time, a different philosophy of raising kids. When she would become upset with something I said, she would sternly say to me, "Children should be seen and not heard!" I ask my workshop participants if any of them also heard this comment when they were growing up. Inevitably, it's my fellow boomers who raise their hands. It was a mantra from the Silent Generation parents for their precocious boomers who wouldn't stay silent—many of whom became so outspoken they would later rail against the establishment and burn their draft cards to avoid going to Vietnam.

Gen Z and Gen Alpha, on the other hand, have been raised in a much kinder, more participatory model. According to one marketing study,

- Millennial parents feel closer to their children than they think their boomer and Gen X parents were to them.

- Millennial parents are more afraid of disobeying their boomer and Gen X parents than Gen Z and Gen Alpha kids are afraid of disobeying their millennial parents.

- Millennial parents consider their Gen Z and Gen Alpha kids to be some of their best friends.

- Seventy-one percent of millennial parents seek the opinions of their Gen Z and Gen Alpha kids when making most purchases—and this number is higher for millennial parents outside the United States. (Gauthier, 2019)

In other words, our students today are being raised in families where the parents are closer to their kids, where the kids have less fear of disobeying them, where parents and kids are best friends, and where kids have more say in family decisions than in the past. Boomers and Xers were told to stay silent, but millennials and Zers were encouraged to speak up.

The millennials and some of these Zers who have grown up and joined our teaching force were raised in a model that put them at the center of the family circle, which helps explain why millennial and Gen Z teachers would want more interaction with authority figures. It also explains why they see themselves as being more equal to the authority figures and are less inclined to blindly adhere to their mandates.

The same can be said for our Gen Z and Gen Alpha students. A study in 2015 found millennial parents were much more likely to praise their children more than previous generations (Suglia, 2017). When I first began teaching in the 1980s, if a Gen X student was disrespectful to me or to some other teacher, most parents would quickly side with the teacher; however, when I last helped lead a middle school a few years ago, I found that while parents of Gen Z students were generally supportive, I found more parents who would quickly blame the teacher, me, or the school system for any problem encountered by their kids. Not all parents did this, but I noticed a significant increase.

A Pew Research study in 2016 found parents also wanted a new emphasis on skills: Millennial parents expect more from schools than have previous generations. There is a general consensus that while academics are still of primary importance in the classroom, students should also be learning practical and personal skills (McBirney, 2018).

Overprotective parenting, for lack of a widely accepted definition, describes a collection of behaviors by parents toward their children that work together in an attempt to prevent children from taking on any risks to their emotional or physical health. Sheltering, constant supervision and micromanagement, prevention of taking responsibility, excessive catering and overconsoling, controlling of the social sphere, and excessive caution are all identifiable behaviors that can be considered a part of the scheme of overprotective parenting. Many people will find most of these behaviors, if not all, to be very familiar simply because they have become more commonplace in today's dialogue and observable in our own personal lives. (Chae, 2019, para. 3)

Chae (2019) also points out that, according to studies, overprotective parenting can lead to risk aversion and an overdependency on the parent, as well as psychological disorders and a lack of coping mechanisms. And it can lead to chronic anxiety, which leads to problems when the young person has to face the realities, which are often harsh, they will find in the adult world.

This describes many of our Gen Z and Gen Alpha students today. Again, this describes many of our millennial and Gen Z teachers.

In our staffs, this means our boomers and Gen Xers grew up as *roamers*, and our millennials and Gen Zers grew up as *homers*. We'll find some wonderful millennial and Gen Z teachers who are huge risk-takers in the classroom, but if we encounter young teachers who are adverse to taking risks, it might be that they are intimidated by our testing system or by the normal travails of learning how to teach, just as their predecessors before them had to learn the tricks of the teaching trade—or it might be because they grew up in a model that minimized risk-taking.

Conversely, when boomer and Gen X administrators and teachers faced adversity as kids, they were told to "suck it up and get back out there." This John Wayne–like philosophy manifests itself in some schools today when boomers and Gen Xers encounter struggling young teachers and think, "You're out of college now. You have a job. What's wrong with you? Be quiet and just do it." But it might not be that easy for Gen Z and millennials, especially if the overprotected lifestyle extended all the way into their university lives.

As an example of the extended reach of today's parents and the power of technology to reshape parenting, it's not uncommon for parents to have tracking apps on their college student's phone so that the parents can monitor and keep track of their child's location for safety reasons—and to know if their child is going to class, where the child is hanging out, and how late the child is staying out. Not all parents do this; it's controversial. Some parents shun the apps because they want to respect their child's privacy (Cianci, 2018), and some mental health experts fear it could prevent young adults from being free to explore more of their college world (Greenthal, 2021).

Either way, some of our youngest teachers are coming to us from a university lifestyle boomers and Gen Xers could never imagine. When boomers and Gen Xers packed their footlockers and headed off to university, they were free from the family nest; today's college students might be partying in the dorm or down at the local bar, but their iPhones are still tethered to the parental nest.

I wonder how many of our Gen Z teachers still have the tracking apps active when they come to our schools for interviews? When I went to my first interview in the early 1980s, my parents were waiting for a phone call so they could hear all about it; parents today still want to hear all about it—but they can see in real time when their child is approaching the school, is inside the school, and leaves the school.

As school leaders, we have high expectations for all teachers, and there's always been a steep learning curve for first-year teachers, but today's newbies might carry some new type of growth experiences in their backgrounds that they need to overcome to be independent professionals.

We saw earlier that millennial teachers are leaving the profession in record numbers. Will Gen Zers also leave? Could it be some of them are leaving because they're broken? Some of our breakable students have now become our young, breakable teachers. As we help struggling first-year teachers, it's no longer just a question of them having the best practices; it's also about helping a few of them to leave part of their sheltered past in the rearview mirror and giving them the confidence to walk into a new future.

Coaching Into Grit and Professionalism

TriNet is a firm that specializes in human resource services for the private sector. It conducted a survey that targeted millennial professionals and how they feel about job evaluations, which could help 5-Gen leaders apply its findings to our young professionals in education:

- A good majority—62 percent—of millennials have felt "blindsided" by performance reviews.

- Almost half say that performance reviews leave them feeling they can't do anything right.

- Over half said they lack confidence in their supervisor to give them accurate feedback. (TriNet, 2015)

Consider how this evaluation information fits with what we're seeing about millennial and Gen Z childhoods and how this could play out in a school setting: As central parts of their family units, millennial and Gen Z teachers had constant communication and feedback; however, when they don't have this communication and feedback in their jobs, and then they receive average or below-average ratings, they feel isolated and feel like failures. They often express their disappointment to their peers (with whom they are in constant communication) and look for a new job where they can feel more accepted. Because of the lack of connection, communication, and input with their evaluator, they lack faith in the evaluator to help them.

This is not to say this scenario plays out for all young teachers. Some of them will adjust and grow quickly. Some young teachers approach their evaluations in the same way boomers and Gen X teachers approach theirs, which is usually with a lower stress level. Also, the fault might not lie with the young teacher; it might be lie with the principal. Maybe the teachers feel isolated because the principal is not a good communicator or is overwhelmed. We've all seen our share of weak leaders, but when they lead a school today, the negative results can become magnified with younger staff members who need even more dialogue, clarity, and competence than their predecessors.

There's still something to be said for encouraging all teachers to work through adversity. Angela Duckworth, a psychologist and the author of the best-selling book *Grit*, believes millennials are lacking the grit found in older generations because the millennials were raised differently, and they just haven't had the life experiences to acquire it. To be an educator, especially today, is to accept one of the toughest jobs in the world; grit is a necessity (Duckworth, 2016).

Now let's take this information about millennial evaluations and think of ways 5-Gen leaders can use it to coach millennial and Gen Z teachers. Let's focus on creating ongoing feedback and dialogue, setting professional expectations, and providing specific, clear feedback (see Figure 3.1).

Are these steps much different from what we would use with today's boomer and Gen X teachers, who really aren't used to being "coached" but are more likely to have been told explicitly what to do and how to do it? Not really. Everyone is better with ongoing, clear feedback, and every teacher deserves specific proof of how an evaluation score is tabulated.

However, one area deserves more emphasis than in the past: professional behavior. The world used to be a place where informal behavior happened in personal lives, and formal behavior occurred in professional lives. All generations, especially millennials and Gen Zers who grew up in the age of Starbucks and Panera, want a more casual work environment, but what does that mean when generations have varying views of what it means to be a professional?

One human resources consultant quoted an office manager who said this about millennial professionals:

> They are intelligent, capable, and technically savvy . . . but they show up not knowing how to behave and engage professionally in the workplace. They have to be told not to curse when speaking to clients, that ripped jeans are inappropriate work attire, and that emails need to be written in complete sentences. (Doss, 2017, para. 2)

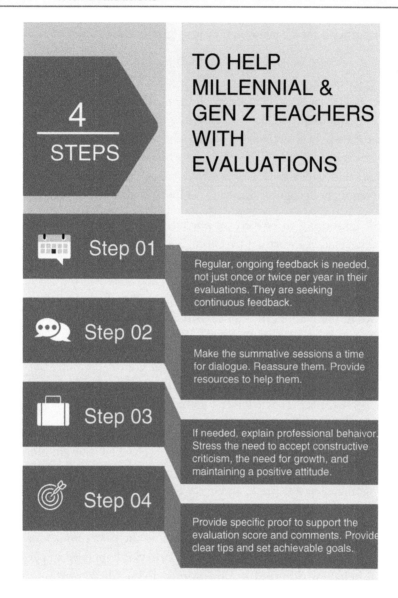

The first point in Figure 3.2, **professional dress,** is not just an education issue; it's a global workplace issue. More people everywhere in all fields want to dress more comfortably, but what does that mean? Where's the line between professional and sloppy? It's hard to define in an era of disparate generational views. One study showed that 38 percent of millennial professionals have been asked by a manager to dress more professionally because they were dressing too casually (Bayern, 2019). More than ever, school administrators need to be proactive in discussing appropriate dress to prevent awkward conversations in the future.

FIGURE 3.2 5-Gen Leadership Tips

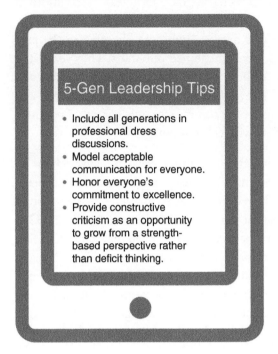

5-Gen Leadership Tips

- Include all generations in professional dress discussions.
- Model acceptable communication for everyone.
- Honor everyone's commitment to excellence.
- Provide constructive criticism as an opportunity to grow from a strength-based perspective rather than deficit thinking.

Some of the areas in the business world that receive the most attention in dress codes revolve around wearing clothing that is too casual, reveals too much skin, and is too wrinkled. Wearing blue jeans can be an issue, and some businesses discourage clothing that reveals too many tattoos (RMI, 2015). But how much is too much? What a boomer considers to be too much might fall well within the norms of a Gen Z employee, especially when we consider that Gen Z is the generation that is the most diverse and the most inclusive of all generations.

We often find teacher dress code issues in schools revolving around the same issues as in the business world. When working with today's teacher force, especially with the number of millennials and Gen Zers in the ranks, dress code edicts coming from the principal or superintendent will not be well received; there must be dialogue between the leaders and the teachers, an understanding of the need to have professional dress, examples provided of professional and unprofessional dress, and a willingness to compromise. I've seen this done in some schools: Teachers and administrators agree to have "Blue Jean Fridays," or teachers can start the week wearing t-shirts while showing school spirit with "Spirit Shirt Mondays" during which they wear t-shirts in the school colors and with school logos. There has been a growing acceptance that jeans, shorts, hoodies, and flip-flops can be worn daily by teachers and even some administrators. Comfort is essential in today's workplaces, including schools. One of the first points I tell new administrators today is "Get rid of the dress shoes. Find some comfortable walking shoes because you'll be on your feet all day!" But dress is still a contentious topic: It has reached a point that it's often defined in teacher union contracts. Most educators of all generations recognize that clothing won't improve teaching, but they need to reach a consensus about what is accepted so it's clearly understood by all generations.

It's especially important when school leaders look at professional dress to reimagine the committee process. In most situations, the leaders rely up on the input of a committee of teachers who represent the entire group of teachers. As mentioned in

Chapter 1, these groups often consist of experienced teachers who have risen through experience to become department chairs, grade-level leaders, or informal leaders in the school; this model is woefully outdated when dealing with teacher dress codes. Think of how teacher dress has become more liberated in the past 10 to 15 years as the millennials and Gen Zers joined our staffs. They've led the way in moving to more casual dress, so they *must* be included in the front lines of the conversations. They need to see a few of their peers on the committee, and their ideas need to help form the policy. If the committees only consist of boomers and Xers, the millennials and Gen Zers will feel shut out.

While conflict around **communication** between staff members has always been an issue, the advent of social media and text messaging has changed the way all generations communicate. Boomers and Xers have been immersed in the professional culture long enough to have a grasp of professional communication, but millennials and Gen Zers who grew up posting and texting might need to be reminded that communication in the workplace is not the same as their communication in their personal lives. Actually, this would be a good reminder for all generations today, but 5-Gen leaders in particular need to prioritize discussing the need to write in complete sentences, to be tactful, and to use periods and other traditional conventions in written messages (Inman, 2020).

Since the data indicate the millennials and Gen Z teachers have grown up in a more sheltered environment, they will need constant encouragement to take risks in the classroom and to survive the challenges of 21st century teaching; they will need a strong sense of **commitment**. Five-Gen leaders should remind them that their boomer and Gen X peers also faced challenges and that feeling overwhelmed and insecure at times is a normal part of teaching, especially in the first years of a career. Now, more than ever, 5-Gen leaders need to provide constant support through dialogue and coaching to help young teachers grow their self-confidence, which brings us to the final point: the need to accept **constructive criticism**. The only way millennial and Gen Z teachers, who have spent much of their life not receiving the level of parental criticism received by previous generations, will accept criticism from a school leader is through the establishment of strong relationships, reminders of the need to constantly improve through various critiquing, and constant dialogue.

"Dialogue"—there's that word again. It's the new secret sauce of leadership in the 2020s.

Rethinking Evaluations

1. I've sent feedback to the principal who shared it with teachers.

2. I've emailed teachers.

3. I've spoken to teachers that day during their conference period.

4. I've spoken to teachers *immediately after the observation* while another teacher, an aide, or a substitute teacher covered the class.

And here's what I've found: Millennial and Gen Z teachers want the last option mentioned—they want real-time, immediate feedback. They would prefer to get the feedback in minutes, not hours or days after their observation. I've also seen boomer and Gen X teachers who prefer this method; however, I sense they are *eager* to hear my points because they want to be better teachers and because they are fearful they will hear negative feedback. They want to know they are not in trouble with the administration.

The younger teachers are also nervous, but they *need* to hear my points; they are genuinely excited to speak with me so their actions can be affirmed. They have more of a need to be reassured that they are being successful. Part of this is being a professional who has a new job, but I sense a huge part of it is their desire to receive praise as they did in their childhood.

This brings us to a difficult point: It's extremely hard for today's overly burdened school administrators to meet with teachers in the minutes after an observation. It's often hard enough just to find time to observe the teachers; providing prompt feedback is an even bigger obstacle. Perhaps we've reached a point in our school development, as the disruptions continue to grow and campus administrators have more items added to their daily routines, that more full-time evaluators be hired whose main, or perhaps only, job is to evaluate and coach teachers. Another solution is this: Just try to find one to three minutes during the day of the observation to give some quick comments to the teachers so they can have an idea of the content of the formal conversation coming later. This can be done in person, in email, or even in a text. This quick note can be something as simple as, "Hey, Alex, I enjoyed being in your class today. You did a great job with your rigor and technology usage. Let's talk tomorrow during your conference period so I can share other ideas and get your input!"

As evaluators, we have to be more ready than ever to defend the **content** of our evaluations and the scores. One day I was coaching in a high school, and it was my second trip into the school. The assistant principal with whom I was working got an email from one of the teachers I had seen on my previous visit and to whom I had given feedback via email. The teacher heard I had returned to campus and was asking the assistant principal if she could have a quick conversation with me. I didn't know what she wanted, but I was happy to chat. At the end of the day, the teacher was able to sit down with me, and she pulled a copy of the evaluation rubric out of her folder, along with the scores I had given her: She wanted clarification on why I had marked her down in one of the categories. She was in her second year of teaching, and probably in Gen Z. Luckily, I give every score and comment with the premise that I might have to defend it, so I was ready; however, it had been a few months since I had been in the school, so I had to dig into my memory to remember specifically what had transpired in the lesson. As I looked over the comments I had given her, the lesson content came back to me. I pointed to a phrase in the rubric, read it aloud to her, and asked, "Did you do this in your lesson?" She paused for a moment, and then she said she thought she had done it. I clarified the phrase: "It says 'all students will have the opportunity to respond.' Did *all* of your students have an opportunity to respond?" She paused again and said, "No." I assured her that's why she had received a slightly lower score, and I gave her some examples of ways she could have solicited responses from all of her students.

As a young boomer teacher, I would never have had the confidence, or the need, to confront a visiting instructional coach whose observation had no impact on my official performance rating or job security. Yet the assistant principal had told me this particular teacher had been insistent on speaking with me. I admired the teacher's courage and tenacity. She was bright, articulate, and a fine young teacher. But she struck me as the type of person who had always been successful in most, if not all, of her academic studies; she had always been a star and wasn't used to being told she had to improve. It could be she happened to have a personality that can be found in any generation that drove her to confront what she thought had been an incorrect score—or it could be she was showing a Gen Z characteristic and questioning my ability to give her accurate feedback. While evaluation scores have to be based on the evaluator's ability to accurately assess what is happening in the classroom, generational views could now be coming into play. The boomers and Gen Xers might accept evaluation scores more readily because of the experience and credentials of the evaluator, but the millennials and Gen Zers need to first be able to trust the administrator.

Moving to a coaching model doesn't mean we have to abandon all of the traditional best practices of teacher evaluations. Actually, some of them can still help us. For example, Grant Wiggins (2012) has written that evaluators need to share feedback that is understood and believed, and they need to share achievable goals. If millennial and Gen Z teachers are less trusting of their supervisors, then evaluators need to be sure they can support the points they're making. They need to be able to point to specific evidence from the lesson to assure the teacher the feedback is correct. A number of video options are also available today with which teachers can video themselves and critique their own performance. It's always good to help teachers set goals to be achieved in the long term, but it's become increasingly important that younger teachers also be given short-term goals. If they have a fragile ego, they need to be given goals they can achieve in the near future so they can see progress sooner rather than just later.

A part of good leadership today is to coach everyone, regardless of their generation.

Providing timely and accurate feedback isn't just a trait to use with millennials and Gen Z teachers; they should be used with boomer and Gen X teachers as well. However, the expected **tone** of the conversations varies between what younger and older teachers expect. As mentioned, younger teachers want to be coached; older teachers are more used to being told what to do. A part of good leadership today is to coach everyone, regardless of their generation. The days of the imperious principal sitting behind the desk while he or she dispenses evaluation scores to teachers have been disappearing, and they now need to be abolished.

One successful school leader who has experienced some of these leadership challenges is Kristy Venne, an administrator in Dublin City Schools in Dublin, Ohio. She has been a teacher, dean of students, assistant principal, and principal. She currently is the district's K–12 career education coordinator. When asked what she has noticed about evaluating and coaching teachers of various generations, she offered her insights.

Note the themes of Venne's words: a need for rapid feedback, trust, and affirmation for new teachers; a needed adjustment for the older teachers who aren't used to receiving constructive feedback; and a reluctance by some (but not all) of the older to teachers to shift their mindsets.

As a building administrator assigned to formally evaluate a few dozen teachers biannually, I have noticed similarities in expectations among teachers of similar age groups. My personal coaching style tends to fit millennial and Gen Z teachers well and sometimes leaves older teachers caught off guard. Younger teachers require my feedback as quickly as possible and seek affirmation and celebration. Once they know I believe in them, they are then able to discuss options I provide for their learning and growth. In fact, they want much more attention on a regular basis with frequent visits and involvement with their classrooms as compared to their experienced peers. Older teachers, when empowered by this coaching model that is new to them, are sometimes confused at first. Often, they have experienced years of traditional evaluations, being passed between many evaluators, receiving high marks, and not being provided constructive feedback. Most end up appreciating and embracing the new coaching approach, but a few of the more senior teachers I have worked with do not come around before soon retiring.

(K. Venne, personal communication, March 15, 2021)

New Channels for Communication

Consider how quickly the world has changed. I remember my first personal email address was through my America Online account, and when I opened my inbox if I had a new email, a recording in the program would excitedly exclaim, "You've got mail!" It's hard to believe we were so innocent as to be excited about getting email. Now I know how my grandparents, who were both born before we started giving names to generations, felt the first time they heard their telephone ring.

But email didn't jump immediately into our workplace. I first began working as an assistant principal in the mid-1990s, before email began to rule our lives. The way I and other administrators communicated with the staff as a whole was to type a memo, make copies on the copier in the workroom, and then get some student office aides to help us stuff a copy into each of the teacher mailboxes. It was a slower world. When I was a teacher, my principal tried to speed it up. He had a rule: Teachers had to check their mailbox in the staff workroom not once, but *twice* each day so they wouldn't miss any time-sensitive memos or handwritten notes from the receptionist about phone calls she had taken from parents, doctors, or the babysitter.

By the early 2000s, email had made its jump into school communication, but not all teachers had embraced it. I remember a conversation I had with one of our technology specialists. He explained to me in 2001 that *every* teacher had been assigned his or her own school email address. It was a big deal. "So how do we get people to use it?" I asked the technology specialist. He thought for a moment and said, "Start sending them some important information they can *only* get in email. They'll have to log in to get the information."

It was great advice.

I did the same thing with Twitter 14 years later. Twitter was already established, and some of the best teaching ideas were being shared there. I wanted more of my staff using it. "Follow me on Twitter," I told them. "It's the first place I'll announce school closures because of icy roads." Teachers who had been reluctant to use Twitter didn't want to miss the big news about snow days. They were suddenly following me and getting used to Twitter.

The lessons for 5-Gen leaders that can still be used today are these:

- Embrace different ways of communicating.

- Help people understand the new channels that will continue to work their way into our lives.

According to one global survey of private-sector employees in 2018 by a U.S. recruitment firm, communication is where generational differences are most apparent. Thirty-eight percent of workers said interacting with colleagues is difficult, often because generations might prefer different ways to interact (Murray, 2020), so 5-Gen leaders can help staffs avoid communication breakdowns with the tips found in Figure 3.3.

> Communication is where generational differences are most apparent.

Here is one of the most important tips: Everyone should accept the need to teach others and to be taught by others (Rivers, 2019). One of the enduring beliefs of educators is that all stakeholders have something to offer; this is especially beneficial in four generations of staff members.

FIGURE 3.3   Communicating Over the Generation Gaps

Communicating Over the Generation Gaps

Give teachers options in how they communicate, such as through email, video chatting, texting, or phone calls.

Remind people that settling disagreements is best done face to face, not through email or texting.

Stress that everyone needs to to understand the different channels so they can all use them.

Different generations need to know the different perspectives on smartphones. Older teachers might not look at them in meetings, but younger teachers might check them constantly. The older teachers might find this annoying, while the younger teachers are just doing what they've always done during most of their lives.

Everyone needs to know the generational perspectives when setting differences. Older teachers are driven more by mission and loyal, but younger generations are driven more by individual praise and guidance.

Working space, especially in large schools can be a barrier to face to face communication. Try to provide common spaces where teachers can meet and mingle.

Relationships and face to face communication still matter. All educators need to be known as individuals by their leaders and peers.

Sources:
• Murray: *The Other 5G: Learning to Lead the Multigenerational Workforce*
• Rivers: *8 Tips to Improve Communication Between Generations in the Workplace*

Every generation has something to offer, and every generation can teach each other generations. This is called reverse mentoring (and it will be covered more deeply in Chapter 5). Younger teachers might be more technology savvy, but older teachers have more years of experience in working with all kinds of students and parents. Boomer and Gen X teachers can be calming influences in difficult times, and millennial and Gen Z teachers can bring fresh energy and perspectives to old initiatives. When establishing work groups, 5-Gen leaders should look at the generations on the team to ensure all are represented. They can help each other. Remind them to *coach* each other. This is where teachers have a solid advantage over their peers in the business world; teachers know how to coach every day.

While 5-Gen leaders have to understand differences in generations, they can't forget the generation commonalities among teachers:

- Teachers of all ages want to connect.

- Teachers of all ages want to be on the same page.

- Teachers of all ages want to be friends and good teammates.

- Teachers of all ages want happy, fulfilling careers.

And it's easier for me to help them all, regardless of their generation, on another commonality: Teachers want to be better teachers so they can help students. Many teachers today, especially the younger ones, want to be coached to greatness.

FIGURE 3.4   Tips for Transitioning to 5-Gen Leadership

Tips for Transitioning to 5-Gen Leadership

15. Be a coach, not a manager.
16. Understand how new parenting models require more attention to be given to Millennial and Gen Z teachers.
17. Remember how stressed younger teachers get over their evaluations.
18. Rethink evaluations: give faster feedback, create dialogue, be specific and clear of what is expected.
19. Stress professionalism to all generations.
20. Help staffs work through communication issues that are caused by generation gaps.

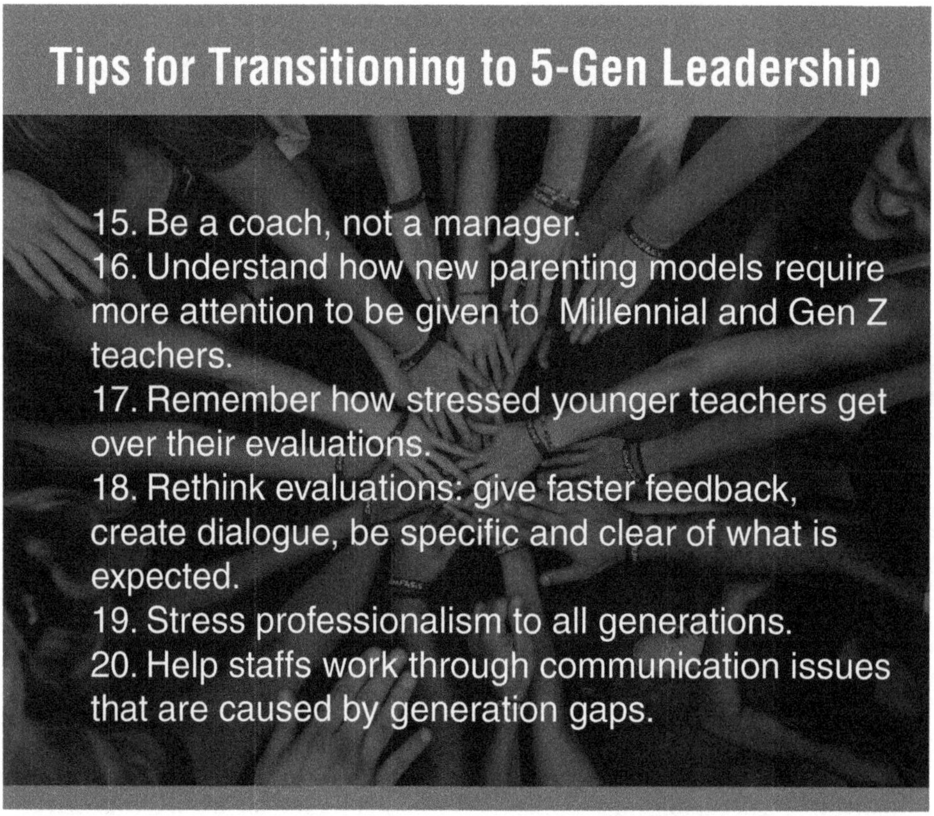

CHAPTER 4

Teaching Distracted Generations

Key Points of This Chapter

- All generations of teachers, not just young ones, are distracted learners today.

- Our Gen Z and Gen Alpha students are also distracted.

- The four generations have their generation gaps, but the four generations also have similarities that have turned them into one new type of audience.

- We need to reimagine our PD and teaching to make them fit the learning styles of this new type of audience.

We've been looking at the disparities in the generations, but we need to recognize another new wrinkle in leading today's staffs: In some ways, all of our teachers, from our boomers to our Gen Zers, are merging into a new type of audience. A distracted one. You might say we are all sharing one brain today.

Let me explain.

In the early 1990s, before technology began to rewire my brain, I taught high school English. I spent my days with Shakespeare and Hemingway. I was a 20th century teacher whose students used note cards and wrote all their papers by hand. My school had just gotten its first computer lab, and I remember sitting down at my first keyboard and typing a sentence in green font on a black background. And then I erased it with the touch of a button and typed another sentence, a longer one. "What . . . is . . . this?" I asked, stunned by my first taste of the digital future.

"It's a system called DOS," the computer science teacher said, referring to that now-defunct operating system that introduced word processing to the masses before it was swept aside by that world changer we call Windows.

I was in DOS heaven. I walked down the hall to my principal's office and said, "I need computers in my classroom for my students. How can we do that?"

"That lab with 30 computers cost over $40,000," he answered, chuckling at my naiveté. "I agree with you, but it'll be a long time until you see computers like that in your classroom."

He was a pragmatist; I was a dreamer.

It has, indeed, been a long journey, but two decades later, the advent of Chromebooks and tablets have made my technology fantasy a reality. Technology availability, and capability, have reached the point that I now say the history of teaching can be divided into two categories: BC and AC—the time *before computers* were first used in schools and the time *after computers* were first used in schools.

But looking back at that momentous day over 25 years ago, I see now it was the beginning of another type of journey, one started in my brain that continues today. That first taste of digital ecstasy started to change how I view the world and how I want to learn. My brain is different today than it was in the early 1990s. DOS was my gateway software.

Our Evolving Brains

The idea that technology is rewiring our brains is not new. It's been debated for over two decades. As educators, we know the power of plasticity, the ability of the brain to rebuild itself and to become stronger. A researcher recently wrote about the physical rewiring of the brain:

> Our brains are truly extraordinary; unlike computers, which are built to certain specifications and receive software updates periodically, our brains can actually receive hardware updates in addition to software updates. Different pathways form and fall dormant, are created and are discarded, according to our experiences. (Ackerman, 2020, para. 8)

Many researchers now think those interactions with computers are changing our adult brain structure (Horvath, 2015), but they're also changing kids' brains. Dr. David Eagleman, a neuroscientist at Stanford who has studied brain development and has been featured on PBS in *The Brain With David Eagleman*, stresses this fundamental fact for educators about today's Gen Z and Gen Alpha students:

> The No. 1 thing they need to know is that kids' brains are physically different from the brains of kids a generation ago because of the way they're taking in information—because of this fast-paced digital intake, which is different from the way a lot of people here grew up. We were reading textbooks in black and white. (Noonoo, 2018, para. 6)

Even most of the boomer teachers, the ones farthest away from the digital revolution, get it: Kids are different today. However, I do encounter one or two boomers every now and then who will tell me, "That's malarkey! Kids are kids. They're the same now as they were 20 and 30 years ago!" Some of these teachers probably pray the internet will one day crash forever (but only in schools) and 20th century chalkboards will be reinstalled in their classrooms.

"Yes," I respond, "in some ways kids are the same: They need nurturing, guidance, and an education. But they've grown up with the internet and started playing games on their iPads when they were two years old. For their brains, the internet is what's always been normal. For the rest of us, it's the new normal."

The data show us the amount of screen time being grabbed by our young people, over 50 percent of whom own a smartphone by age 11 (Jacobo, 2019). A report in 2019 showed American teenagers spent seven hours online each day, and the number jumped to almost 10 hours per day when online books and music were factored into the data—and these were hours outside of school and before the COVID closures of 2020. This means if middle school and high school students are in school for seven hours each day, and then spend another 7 to 10 hours interacting with devices, they are spending up to *17 hours* of each 24-hour school day in school, online, or sleeping. A third of each day is spent staring into devices. It's not much better with tweens, the students between the ages of 8 and 12, who spend almost five hours online each day. According to the American Academy of Pediatrics, tweens should be getting 9 to 12 hours of sleep, and teenagers should be getting 8 to 10 hours of sleep each day (Jenco, 2020). Most young people today don't get enough sleep, and it's partly because of the time spent online. Sleep deprivation in young people can lead to "increased moodiness, trouble staying awake in school, drowsiness while driving, disinterest in activities that used to introduce them, depression-like symptoms" (Campbell, 2019). Experienced teachers today tell me today's kids are more reluctant to read, do their work in class, and pay attention.

Perhaps it's because they are thinking of what they are missing online. But I have to ask, "Is the same thing happening with all of our generations in the teaching staffs?"

Distracted Students, Distracted Teachers

In 2015, Microsoft released data showing that the average attention span for adults had dropped to eight seconds, which is down from 12 seconds in 2000 (McSpadden, 2015). It's not that people can't pay attention; it's just that if they don't find you interesting in the first eight seconds, then they are start dreaming of something else they want to do.

A decade ago, Nicholas Carr, in his 2011 Pulitzer Prize–nominated book *The Shallows: What the Internet Is Doing to Our Brains,* chronicled the overall effect of interaction with technology, including how it's shortening our attention span. He blamed Google:

> "Every click we make on the Web marks a break in our concentration, a bottom-up disruption of our attention—and it's in Google's economic interest to make sure we click as often as possible," he writes. "Google is, quite literally, in the business of distraction." (Snyder, 2010, para. 6)

I don't know the length of the attention span for students, but it can't be much better. Perhaps it's worse because they have spent their brain-formative years locked into a screen. One of the topics I discuss in my trainings with teachers is relevance: More than ever, today's teachers of all generations need to know what is relevant for their Gen Z and Gen Alpha students. Or else our students won't find us relevant, and their minds will wander off into the cybersphere.

To introduce relevancy, I often have the workshop participants do a Mentimeter word cloud. Mentimeter is an online tool that allows teachers and students to do some amazingly cool things, from answering open-ended questioning to making word clouds to online voting. In this exercise, I have the teachers submit information that goes into a word cloud; the more times a word is entered, the bigger it shows up in the word cloud. The question I ask is "Which three adjectives would you use to describe your students?" The teachers use a code to get to the site, they submit their answers, and then wait for me to hit the "show screen" button so we can all see the results. I often keep the results hidden as teachers enter their choices; that way they won't be influenced by their peers as they enter their own choices. I first did this exercise several years ago at a high school in Southern California, and here's the resulting word cloud (see Figure 4.1).

"Distracted" was the word entered the most times by the 19 teachers. I went back to the same district a few weeks later, but to a different school. I did the same

FIGURE 4.1   Distracted Word Cloud, Los Angeles, May 2018

exercise to see which words would pop up; I did *not* show them the word cloud from their peers a few weeks earlier. Here is their word cloud (Figure 4.2).

Distracted. "Okay," I thought, "this is high school. I know high school students can be challenging to teach in May. Perhaps that's why the students are distracted." These were students in a school with high poverty and a high percentage of English learners.

But a month later, I did some training at a high school in a suburb of Houston, one with a very low poverty rate and few English learners. Here's what I got (see Figure 4.3).

Distracted. *Again.* And the school year was over. It was no longer May. All the participants had had a few weeks off to decompress before they participated in this

FIGURE 4.2   Distracted Word Cloud 2, Los Angeles, May 2018

FIGURE 4.3   Distracted Word Cloud 3, Texas, June 2018

training. Their "distracted" description wasn't a May product; it was description of how they saw their students throughout the year.

A month later, I worked with a group of 25 PreK–12 educators in New York, in an area where they said their students' economic status ranged from "impoverished to *Lifestyles of the Rich and Famous.*" Do you want to guess what their word cloud said (see Figure 4.4)?

Distracted. *Yet again.* This time at the PreK–12 level in another part of the country. Our students were distracted from LA to Houston to New York. Coast to coast distraction.

I still do this exercise, and I could show more examples with similar results. I want to stress I don't always get "distracted" as the largest descriptor. Sometimes, I see "enthusiastic" or "creative." Here's an example from a New York City elementary school with an extremely positive culture (Figure 4.5).

FIGURE 4.4   Distracted Word Cloud 4, Long Island, July 2018

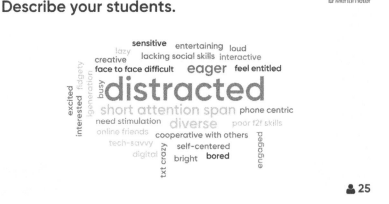

FIGURE 4.5   Curious Word Cloud, New York City, August 2018

However, "distracted" is the most frequently shared response when I do the exercise. I've noticed it usually happens when the audience is made up of secondary teachers, especially high school teachers.

Something's going on here with our students; they are distracted, and again, very experienced teachers are telling me it's harder to hold their students' attention than it used to be. This is something to remember as we help our teachers find engaging content. I wonder, "Are students becoming more distracted as they get older and become more independent and spend more time with their personal technology?"

But this idea is also what we have to remember as we train our four generations of teachers. They, too, are distracted. They, too, are all interacting with technology. Look at how the use of smartphones has grown and how they have taken on central roles in our lives. The first iPhone was introduced in 2007; now 81 percent of adult Americans own smartphones (O'Dea, 2020), and 96 percent of adult Americans have a cell phone of some type. Almost half of all Americans check their smartphones before they get out of bed each morning (Keating, 2020). It used to be we'd wake up thinking about making a fresh start to the day. Now, we wake up to see how many "likes" we got on last night's social media posting or what we missed in other parts of the world as our brains took their brief cyber sabbaticals. And it continues throughout the day. Americans check their smartphone 96 times each day (Asurion, 2019). In 2019, American adults spent three-and-a-half hours each day on the mobile internet, and that number is expected to increase to four-and-a-half hours by 2021 (Molla, 2020).

We are so concerned about this addiction to smartphones we can buy Light Phones that don't have texting or app features, or we can check into some luxury hotels that offer digital detox packages. We can even join a digital Sabbath movement that encourages people to ditch digital technology one day each week (Roose, 2019).

This cell phone interaction of the last decade—along with screen time on tablets, computers, and other devices—has given people individual choices in which movies they watch, the music to which they listen, the news sites they read, and the social media platforms they use to keep up with their friends. They also can choose the amount of time they spend in each site and where they do it.

Here's an important note for 5-Gen leaders: This is not just the young teachers. This addiction crosses generational lines.

In one of my PD sessions, I was talking with teachers about our need to be connected to our smartphones and how lost we feel when we're offline. "How did it feel that last time you got to work and forgot your phone at home and spent a whole day without it?" I asked.

"I don't know," a middle-aged teacher said. "The last time I forgot it I turned around and went home and got it!"

The other teachers laughed. Many of them nodded their heads in approval.

"Were you late to work?" I asked the teacher.

She smiled. "Just a few minutes late. No problem!" There was even more laughter.

This story has several lessons. This teacher was a baby boomer, not a millennial. When we think of digital addictions, we tend to first think of millennials and Gen Zers. While these two young groups have lived with technology more than other groups, we have to remember that smartphones and the internet have crept into the lifestyles of people of all ages. For older educators like me, the smartphones first were gimmicky novelties that made us laugh and "ooh and aah" over all the things it could do. But those frequent searches for restaurant menus and our need for Google maps has allowed smartphones to move front and center into our daily lives—to the point that we are willing to be late to school to avoid the discomfort of not having that phone in our hands throughout the day. Even some members of America's oldest age group, the Silent Generation, have jumped the digital fence. Great-Grandma has an iPhone and a Facebook account, and she's not giving them up.

Clues in the News

Digital waves have washed over all the generations. And it's not just our cell phones that are changing us. Besides blaming our smartphones, 5-Gen leaders can find clues of what's changed their audience and what they can do to improve teacher training in a most unusual place: the cable news networks. The networks have analyzed the distracted digital masses—and have adjusted their presentations to try to hold their attention.

We can start with Walter Cronkite.

For younger readers who don't know of Walter Cronkite, he served for decades as the anchor of the *CBS Evening News* and was an icon of American society. A poll in 1972 showed he was the Most Trusted Man in America. Members of the Silent Generation and the boomers came home each evening from their jobs in the factories and offices and turned on their pre-cable television sets so Walter, as he was called by the masses—as if referring to their favorite uncle, would tell them what was happening in the world. He sat behind a desk on a bare set, a lone face looking seriously into the camera, reading reports about Vietnam, Watergate, and a world when the internet and social media could only be imagined by a handful of futurists and dreamers.

While he told us of the complicated stories of the time, it was simpler, digital world. Notice in the shot of Walter Cronkite (see Figure 4.6), we see three items: him, a screen in the background, and parts of some decoration in the background. There wasn't much to see. He was the focus.

Compare that with what we see today on cable news programs today from CNN, Fox News, MSNBC, or HLN. The news programming has become an arms race of color, movement, and sound. Each station wants to outperform the other ones, which means they bombard our senses to keep us watching. Figure 4.7 shows a shot of a CNN newscast from 2018—and there are at least 14 different items to grab the viewers' attention.

We hear the words of the journalist, and everything is in vivid color: The donkey and the elephant are squared off in combat with the U.S. Capitol in the middle; the Democrats and Republicans are represented with giant gold numbers; the date of a poll is given; it's from the "*NBC News Wall Street Journal* Poll"; this is "America's Choice 2018"; we're reminded the election is a day away, and it's high stakes; the president is going "all out with five rallies"; a digital countdown is running until they get to "Election Night in America," with the countdown spinning down the seconds; CNN reminds you that you're watching CNN and also gives you the time of day; and finally, across the bottom of the screen is a never-ending stream of headlines, with dramatic words like "stoked fear" and "takeover."

FIGURE 4.6   Walter Cronkite

FIGURE 4.7   CNN Broadcast, 2018

An example of how today's news is presented with colors and a wide mix of information.

FIGURE 4.8   CNN Broadcast, 2020

The screens are becoming more crowded. Here's a shot from 2020 in which there are at least 28 items vying for our attention (see Figure 4.8).

But this screen won't stay here for too long. It will be replaced by a looping video of an airplane crash, a hurricane coming ashore, or some other dramatic event that will be running in three- or four-second continuous loops, drawing our attention to it over and over again. We see the journalists in the studio. Their set is a mix of dazzling colors, and dramatic, cinema-like music plays as the show cuts to a commercial and plays again when it returns, as the camera zooms dramatically in toward the anchor. A "BREAKING NEWS" banner might be on the screen—for hours—as the station keeps changing the content and updating the story to keep you tuned in to what the "breaking news" is. We're urged to stick around because we don't want to miss the next breaking news and be left behind. Perhaps two people are talking to us, or there might be four, five, six, or seven commentators taking turns, sometimes with different viewpoints. Maybe they're arguing and talking over each other.

We've gone from watching lonely Walter Cronkite reading the news to being spectators at a nightly event where the reporters and consultants spar like info-gladiators. It's dizzying. Will we reach a point where the screen will be so crowded that all we see is a round face surrounded by numbers, images, and words? When I show these slides of today's newscast in my trainings, teachers tell me they sometimes feel overwhelmed by the cable news and have to turn it off. This is a metaphor for our world; there's so much coming at us, sometimes we just want to screen it out. Our brains are on digital overload.

All of the generations in our teacher force now have a variety of digital options in their personal lives that can cater to their whims. They have home entertainment systems with wireless speakers where Alexa can play their favorite tunes or take them to a personalized Pandora station. The televisions are flatter and clearer, and teachers can choose from hundreds of cable stations; or if they've "cut the cable" and only receive their programming through the internet, they can choose which platform they want to use, like YouTube, Apple TV, Hulu, or Netflix. If they're driving, they can stream satellite radio into their cars. When they're walking or between classes at work, they can log in with their smartphones for movies and music on the go.

Notice how this description could fit the lifestyles of Gen Z and Gen Alpha? Teachers of all generations, like their students, are living a digital lifestyle. The millennials and Gen Zers grew up with it, but research is showing boomers and Gen Xers are embracing technology at home and closing the gap (Digital Media Solutions, 2019).

Now, consider how these digital lifestyles are affecting teachers in our PD sessions: They want the same presentation methods in PD they get in their personal lives. I've trained thousands of educators in the past five years, and I can attest they want fast-moving, interactive, choice-driven, rigorous, relevant, useful PD. And it needs to have a strong technology element to fill their cravings to use technology.

Think of it as a tug-of-war: We yank them by one hand in our PD as they hold their constantly connected, often-vibrating-with-notifications smartphones in the other hand. And if we somehow get them to put their smartphones away, they will still be tempted by their school-issued laptops or tablets, and their email and Amazon are just a happy click away. In today's PD, teachers might be facing us, and they might be half-listening to us, but it's oh-so-easy for them to bury their faces in the screens and get sucked quietly into the cybersphere.

I've seen it. I've lived it as a trainer, and I must admit there have been a few times when I've been in meetings or trainings and my cell phone apps have called me like sirens onto the Rocks of Distraction. In today's PD, the digital sirens are hard to beat.

To open this chapter, I mentioned BC schools and AC schools: schools before and after computers. I believe the history of PD can also be divided into two eras: BT and AT—*before* technology and *after* technology started changing our brains. That's how big this shift has been. As we have sunk deeper and deeper into our gigabyte sea, the parts of our brains that were once happy with three channels of black-and-white television are now demanding constant interaction, stimulation, and choices from a myriad of sources. Like our students, our teachers still need guidance, nurturing, and education, but they have turned into an audience that learns differently. In other words, our boomers and Gen Xers are becoming more like our Gen Z students.

I call this the *Rise of Teacher* Z. Audiences in our PD sessions have never been more diverse and, paradoxically, similar. They are all distracted. As 5-Gen leaders train the four generations, they need to know how to rework their PD methods to match the way their teachers' brains want to process the information.

We need new tactics.

FIGURE 4.9   Tips for Transitioning to 5-Gen Leadership

Tips for Transitioning to 5-Gen Leadership

21. Remember that all generations of teachers are more distracted than in the past, which makes them harder to train.

22. Know our Gen Z and Gen Alpha students are more distracted than in the past, which makes them harder to teach.

23. Recognize the constant interaction with technology is changing brains and how people want to be taught.

24. Know the four generations of teachers have different views and needs, but the four generations share new similarities because of their digital lifestyles.

25. Look to different fields outside of education for tips on how to connect with Teacher Z.

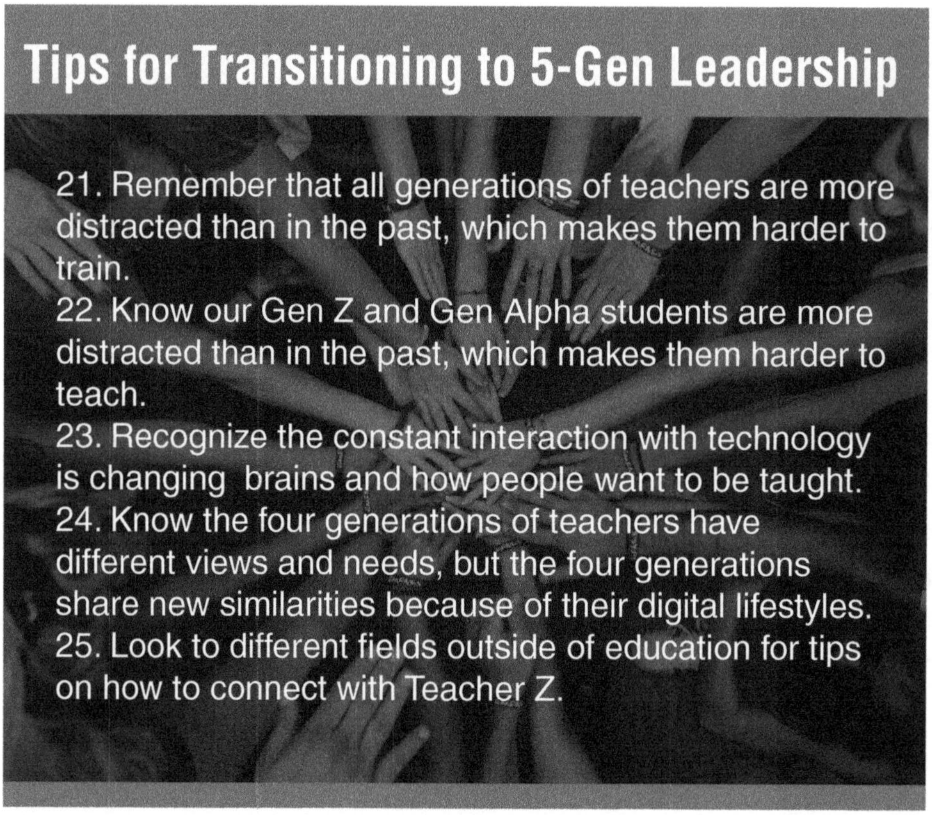

CHAPTER 5

Tactics for Creating Multigenerational PD

Key Points of This Chapter

- PD leaders must determine which teachers are in which generation.

- Teachers of different generations will view PD topics in different ways.

- PD leaders should focus on four key areas while training: communication methods between generations, what motivates each generation, reverse mentoring that allows young teachers to share their talents, and bridging the technology generation gaps.

- PD leaders must find ways to differentiate PD for the different generations and to use common teaching methods that appeal to all generations.

First, a PD mea culpa.

I've been leading professional development (PD) for a long time—since the days when Ronald Reagan unleashed *A Nation at Risk* and started us down the long assessment tunnel that has led to America's current PD system, and I must admit not all the professional development I've led in my career has been good. In fact, some of it has been bad. I, like other well-meaning school leaders, have designed my share of boring, ineffective training sessions, the type that made great teachers scratch their heads and say, "Hmmm, that could have been so much better if he had *just* . . ."—just done this better or that better, done a lot of things better. In other words, I've been part of the PD problem.

But I've learned a few things, especially in the last few years as the world has accelerated and the internet has changed our lives—and our generations. I've tried to take a drone's eye view of what's happening with the world, American society, and its schools. As a boomer set in his ways, I was able to evolve in how I plan and present PD to teachers.

And If I can do it, others can do it.

Acknowledging the PD Problem

Before looking at multigenerational PD, trainers need to acknowledge the PD problem: the PD often isn't very effective (Zarrow, 2020). Unfortunately, I've worked with a lot of people leading the training who don't realize their content just isn't sinking in.

I was on the phone recently with a district's professional development director and one of the district's technology specialists. We were discussing some PD they wanted me to lead. It was my first time to work with the district.

"We have great PD!" the PD director, a Gen Xer, told me proudly.

But later in the same conversation, I heard something else from her: In their last two optional PD offerings, which were over a high-interest topic (how to use technology in the classroom), only *two* teachers had signed up to attend—*out of over 700 teachers in the district*. I looked at the district's accountability ratings given to it by the state: a solid "C." Not a bad district, just an average one. With average PD.

I frequently hear the comment "We have great PD," but when I visit the district or work with the teachers, I don't see the results in the teaching and learning. Even in the most dysfunctional districts, I've yet to come across any high-level administrators who don't speak highly of their PD. People will say, "We have budget issues . . . We're working on our curriculum pacing . . . We're putting in more formative assessments . . . ," but they don't ever say, "Our PD is not very good." Instead, they'll usually brag about their PD. But when I talk with the teachers about their PD, out of earshot of the administrators, they often give me a completely opposite view of what their administrators are saying. The teachers tend to smile politely, shrug their shoulders, or come right out and tell me how bad their PD is in the district.

It's a widespread and expensive problem. According to a study of school PD by the highly respected consulting firm McKinsey,

> Many (school) systems invest significant sums in PD programs but do so as a habit, tending to offer the same set of training courses each year without regard for how they might fit into a comprehensive program or how effective they are—even when teachers complain that some of the courses are not useful. According to a recent survey, 59 percent of

teachers found content-related learning opportunities useful; fewer than half found PD on non-content-related areas useful. (Jayaram et al., 2012, para. 1)

That means at least 41 percent of the teachers don't find the content-related PD useful, and over 50 percent of the teachers don't find non-content-related PD useful.

Here's what I know is happening. The people who design the PD are sharp, knowledgeable, hard-working, and can clearly lay out their PD plans and objectives. They are pedagogically sound. They care. But their PD is ineffective because the delivery of the content is weak and/or there's not enough follow-up after the PD to help teachers implement the changes. The PD designers have a clear idea of what they want to achieve, but it's not working. They deliver the PD in a traditionally, pedagogically sound manner, but the teachers aren't buying in, especially Teacher Z, who wants to learn differently.

I came across this view of PD in an *Edutopia* article by Pauline Zdonek in which she summarizes the feelings of too many teachers:

> As I prepare for another afternoon of district-provided professional development activities, I always make sure that I bring plenty of work to do (papers to grade, lesson planning, etc.). This isn't because I have a bad attitude and hate professional development (PD). A great PD event can really energize me to improve my classroom instruction. However, the sad fact is that the majority of PDs I attend are repetitive, simplistic, or downright boring. I bring other work to do so that I don't get irritated when I feel that my time is being so carelessly wasted. (Zdonek, 2016, para. 1)

A waste of time. There's no bigger sin in educational leadership than to waste a teacher's time. The good news, and this is huge, is that she said great PD can energize her. There's still hope.

> There's no bigger sin in educational leadership than to waste a teacher's time.

I mentioned I had evolved as a trainer. I recently met a teacher like Zdonek. I had been leading a day of PD, and a teacher approached me at its end. "I admit I didn't want to be here," he said. "I didn't want to spend hours making a full day of lesson plans to attend a PD session that would mean nothing to me. But this was the best training I've had in years."

And I thought, "What's happening here?"

This teacher had been attentive throughout the day. He had participated actively and positively. He had been engaged. I could tell he was a fine teacher, the kind

I had wanted on my staff when I was a principal and superintendent. How is it, I wondered, that we've reached a point where educators like this one, people who have dedicated their professional careers to teaching and learning, dread attending their own learning sessions?

Something's gone wrong in how we train today's teachers. Besides examining the methods and the overall design, we should also answer this question to find part of the answer to building better PD: "In which generations are the PD designers?" In many schools and districts, the PD designers are curriculum specialists, principals, and assistant principals who have risen through the ranks, and many of them are boomers and Gen Xers. To improve PD today, let's also look at it through a generational lens to design more useful systems and training methods.

A Global Leadership Question: "How Do We Train These Different Generations?"

Here's a message of reassurance for school leaders: We're not the only ones trying to figure out how to train today's employees. It's a new world for corporate trainers too.

Knowledge Anywhere is a firm that designs systems to help companies train their employees, at least three million workers worldwide. It, too, recognizes the challenges of training different generations, and it makes four recommendations.

1. Trainers have to recognize "the elephant in the room" (Johnson, 2017), which is the negative perceptions the four generations often have of each other. The younger generations see the older ones as being behind the times and hanging on, while the older generations view the younger ones as being lazy and spoiled. They need to blend and work together.

2. Trainers need to use various learning styles that appeal to various generations. They should provide face-to-face activities to appease the older generations but also provide online opportunities for younger generations.

3. Trainers need to know what motivates the different generations. They should let everyone see how the training will benefit them, but they need to give the younger generations more feedback and encouragement.

4. Trainers should tap into the strength of the different generations. They should blend the working groups to bring out the expertise and experience of each generation (Johnson, 2017).

What can 5-Gen leaders learn from these corporate points? They should recognize the generational conflicts and misunderstandings between older and younger teachers; the need to mix different training methods that appeal to different generations of teachers; how to motivate teachers of different generations; and the need to find ways to blend the talents of the different generations in the staff.

Training matters. Another company in the private sector, APQC, which aims to deliver "best practices and strategic guidance amid disruption" (APQC, 2021) has studied the number of days employees are trained each year and how it correlates with the success of that company.

Here's what their study found:

- Companies that train their employees **seven** days each year are in the top 25 percent of their fields in performance.

- Companies that train their employees **five** days each year are in the middle 25 percent to 75 percent in performance.

- Companies that train their employees **four** days each year are in the bottom 25 percent in performance. (P. Wiggins, 2018)

So we can see in the private sector that employees who get more training—in this case, at least seven days each year—help their companies outperform other companies.

Now, let's look at the number of days teachers spend in professional development. The number varies widely. A survey of 10,000 teachers in 2015 showed they averaged 19 days, or around 10 percent of their time, each year (TNTP, 2015). That would be a higher number of PD days than in many districts, where teachers start the school year with a day or two of PD, followed by another day in the fall and one in the spring. These teachers might have a total of four or five PD days set in the calendar, with options to sign up for more during the year or during the summer. Other districts might have a week or more of PD to start each year, and they might have regular, established PD days or hours established throughout the year. There are other snippets of time devoted to PD: perhaps 20-minute segments in staff meetings, some PLC meetings during school days, and an hour or two found occasionally when time can be squeezed between other activities.

But is the PD working? Is it leading to better teaching and learning?

Researchers at the American University School of Education reviewed articles about PD and found commonalities. According to their research, teachers support the idea of professional development, but many of them find their PD to be "useless." Why? Because some basic elements of good teaching were missing: time spent on instruction, support, and relevancy of the content. The researchers

(American University, 2018) found that for PD to be effective, it should have these three elements:

1. The PD must be ongoing and consistently focused to help teachers as they grapple with new ways of teaching. The researchers state an "analysis of 1,300 pieces of research found that PD programs of 14 hours or less did not affect student achievement at all—in fact, they failed to even change teachers' practices" (para. 4).

2. The PD organizers must provide support after the PD when teachers implement the new ideas. The researchers cite research that says "teachers require an average of 20 distinct moments of practicing a new skill before it comes easily to them. They need support after PD sessions are finished—but while they're still in this practicing mode" (para. 5).

3. The PD must be relevant and useful for teachers. They need content they can use when they return to the classroom. The researchers cite studies that say the top priority of teachers is to gain "information and tips about the specific content they teach" (para. 6).

If 5-Gen leaders are going to create 5-Gen schools, they need to provide consistent, ongoing, focused PD; they need to implement support systems as teachers implement new ideas; and they need to make sure the teachers see the relevancy in their PD content. Remember that eight-second attention span? Teacher Z needs to see the relevance in a hurry.

Relevancy in PD

I recently participated in virtual PD for a school district in the Pacific Northwest. It was a PD day for the entire district, and the teachers were able to choose five one-hour sessions throughout the day from a long list of breakout sessions. In my session, I presented information on how to use education apps to deepen engagement and efficiency in remote learning. Teachers didn't have to register beforehand for the sessions; they just chose sessions that day and logged on with a Zoom link. I didn't know how many people to expect in my sessions, the grade levels they taught, or their technology ability.

I would open each session in gallery view so I could see the faces of my audience (only about half had their cameras on), and I noticed in the last session a teacher who was probably a boomer, who appeared to be about my age, and who probably had decades of experience. I remember thinking, "I'm glad he cares enough to be in this session. Is he new to technology? Is he advanced? Is he catching up or leading the way and searching for new apps to use?"

In the session, I quickly led the teachers through eleven different apps. Yes, eleven apps in under 60 minutes. When dealing with distracted audiences, as detailed in Chapter 4, speed is essential. An old slogan created to deter reckless driving is "Speed kills." In PD, I say, "A *lack* of speed kills." I know I have to keep it moving. In the first and second sessions of the day, I asked the teachers at the end, "Was I moving too fast?" And they emphatically said, "No!" They liked the fast pace. In the third and fourth sessions, when I didn't ask about the pace, I noticed several teachers thanked me without prompting for delivering the information rapidly.

Another essential element: I would open the apps, briefly explain what they all did, and then send them into Zoom breakout rooms where they could explore a tool or two of their choosing. I call this the "Digital Sandbox." Two points detailed by American University (2018) are that teachers need support and need to see how they can use the information; in letting teachers play with the apps and jumping between breakout rooms to answer questions, I was providing some support as they applied the apps to their own teaching, which created relevancy.

When I entered the breakout room with the boomer teacher, I asked if anyone had any questions, and he said, "I've been exploring *Insert Learning* (a Google extension that allows teachers to turn web-based articles into interactive documents). I've been looking for something like this for the past few months, and here it is. It's probably going to change the trajectory of the rest of my career."

Wow. Isn't that what we live for as trainers? To know our training is impacting teachers and will positively impact hundreds or perhaps thousands of young people? But here's the bigger point: This was a boomer teacher who found deep relevancy in his PD, and it was centered on technology he could use immediately with students. Relevancy is a common thread of effective PD for all generations.

I've seen all kinds of PD in my 30-plus years as a department head, school administrator, and consultant. Let's take a look at the types of information usually covered in PD sessions or staff meetings. Some of it is more relevant than others. As you read it, think of the PD you design and where it fits in these groups.

Exterior information is information that is presented in meetings from exterior sources. Examples could include motivational speakers that might or might not be effective, visitors from exterior agencies such as the local police or fire department who explain how they interact with the school, or a fundraising drive hosted by a local or national organization that involves the school.

(Continued)

(Continued)

Nonessential organizational information is information from within the organization that doesn't affect the teacher directly. Examples could include new food nutrition guidelines for the cafeteria, new busing procedures within the district, new organizational charts about district personnel or procedures, and new information about the state testing system and how it will affect the entire state but not necessarily the school or the teacher.

Essential organizational information is information for the teachers to function efficiently within the local school system. Examples could include the new information management system, new substitute systems, whom to call when the copy machine needs paper, and this year's new and improved standardized testing procedures for the school or classroom.

Standardized test prep information is information needed to survive and thrive in the state's standardized testing system. Examples could include information about the school's data, individual classroom data, practices specifically designed to improve test scores, unpacking curriculum standards, and any other information about ways test scores will impact the school and individual teachers.

Safety information is information meant to help teachers and students survive school shootings and other 21st century dangers. Examples could include information about whom to call to help break up a fight, the latest lockdown procedures, and how to flee a school in the event of an emergency or active school shooter. This could also be information about how to help students who are being abused, are homeless, or are facing some other life-threatening crisis.

Teacher evaluation information is information about the latest iteration of the state or district teacher evaluation system. Examples could include guidelines and formulas that affect teacher ratings and employment.

Subject matter and teaching information is information that allows the teacher to more effectively teach specific lessons or subjects for the sake of better teaching and not necessarily for better standardized test scores. Examples could include unit and lesson revision, new literacy and math techniques to use in specific lessons, and how to use a new device or teaching app. This information tends to be useful in the short term but might not be useful for long periods of time as new apps, devices, methods, and textbooks are created to replace the previous ones.

Profound information is highly rigorous and relevant information that has a profound, broad impact on teachers' careers. Examples could include how to raise rigor in all lessons, how to make all lessons more relevant, information about Gen Alpha and Gen Z, how to thrive as an educator in hyperchange, and understanding other trends that are affecting 21st century teaching. ∎

The PD and its impact doesn't always sort themselves cleanly into one of these categories. For example, PD I led that day in the Pacific Northwest was about apps teachers could use in their subjects, so for most teachers, it would be placed in the "Subject Matter and Teaching Information" category; however, the teacher predicted it would profoundly impact his career, which could move the PD into the "Profound Information" category. All of these categories can be essential and effective; they could vary by topic, by individual—and by generation.

Relevancy in teaching and learning is an ancient essential concept. In the 20th century, in the days when I first began to lead PD sessions and generations were more similar, the teachers also wanted relevant information. But the diverging generations today have brought about a slightly diverging view of what is relevant for each generation.

Let's take another look at these eight PD topics, but let's look at how different generations, with different interests, might view them.

TABLE 5.1   PD Topics by Generations

PD TOPICS	INTEREST LEVEL IN THE GENERATIONS
Exterior information	This used to clearly be the least relevant of topics; however, millennial and Gen Z teachers will be more focused on community causes and creating values-driven organizations, which means they will find relevance in exterior information related to partnerships with outside groups and other initiatives that enhance the community. While boomers and Xers could care about these topics, they often won't share the urgency of the younger teachers.
Nonessential organizational information	What is nonessential for one group might be essential for another group. While boomers and Gen Xers are used to hearing general district information, they tend to be more cynical because they've seen through the years how the information is constantly changing. Millennial and Gen Z teachers, on the other hand, might find some of the information essential because of their different interests, such as the nutritional content of the cafeteria food and the amount of time certain students are spending on buses compared to other students.
Essential organizational information	All generations will find information about the organization to be relevant; however, they could have different approaches to the topics. For example, younger, more tech-savvy teachers could request new systems have a technology component. This is an excellent area to foster collaboration between the generations: Younger teachers could assist older teachers as they navigate new digital platforms, and older teachers could assist younger teachers by using their experience to connect the new organizational ideas to the previous ones so it makes more sense.
Standardized test information	This is a great area to foster leadership in experienced teachers of all generations as they unite to help the less experienced teachers. Because of the accountability placed on test scores, all generations will find this information relevant. Five-Gen leaders can remember that some of the generations had different test experiences growing up. Boomers didn't have many tests; Gen Xers were in school when the state test initiatives began; millennials were the first generation to feel the full weight of standardized testing; and Gen Zers who attended public schools spent much of their K-12 careers in systems tightly refined and fully focused on test scores.

(Continued)

TABLE 5.1 (Continued)

Safety information	Safety is a constant concern for everyone in a school building, which means all generations will find this information highly relevant. Five-Gen leaders should remember boomers and Xers grew up before Columbine, and millennials and Gen Zers grew up with lockdown drills and evacuation routes.
Teacher evaluation information	Stress levels will rise for all generations when studying this information; however, we've already seen how evaluations affect millennials (and probably Gen Z) teachers. Younger teachers will be more stressed than their older peers.
Subject matter and teaching information	All generations want to constantly improve their teaching, so they will find subject matter and teaching method information relevant. But they could be viewing the content through different sorts of lenses, especially when looking at how to use new types of devices and education apps. Younger teachers will more quickly embrace them. Older teachers will also be open to using them, but 5-Gen leaders should remember the older teachers will be in more varied stages of development and will be more selective in choosing which technology to use.
Profound information	Information that has a long-term, profound impact on teachers will be relevant for all generations, and they will find common ground in studying this content. For example, when teachers look at rigor in their classrooms (as in applying Bloom's taxonomy to their teaching), they will all see it's ageless. However, boomers and Gen Xers might be more inclined to be counting the years until they retire, which could reduce their urgency in changing their methods and teaching styles.

Finding the Generations in the Staff

In the last chapter, we looked at how teachers are all forming some common learning styles—how they are all turning into Teacher Z because of their affinity for their cell phones and digital lifestyles. Yet we still will find significant gaps between the generations, especially in looking at their learning preferences in PD sessions. So as 5-Gen leaders, we need to know how many teachers of each generation are in our staffs and who they are. We can't apply generational characteristics to solve problems unless we know who is in which group, so we have to have an idea of when the teachers were born.

Important note: Birth years are tricky subjects. We need to be sensitive to the feelings of the teachers, and we need to let the teachers know generational problem-solving is being done to help the staff and the individual teachers be more efficient. Many teachers are comfortable as being identified as being a part of a certain generational group—but not by giving their exact birth year. For example, I've found boomers are more willing to laugh and say, "I'm a baby boomer, and I remember when . . ." than to say, "I was born in 1960, and I remember when . . ." If they are allowed to identify as the most experienced teaching generation and not as a teacher born over 60 years ago, then they feel more respected. (Total disclosure: As I write this book, I am 60 years old . . . or 60 years young.)

One of the easiest ways for a leader to classify a teacher by generation is to consider how many years of experience the teacher has accrued; this will often provide an estimate of the teacher's age. This is an unscientific method, but if the leaders know the teacher's years of experience, the leader can more accurately guess the teacher's generation.

After they determine how many teachers are in each age group, here are some internal questions leadership teams can ask about their staffs:

- In which generational group are most of the teachers?

- Which generational group is the smallest?

- How many boomers are still on the staff?

- How many Gen Z teachers have joined the staff?

- Are the Gen Xers and millennials about even in their numbers?

- Are recently hired teachers mainly in the millennial and Gen Z groups?

In Chapter 1, I mentioned a PD activity that I use to introduce the idea of getting teachers to look at their peers and school issues through a multigenerational lens. Let's look at how this exercise can introduce multigenerational dialogue into a school staff—and how we can work multigenerational PD techniques into its design.

Mind the Gap!

Anyone who has traveled through a city by subway has probably seen signs that say "MIND THE GAP"—those universal warnings not to step or fall into the gap between the subway platform and the subway car. The same warning can be given for educators today: They need to mind the generation gaps so they can avoid misunderstandings, know how to better assist each other, and do a better job teaching today's Gen Z and Gen Alpha students.

So this exercise is called *Mind the Gap!*

Many teachers have known there are generational differences. It might be that boomer or Gen Z teacher looking around and saying, "Some of these people are just different from me," or "Why is that boomer still doing it that way when this new way is so much more effective?" or "Can't that Gen Z teacher see that's not going to work?" The *Mind the Gap!* activity is a fun way to introduce the idea of looking at each other through a

FIGURE 5.1 Mind the Gap

Photo by Suad Kamardeen on Unsplash

multigenerational lens. When designing PD, we need to have clear objectives, so here are the objectives for *Mind the Gap!*

Objectives

1. Teachers will have a better understanding of the characteristics of the four generations in today's teaching force.

2. Teachers will have a better understanding of the generational characteristics of the individuals with whom they are working on their team, in the department, and in their school staffs.

3. Teachers will see how technology shaped them and the formative years of their colleagues.

4. Teachers will have a better understanding of the generation gaps that exist between them and their colleagues.

5. Teachers will gain ideas of what they can do to understand and assist each other as they communicate and solve problems.

6. Teachers will gain ideas about teaching methods they can use when teaching Gen Z and Gen Alpha.

Opening Points

To introduce the exercise, leaders should cover two key points. First, they should let the staff know business and school leaders are now addressing generational issues within organizations. This will be a new concept for many teachers. They've known there are generational differences, but they've never realized that they are drawing serious attention in today's organizations.

Before leaders discuss the generational differences, the leaders should remind teachers that they are speaking about generational characteristics accepted by many companies and researchers, but these generational differences might not apply to everyone; individuals in the audience might feel they are exceptions. Many teachers will laugh and agree when they see how their generations are described, but some might disagree and say, "No, that's not me at all . . ." Perhaps that teacher is not like the characteristics or perhaps the teacher has more of the characteristics than the teacher realizes. It's okay to feel this way. Leaders need to respect the feelings and individuality of the teachers.

The Prompt

The exercise is built around the common thread running through all of the generations, the one that has had the greatest impact on changing each generation from the previous generations: technology. So the question for the activity is "What new technology changed your life when you were growing up?"

A Model for Introducing Mind the Gap!

Here's how a PD session around this exercise could be put together in a way that could fit the disparate needs of the four generations while addressing the new common threads of the entire group, Teacher Z. In this fictional school, named Hope School, the principal is a Gen Xer named Linda Change. Ms. Change has studied the generations and wants to introduce the topic into her staff in a PD session.

A week before the PD session, Ms. Change convenes a meeting of eight teachers: two boomers, two Gen Xers, two millennials, and two Gen Zers. She discusses some of the points she's read about the four generations and seeks their input. When the teachers hear about the generational characteristics, they share some of their personal stories about generational differences and conflicts they've observed within the staff. They agree it will be a good topic for their upcoming PD day.

Two days before the PD day, Ms. Change sends out an agenda to the staff, and she tells all teachers to feel free to offer suggestions on improving the agenda or the layout of the day. She lists the multigenerational dialogue as the first item on the agenda. She wants this item first on the agenda because she will be using multigenerational techniques for the rest of the day.

When the PD day begins, the staff walks into the room and sees that coffee, water, and snacks will be available throughout the day.

Ms. Change begins the Mind the Gap! *activity by telling a story of a recent epiphany*

5-Gen Leadership Points

The leader solicits input from all of the generations, including the staff's youngest members—the millennials and Gen Zers—who feel they are an important part of the organization.

The leader also learns the staff members will be interested in the topic, which is important since today's audiences tend to be distracted, and it's important for them to see relevance in what they are doing.

In sending out the agenda beforehand and seeking more input, the leader has involved all teachers in the day's design. Even if most teachers don't respond, they know they are part of a team.

The leader wants multigenerational awareness to be a part of the staff culture, so she will refer to it throughout the day and in future events.

The leader understands food, water, and coffee are ingredients that give teachers energy and provide a common area for generations to gather and to bond.

The leader interjects herself into the dialogue by using a personal story about her own growth. She is modeling a transformative mindset and showing she is learning alongside her teachers.

The leader uses a common piece of technology, an app, to grab the attention of the teachers.

As she works the topic into the PD agenda, the leader also lets the teachers know they will be addressing a topic they can use immediately in their classrooms. She is also pointing out today's students are new types of learners.

The leader uses technology early in the session. In this way, she involves all members of the audience in an interactive activity, and she is allowing millennial and Gen Z teachers an opportunity to respond in a way in which they are very comfortable.

The leader anticipates technical challenges in older generations and provides prompt assistance.

The leader encourages teachers to help each other with technology challenges, which allows younger teachers to use their skill set to assist peers, and when boomers and Xers help other boomers and Xers with technology, they can see that older generations can also successfully use technology.

In asking for a group verbal responses, she is ensuring the boomers and Gen Xers are using a communication method with which they are comfortable.

Instead of telling the teachers about common challenges, the leader allows the teachers to recognize some of the multigenerational issues on their own. This makes them a part of the solution.

The leader understands the importance of humor. When teachers laugh, they are entertained, which is important for training Teacher Z.

she had about herself. She tells them she recently downloaded a new app onto her phone and was surprised at how useful it was. She then points out that the younger staff members might not have been so surprised because they've lived with increasingly more powerful apps most of their lives. Then she says, "I began to wonder how our generations in our staff are different and how our Gen Z and Gen Alpha students should be taught today."

Ms. Change then asks, "Have you noticed any way you might be different from other generations?" But instead of seeking verbal responses, she has them answer through an education app. She gives them a code, and they submit their answers digitally; then the answers are displayed on the screen in front of them for the group to see.

Ms. Change quickly scans the room see if any teachers are having difficulty. In particular, she is looking for two boomer teachers she knows are technology challenged. She sees them struggling and moves to assist them, and she also says, "Everyone, look around you and help anyone who might need some assistance."

When all of the answers are submitted, she encourages the teachers to analyze the results and to speak out with their findings. Popular answers might include "I'm not as good at using technology," "I use more technology," and "I have a slightly different view of the world." The teachers laugh good-naturedly at their responses.

Then Ms. Change asks, "What are birth years and characteristics of the four generations in our staffs today?" She allows teachers to answer. After a few teachers offer ideas, Ms. Change then tells the group they are going to learn more about the four generations. She *gives them three options in how they can access the information:*

1. *They can come to the front of the room so she can show them some slides she's prepared.*

2. *They can access a link to a Google doc that has the information in it.*

3. *They can Google "four generations in the workplace" and find their own articles to read.*

Teachers are allowed to stand up, move to another part of the room, go into the hallway, or go to another room to do their research.

The teachers are told they can work independently or in groups of their own choosing. In some later exercises, she will assign teachers to groups to ensure the generations are represented.

After 15 minutes, the whole group reconvenes, and the leader asks a teacher to lead the debriefing (the teacher was chosen beforehand and agreed to lead). The slides prepared by the teacher are filled with bright images and large, colorful fonts, and a video is embedded within the slides.

Ms. Change is sure to compliment and praise all teachers, particularly the millennials and Gen Z teachers.

Ms. Change reminds the teachers they must also understand their Gen Z and Gen Alpha students so they can do a better job of teaching them, which is their mission as educators.

Ms. Change then asks, "Why do we have different characteristics for the generations, including today's students?" The teachers respond that researchers point to different

The leader differentiates by giving them choices in how they learn.

Some teachers can have direct instruction, which serves the needs of some boomers and Gen Xers.

Some teachers can use technology to find information already prepared. This will benefit millennials and Gen Zers who want to learn on their own, at their own pace.

Some teachers can use technology to choose their own content and pace.

The leader allows teachers to choose the space in which they are most comfortable, and the leader encourages physical movement.

The leader knows some teachers might want to work alone. The leader allows some choice in groups to allow teachers to feel comfortable, but she also is sure to mix the groups at other times so the teachers can work on relationships and communication skills as they bring their different skills sets to the group.

The leader shares leadership with teachers who can be chosen from a variety of generations.

The leader knows millennials and Gen Zers respond well to praise and affirmation.

The leader motivates boomers and Gen Xers by reminding them of the mission.

The leader has moved from having teachers studying abstract generational information to having the teachers apply it to themselves and to their students. This increases relevancy and engagement.

The leader transitions into the prompt, technology, and provides a common thread for generational dialogue.

growth experiences, particularly with different types of technology.

Ms. Change explains that they are going go begin to develop their multigenerational understanding by doing a group exercise called Mind the Gap!

The Activity

As Ms. Change led her teachers into the *Mind the Gap!* activity, note that she was inclusive in her leadership, distributed her leadership, and differentiated her leadership; however, she did not abdicate her leadership. She controlled the flow of the lesson.

Here are the steps of the *Mind the Gap!* activity. The teachers on Ms. Change's staff have already done Step 1, researching the generations. Now, it would be time for them to move to Step 2 (see Figure 5.1).

What to Expect

This activity is fun and useful for a number of reasons, principally because teachers will find commonalities in their generations and see how they differ from other generations.

The boomers, Gen Xers, and millennials will look back at their youth and laugh at the technology that seemed so advanced at the time. Examples of bygone technology from the generations will include things such as rabbit ear antennas on television sets, eight-track tapes, Atari video games, America Online (now known as Aol. or AOL), and encyclopedias on compact discs. When they report, there is often a mixture of nostalgia and awe at how the world has changed.

Gen Z teachers only need to look back a few years. For many of them, getting their first smartphone was a big moment in their growth—and this is an essential point: A boomer teacher will realize the Gen Z teacher grew up with today's technology, and the Gen Z teacher will realize the boomer teacher has had to adjust through multiple decades and many technology iterations; yet they might be teaching next door to each other. They grew up in different worlds and bring very different life experiences to their profession. If they all see the differences and similarities, they can start the generational dialogue.

Next Steps for Effective PD

Now that the generations have a better understanding of each other, it's time to help them work together and learn together in their PD. Here are four areas of focus 5-Gen leaders can stress at the conclusion of the *Mind the Gap!* activity.

FIGURE 5.2 *Mind the Gap!* Activity

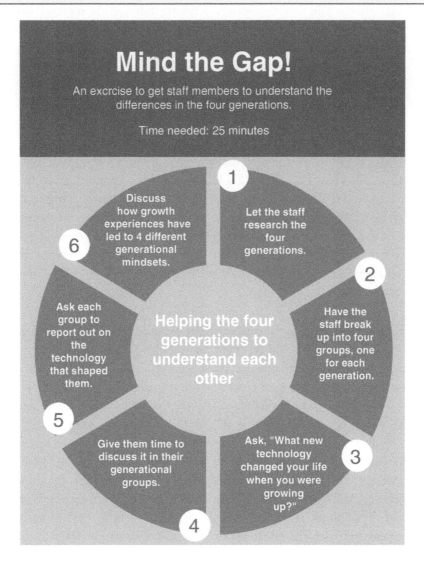

Mind the Gap!

An excrcise to get staff members to understand the differences in the four generations.

Time needed: 25 minutes

Helping the four generations to understand each other

1. Let the staff research the four generations.

2. Have the staff break up into four groups, one for each generation.

3. Ask, "What new technology changed your life when you were growing up?"

4. Give them time to discuss it in their generational groups.

5. Ask each group to report out on the technology that shaped them.

6. Discuss how growth experiences have led to 4 different generational mindsets.

1. **Communication**: Five-Gen leaders should let all of the teachers know they have different communication strengths. One study of millennials and Gen Zers found they considered in-person, face-to-face communication to be their weakest mode of communication, and they consider video and text messaging their strongest form of communication (Morgan, 2015). This tends to be the opposite of boomers and Gen Xers, who like to converse in person. All four groups must now be able to speak face-to-face, text each other, and know how to use video apps to communicate.

2. **Motivation**: Five-Gen leaders should constantly remind the staff that while older teachers tend to value stability and the younger generations tend to be focused on personal growth and contributing to the common good (Fuscaldo, 2020), they can find common ground in schools: helping kids. All teachers entered the profession to have a positive impact on the lives of students.

3. **Reverse mentoring**: Five-Gen leaders must stress the need for reverse mentoring—the idea that all generations can help each other (Quast & Hedges, 2011). This allows all of the generations to feel valued, and it allows the entirety to tap into each other's strengths to advance the school's mission of helping students. Reverse mentoring should be used in committees, grade-level teams, departments, and even in the traditional new teacher/mentor relationship—perhaps the young teacher can find ways to mentor the more experienced boomer or Gen Xer.

4. **Technology**: As 5-Gen leaders model technology usage in PD sessions, they must remind teachers the world is becoming more digitized, which means all teachers must develop digital mindsets. While millennials and Gen Zers tend to embrace technology more quickly than boomers and Gen Xers, studies are showing boomers and Gen Xers are embracing more technology than in the past (Vogels, 2020). The older teachers tend to be more selective and need to see a reason for using the technology, while the technology is a way of life for the younger teachers. In PD, 5-Gen leaders should constantly show boomers and Gen Xers how technology can improve their teaching, and they should allow millennials and Gen Zers to have time to experiment with the latest apps to see how they can be used in the classroom.

Presentation Methods for Teacher Z

There's yet another element needed to ensure PD is successful today: using presentation methods that match the learning needs of Teacher Z. The fictional principal, Ms. Change, modeled some of these methods in her introduction to the *Mind the Gap!* activity. In the classroom, we say it's not just the content that matters but also how we teach the students. The same thing can be said for PD; 5-Gen leaders differentiate their PD *and* use methods that appeal to their 21st century, distracted Teacher Z audience.

As mentioned in Chapter 4, all the generations of our teacher force, like the workforce in the private sector, have what I think of as "digitized attention spans." We must use methods that appeal to teachers who

- Are used to interacting with screens

- Are constantly exposed to colors, images, and videos on their screens

- Play digital games

- Are constantly on social media

- Hang out in Starbucks

- See lots of infographics online

- Need time to collaborate

- Need time to work alone

- Might have been raised with different parenting styles, which affects their need to be a part of the PD planning

So how do we do this? Make sure we use the methods we've been promoting in teaching and learning for the last decade—and add a few new ones, such as gamification of some of the content, using social media to celebrate and share PD ideas, and place an emphasis on the use of space in the PD.

Five-Gen leaders should also remember the ancient glue that can bond the generations: food. In my training sessions, some of the schools provide snacks, coffee, and water throughout the day, or they provide breakfast and lunch. I've felt a different mood in the room when food is available. People are happier and more likely to interact. They're easier to coach.

While busy administrators have often acknowledged these presentation ideas, they haven't always worked them into their PD plans (see Figure 5.2). With Teacher Z, these methods are no longer optional; *they are mandatory*.

Five-Gen leaders do more than just use these methods in their PD; they expect to see teachers using them in their classrooms as they teach Gen Z and Gen Alpha. And if Ms. Change were speaking to us, she would advise us to take the next steps needed in effective PD as recommended by the American University (2018) article. Ms. Change would say, "Make sure you return to generational topics in future trainings to provide consistency, and provide support structure as the teachers implement change."

FIGURE 5.3 Teacher Z PD Checklist

Teacher Z
PD Checklist

Tips for PD Success!

Incorporate these ideas into PD to engage Teacher Z.

√ Activities are included to make the PD engaging and fun.

√ Teachers will be allowed to share stories to make the content more relevant and engaging.

√ If slides are used they have large font and bright colors.

√ Photos connect the participants to the content.

√ Infographics help the content be more understandable.

√ Videos are used at key times to engage the learner and deepen learning.

√ The pace is effective and information is chunked appropriately.

√ Opportunities for participation in multiple ways are offered throughout the agenda.

√ Activities that require movement are inserted at key times.

√ Technology is used by the participants to make the PD more effective and as a model for classroom usage.

√ Some or all of the activities are differentiated to accommodate for generational differences, learning styles, and interests.

√ Social media or online learning platforms are used to capture the main ideas and allow for 24/7 follow-up activities.

√ Gamification is used to present material in a fun format.

√ The PD space is designed to promote comfortable seating, high-quality presentations, effective collaboration, and creative thinking.

√ Time is given during the session to reflect, brainstorm, and incorporate the ideas into lessons.

√ Teachers are consulted before, during, and after the PD so that actives and future steps can be adjusted.

FIGURE 5.4   Tips for Transitioning to 5-Gen Leadership

Tips for Transitioning to 5-Gen Leadership

26. Examine the effectiveness of the PD.
27. Know that companies in all fieds are searching for effective ways to train professionals.
28. Create effective PD initiatives by ensuring they are ongoing, that coaching and support are provided to teacgers, and by providing relevant content.
29. Understand the eight types of PD and their relevance for the different generations.
30. Know which teachers are in which generation.
31. Plan PD through a multigenerations lens.
32. Differentiate PD by generation.

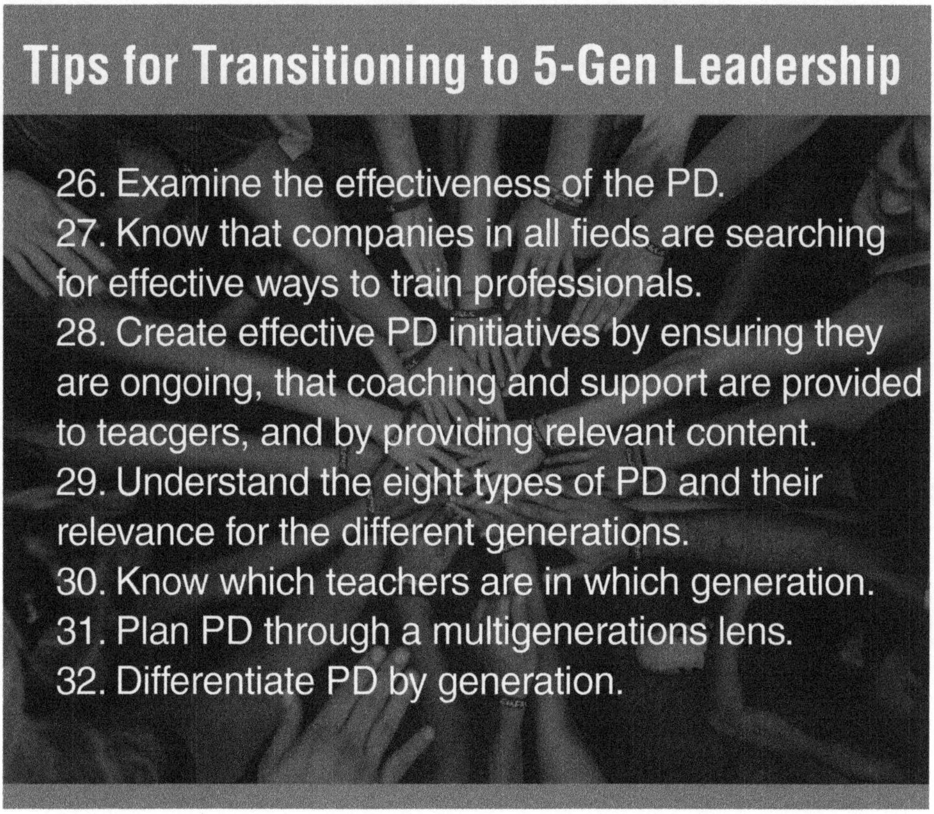

CHAPTER 6

Generational Lessons of COVID-19

Key Points of This Chapter

- The COVID-19 school closures of 2020 reset the education landscape, with technology taking a more prominent role for all generations of teachers.

- Having access to the internet is now a fundamental right for Gen Z and Gen Alpha students, regardless of income or location.

- The school closures exposed a new digital divide, one often found along generational lines, between teachers who can use technology and those who can't.

- Five-Gen Leaders must be technology savvy; they must model technology in PD and close the gaps between their own ability and the ability of their finest teachers.

In March of 2020, I was leading a training session at a high school in Southern California, aka SoCal, where some teachers of all generations ride their skateboards to work. The COVID-19 virus had grabbed a foothold in America, and it had begun its long march through the nation's schools. One of the teachers in the workshop was obsessed with getting the latest COVID-19 updates. She told the group about a satellite radio station that ran COVID-19 stories 24/7. She kept looking at the COVID-19 news bulletins, announcing every bit of data and the latest medical opinions about the new virus as they flashed across her phone. Then in the afternoon she said, "The Ohio governor just closed their schools." The room of teachers became scarily quiet as they wondered if they would be next school system to close.

The closings in sports and entertainment had been coming all week. First, it was the NBA, and then Broadway theaters and Major League Baseball, and then the

NCAA's March Madness. We had heard schools might have to close, but would they really? A world where kids are told *not* to come to school? This school apocalypse was almost beyond our imagination.

As I left the school that day, I tried to check in with an administrator to give her a summary of the day's training, but she and the other administrators were huddling in a hastily called meeting, discussing how to announce their school district was closing the next day. Within a week, the doors of most American schools were locked, and American educators were teaching in their sweatpants at their dining room tables. The COVID-19 school dominoes had begun to fall—and they are still falling.

In July of 2020, in what I think of as the COVID Summer, I was in a Zoom session with Dr. Willard (Bill) Daggett, the founder of the International Center for Leadership in Education. Daggett has been observing and leading in American education for decades, and he's long been one of the most respected voices in our field. When Bill Daggett speaks, I listen. This is what he said: "I think when we look back, we'll say COVID-19 has had a greater impact on reshaping American schools than No Child Left Behind, the recession of 2008, and all the other reform movements *combined*."

Combined. That's a serious, and credible, prediction.

I thought of the words of Mark McCrindle, how he said we are in the most transformative days for education since the 1400's, and when I paired them with Daggett's prediction, it struck me that unprecedented historical forces were now converging in the foyers of our schools. Hyper-change and the growth of AI, the demands of the 21st century economy, and our Gen Alpha and Gen Z students are all being mixed together in a concrete mixer of change—and the COVID-19 fallout became a catalyst that is reshaping American education and other education models around the world. And I thought, "What's this going to mean for 5-Gen leaders?"

When a building is burned and detectives determine the fire was intentionally set, they often find evidence of an accelerant, something used by the arsonist to start the fire. We should think of COVID-19 as an accelerant that has started a fire in our education system. Some parts of the system will be burned down while others will be left standing. Technology, already valued in schools but often underused, has now taken a starring role and will never leave the spotlight. Standardized testing was postponed in the spring of 2020, and most school leaders, teachers, students, and parents didn't care; it's now being questioned with renewed vigor. The negative and positive implications of online learning will be studied from new perspectives. And while many students missed being in school for academic and personal reasons (The Learning Network, 2020), I heard firsthand of some older students who were questioning if they really needed to be in a classroom all day, every day—or if ever again. It's not just students who want to stay home; I personally heard of teachers who would be perfectly happy teaching from home for the rest of their careers.

As the schools struggled to open for the new school year in the fall of 2020, educators and parents everywhere implemented hybrid education models and looked for more options. Some parents took education matters into their own hands as they collaborated to create learning pods of students who could have daily face-to-face instruction with a contracted teacher in their neighborhood (Blum & Miller, 2020). Some students and teachers didn't want to return to regular school—some because of health concerns, but others because they felt remote learning was more attractive than the traditional model. An eighth-grade Gen Z student in New York City wrote an opinion piece for *The New York Times* in which she preferred learning at home and advocated for deep, systemic changes in the system if she was forced to return to it (Mintz, 2020).

The second book I coauthored with Dwight Carter, *Leading Schools in Disruptive Times* (2018), in which we give tips to school leaders for surviving new and unprecedented school disruptions, became the urgent focus of administrative book study groups around America. We quickly did a second edition (2021) updated around the pandemic. How difficult had school leadership positions become in 2020? Here's what we wrote:

> In five system-shattering months, school leaders saw their already busy world turned upside down. In August of 2020, as the new school year was about to begin, school leaders were asked to do perhaps the most difficult task ever laid before them: to restart their schools with face-to-face instruction or remote learning (or both) as they dealt with a raging pandemic, savage political divisions, conflicting virus data, and severe budget restraints, all while worrying that they, some of their students, and some of their teachers could die because of their decisions.
>
> Let's frame that to understand its significance: Prior to 2020, school leaders just worried about school safety, test scores, and social media problems; *now they had to decide if their decisions might kill themselves, their families, their students, and their teachers.*
>
> How much are we paying these school leaders? Not enough. (Carter & White, 2021, emphasis in original)

The COVID-19 pandemic reset education; 5-Gen leaders who were racing to keep up with the demands of the 2020s suddenly had to educate Gen Z and Gen Alpha in the worst pandemic in over a hundred years and navigate incredibly dangerous new barriers to keep them alive.

The pandemic's impact will be felt forever by all of the generations. But as I looked at all of the accelerations and disruptions reconfiguring our world, it occurred to me that the pandemic, which started in a small market deep in China and quickly spread around the world—so quickly that it stunned scientists with its speed—shouldn't be viewed so much as an aberration but a sign of the new normal for 5-Gen leaders. In the second edition of *Leading Schools in Disruptive Times* (2021), we wrote about the constant and accelerating flow of disruptions buffeting our schools, and we proposed a new framing model: cope, adjust, and transform (CAT). School leaders often cope with new disruptions and then might adjust their policies or actions, but to survive today, they also need to *transform their leadership mindsets* to learn from the disruption—and to prepare for the next disruption, which will often be built upon the first disruption.

Let's picture it as a tree of disruptions. Each limb growing out from the tree will create new, smaller branches that will grow out from the limb, and they will all become increasingly larger. Now, think of the COVID-19 pandemic as a new limb in American education; the resulting changes will be the new branches stemming from it that will help reshape American education throughout 2020s. Some of these changes will arrive immediately, and some will morph out of new sprouts that eventually turn into robust branches. A writer for Brookings (Harris, 2020) highlighted some changes that could be brought about of the post-COVID education reset:

- Schools saw the power of some of the digital tools used in the closures and will continue to use more of them in the future.

- As the teachers use more digital tools, they will more likely see their roles shift from traditional instructors to facilitators.

- More virtual options for students and parents could result in families seeking their own education solutions that fit learning needs and lifestyle preferences.

And educators will race to stay ahead of Gen Z and Gen Alpha's efforts to use technology in the new ways; in 2020, some teens already figured out technology could help them skip school:

> Crafty teens figured out that they could cheat the system while attending online classes by looping a video or just adding a still image as their custom background in Zoom Rooms. While Mrs. Such and Such drones on about Franz Ferdinand, teens can leave their laptop running while enjoying Animal Crossing on Nintendo's Switch or watching porn or whatever it is kids do these days. (Clark, 2020, para. 4)

Note the common thread running through these disruptions: technology. It's the sap running through the tree limbs. The pandemic accelerated the need for education in the 2020s to have technology as a core component. Shifting into deeper uses of technology, *for all teachers*, is not optional anymore. Remote learning and new hybrid school/learning models have given our Gen Z and Gen Alpha students visions of what education might be in the future. While the remote learning model of 2020 was often ineffective, the school closings showed us how quickly schools can shift into a new model, and it gave us glimpses of our potential to reshape schools for the future. New school models are on the way, and the 5-Gen leaders must forge the path.

But they must also address another new challenge: closing the learning gaps brought about by the closures of 2020. Gen Z and Gen Alpha will feel the impact for years—perhaps for the rest of their lives.

> *Shifting into deeper uses of technology, for all teachers, is not optional anymore.*

Gen Z and Gen Alpha: The New Lost Generations?

In the 1920s, Gertrude Stein referred to young survivors of World War I as the "lost generation," a term she had heard used by one of her acquaintances, because they had lost their youth in the war; they had lost the years in which they could build their dreams. Ernest Hemingway then made the phrase famous in his 1926 book *For Whom the Bell Tolls* (Editors of *Encyclopaedia Britannica*, 2019).

In the era of remote learning, did the education bell toll for too many of today's Gen Z and Gen Alpha students? What will be the long-term impact of the pandemic on them psychologically and academically, especially for students living in poverty? Some are wondering if today's K–12 students will form a new "lost generation" (Kelly, 2020) because of the prolonged school closures. John King Jr., the president of the Education Trust, has said,

> [W]e know that when we have summer learning loss, it is a significant driver of our achievement gaps for low-income students. . . . Rather than two months away from school, we're looking at five or six months away from direct instruction in the classroom. Even in places that do distance learning well, we can expect that students will lose significant ground. (Kelly, 2020, para. 5)

King summed it up well. The positive impacts of remote learning were minimal, and even when schools did it "well," students lost "significant ground," especially our students from poverty and many of our students of color.

A study begun in 1992, the *Great Smoky Mountains Study*, showed the impact of family income on student achievement. If families have money to escape poverty, their kids are more likely to be successful academically in school (Costello et al., 2016). While the study has always been recognized for its findings, it's getting even more attention in the post-COVID education world as American families experience the worst economic depression since the 1930s. Another study by the National Academies of Science Engineering Medicine shows "a wealth of evidence suggests that a lack of adequate economic resources for families with children compromises these children's ability to grow and achieve adult success, hurting them and the broader society" (Duncan & Le Menestrel, 2019).

Today, that money buys a decent Chromebook and internet access.

But even new Chromebooks and a fast connection couldn't guarantee a quality education for many Gen Z and Gen Alpha students from poverty during the pandemic, mainly because the home situations in impoverished households are often unstable, and the parents might not have the ability to assist their kids with their studies because they are working multiple jobs or don't understand how to use the online programs (MacGillis, 2020).

Of 54 million American school students, nine million couldn't access their online assignments. Students who didn't have technology were often reduced to completing worksheets and doing assignments the teachers printed out from their online lessons. Students of color were especially hard hit in remote learning. The greatest number of digitally disadvantaged students could be found in underserved students—Native Americans, Blacks, and Latinx (USA Facts, 2020)—causing fears of disengagement and higher dropout rates, which could have long-lasting impacts on their lives and on the entire U.S. economy (Dorn et al., 2020).

When and how will this inequity be corrected? Finding answers has moved to the top of the priority list for 5-Gen leaders.

To compound the challenge facing Gen Z and Gen Alpha, the consulting firm McKinsey and Company asked over 800 business executives how the business world would be reset by COVID-19, and it shows the economic mountain just got higher. One of the findings is that "since the start of COVID-19, adoption of digitization and automation technologies has accelerated" (Dua et al., 2020). The Gen Z and Gen Alpha students who are being educated off the grid will be entering the same transformative economy as their more affluent peers who have access to technology, an economy that has dug even more deeply into the digital landscape. As the offline students do their worksheets with pens and pencils, their online peers are typing and surfing. The most vulnerable kids are being left behind—again— this time by a 21st century world relegating them to a 20th century learning mode.

In my workshops with teachers, I often tell a tale from my youth, of the night my parents sat down at the kitchen table and ensured my brother and I that we would have the knowledge needed to be successful in the 20th century. How did they do it? They decided to buy a set of *World Book Encyclopedias*.

But first, they debated whether or not they could afford the monthly payments. It was the 1960s, and while I was still in the primary grades learning my foundational skills, my parents knew owning a set of encyclopedias allowed kids to access information about the world at home; I would not be at the mercy of library hours. I would have the information I needed at my fingertips to thrive in my elementary, middle school, and high school classes. My mother finally settled the money debate with an emphatic statement: "We need to do this!" Then she turned to me and exclaimed, "Now you're going to college!"

And I did go to college, partly because I was lucky enough to have access to one of the most important learning tools of the era: a set of books filled with facts that were never updated. Today, the internet is the new *World Book*. It's updated by the minute and opens the doors to the future for our Gen Z and Gen Alpha students. In the 2020s, learning online should no longer be a privilege—it must now be recognized as a *fundamental right*.

Our American society will never reach its potential until it prioritizes internet access for every student in America. Five-Gen leaders must be more resolved than ever to find ways for every student, regardless of income or location, to access the internet.

But today's Gen Z and Gen Alpha students have another new, fundamental right: They deserve to have teachers who know how to teach in the digital space, which brings us to the next challenge for 5-Gen leaders: helping every teacher be digitally proficient.

The New Digital Divide

The COVID school closures exposed yet another digital divide in our schools— between those teachers who can use technology and those who can't, specifically those teachers who know how to let their students use technology. This new type of digital divide became exposed in March of 2020, and it was found in our generational teaching ranks. In April of 2020, I quizzed some administrators and teachers I knew in various parts of America about what they were experiencing with beginnings of online learning.

- I heard again and again from teachers and administrators during the closings that it was the older boomer and Gen X teachers who had the most difficulty in moving into remote learning because of the technology aspect.

- I heard from a teacher in the Northeast, an older teacher, who wished she'd paid more attention when the technology specialists were leading professional development sessions.

- I heard from an older teacher who was determined not to be left behind again and would quickly try to catch up with her peers and be more proficient in the next period of remote learning.

- From the New York principal, I heard of a divide—like a curtain—between teachers who could quickly transition into remote learning because they had already been using technology in their classes and those teachers who had shunned technology and fumbled away days and weeks of instruction time as they wrestled with Google Classroom or Nearpod or some other platform that could have made learning so much more effective (and their teaching jobs easier!).

- I heard the frustration of another principal (who was born late in the Gen X period, making her officially a young Gen Xer, though she thought of herself as more of a millennial leader) as she described the digital challenges encountered by her Gen X and baby boomer teachers. I did some follow-up training with her staff via Zoom sessions, and I, too, saw how some of the older teachers had trouble with the most basic of functions, like clicking on links and opening a new window in their search engine. As I looked at the gallery view in the Zoom sessions, I saw some of the younger teachers staring forlornly into their screens, waiting for their boomer and Gen X peers to catch up so they could continue the training.

So how is this new digital divide, often found between the older and younger teaching generations, affecting our Gen Z and Gen Alpha students?

Consider this: Two students could be in the same grade in the same school. Maybe their classrooms in school are side by side. Both students have top-of-the-line computers at home with robust, fast internet access. Yet only one of the two students has a teacher who knows how to navigate learning platforms and use education apps that allow for online formative assessments, collaboration, enhanced direct instruction, and digital creativity. The other student has a teacher who, for whatever reason, never got around to learning how to use much technology in the classroom. One student logs in and is able to use all sorts of programs to vary the learning and accomplish different objectives in various ways; the other student just logs in and watches the teacher lecture and then does a lot of worksheets downloaded onto the teacher's webpage.

If the two teachers are equal in knowledge of the subject, attitude, work ethic, and pedagogical best practices, which student has the advantage? The student whose teacher knows how to let his or her Gen Alpha or Gen Z students plug into technology. The Gen X principal I mentioned who saw the digital divide in her staff told me she was already seeing the divide in student achievement.

I thought of a line from Winston Churchill. In 1946 he famously said, "From Stettin in the Baltic to Trieste in the Adriatic, an 'iron curtain' has descended across the continent" (Westminster College, n.d.). In the spring of 2020, as schools closed and learning went online, a digital curtain descended between the houses of students who had technologically proficient teachers and those who didn't.

A Flipping of the Paradigm

Think of how technology proficiency has dismantled the seniority paradigm in the teacher ranks (see Figure 6.1).

It used to be more experienced teachers were the ones to whom the younger ones turned for guidance. While boomer and Gen X teachers still have a wealth of

FIGURE 6.1 The Impact of Digital Ability on Teacher Seniority

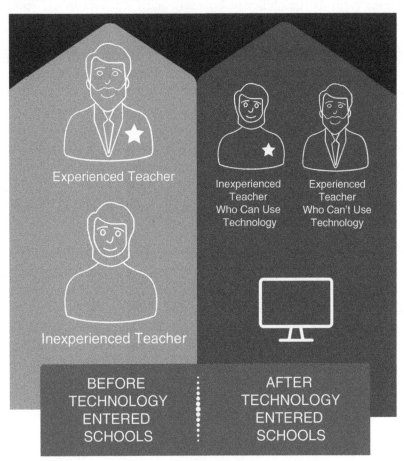

The Impact of Digital Ability
on Teacher Seniority

knowledge to offer, their lack of technology prowess, along with the fact that millennial and Gen Z teachers have more in common with their Gen Z and Gen Alpha students, has evened out the paradigm. Boomers and Gen Xers are like Santiago, the protagonist of Hemingway's *The Old Man and the Sea*: They know many tricks of the trade, and they can pass them on. But the younger teachers know many of the *new* tricks of the trade, specifically how to quickly move into a new online platforms and apps.

In previous decades, experienced teachers were far enough ahead of younger teachers in the traditional best practices that the older teachers could avoid incorporating technology into their practices, but the school closures of 2020 exposed this attitude as a career-altering deficiency. They fell behind their peers in this emerging, critical area, and consequently, their students fell behind their peers in the number of learning options.

Kristy Venne, the Ohio school leader who offered insight into coaching all generations in Chapter 3, saw her younger teachers helping to bridge the digital divide. Venne also reaffirms the ability of boomers and Gen Xers to use technology effectively—if they have the right mindset.

> As an educator with a growth mindset, I believe all teachers can learn to use technology well in their classrooms, regardless of their age. Prior to the pandemic, the divide between teachers using the latest education apps and district Learning Management System was significant. Once those technologies were no longer optional, the shift happened quickly. However, those who were already making strides were able to fully transition smoothly and ended up in an informal tech support role for their older colleagues. The older teachers that were the exception to this were the staff that tended to demonstrate a strong growth mindset, resourcefulness, and grit. (K. Venne, personal communication, March 15, 2021)

This same generation gap was also found at the university level in the spring of 2020 when younger staff members led the way into remote learning as the universities shut down. For example, at the Rutgers Business School in New Jersey, the younger professors took the lead in helping the older professors learn how to use technology and platforms. It was recognized that the younger professors had grown up with the internet and were much more comfortable using technology (Murray, 2020).

This technology deficiency had already been noticed in the private sector. In 2019, the United Kingdom recruitment company Robert Walters conducted a survey of business leaders. The study found 20 percent of the employers didn't see much value in having older employees in their companies, and "59 percent of workers had experienced intergenerational conflict in their jobs" (Robert Walters & Totaljobs, 2019). Even before the pandemic and employees were told to work from home, some companies were already putting an emphasis on recruiting younger employees because of their digital skills (Murray, 2020). As companies hire new employees in the stay-at-home world of the 2020s, will there be an even heavier emphasis on the applicant's ability to use technology? Will applicants who lack technology skills find it even more difficult to find employment? Will the same thing happen in education?

We don't have much time to get teachers caught up on their basic technology skills. Principals need teachers of all generations who can teach well in the classroom—and who can all quickly adapt when the next pandemic strikes, the next great education app arrives, or new AI enters the teaching space.

But it's not that easy. These technology-deficient teachers are in our staffs now. We've already seen there's a shortage of teachers, so easily replacing them is not an option, especially in places where removing weak teachers is a contentious, costly, time-consuming process. Plus, we have to remember teaching requires a wide skill set often developed through experience—and boomer and Gen X teachers often bring skills to the classroom their younger protégés are lacking. The 5-Gen leader must bring out the talents of each generation and allow them to help each other through mentoring and reverse mentoring. In the post-COVID reset, 5-Gen leaders must also deepen the technology skills of their older teachers to rip down the new digital curtain separating the generations.

> *The 5-Gen leader must bring out the talents of each generation and allow them to help each other through mentoring and reverse mentoring*

But first, they have to get these technology-deficient teachers to *believe* they can do it.

Adjusting Mindsets

I've mentioned that as a boomer teacher I used to teach high school English in the 1980s. The term "language arts" was just coming into our education vernacular. When I began my career, I saw myself as the defender of the canon, the one charged with drilling literary facts, themes, and titles into the heads of my students. I was old school. More like OLD SCHOOL. I look back at those days and think of an apology the author Kurt Vonnegut made for his generation's reliance on fossil fuels: "Dear future generations: Please accept our apologies. We were rolling drunk on petroleum." I say now, "Forgive me, former students. I was a boomer teacher rolling drunk on a history of education tradition."

Those days, thankfully, are gone because the world has changed, the economy has changed, our students have changed.

And I've changed. I began my journey down the winding Transition Road over two decades ago, and now I use more apps in my trainings than most millennial and Gen Z teachers use in their classrooms. Now my mantra to my boomer peers is, "If I can do it, you can do it!" Training boomer and Gen X teachers in how to use technology helps reduce the digital divide, but as Venne mentioned, the most important element is mindset: The older teachers have to be determined and willing to take chances.

While some boomer and Gen X teachers have transitioned well with technology, most younger teachers clearly have an advantage because technology's been a constant part of their lives; they are more likely to seamlessly and more quickly incorporate the technology into their new routines (Vogels, 2020). It's not that boomer teachers and Gen X teachers don't use technology in their personal lives; they use a wide variety, including computers, laptops, iPads, social networks, online banking sites, Kindles and other types of e-readers, new home entertainment devices, home health care technology, and GPS systems on their phones (Scheve, 2011).

But I've found older teachers are less inclined to quickly incorporate new technology into their professional lives. Sometimes when I train groups of teachers to use education apps, I hear these comments from boomer and Gen X teachers: "I have my established ways of doing things, so I don't need to use technology," or "Technology is great for other teachers, but not for me," or "I'm too old for that new stuff." As a boomer, I must admit that I, too, have those thoughts when I come across a new way to use technology to do something I've spent my entire life, six decades now, doing without using technology. I think, "But I've been just fine without it, so do I really need to use that app to do this?"

Boomers and Gen Xers are more likely to have to see a *need* to use the technology.

Here's an example. I live in Florida, which, for better or worse, was one of the first states to reopen during the pandemic, meaning I was one of the first ones in America who could go back to my favorite Starbucks to grab a coffee in the morning. I didn't want to hang around inside the store. I didn't want to stand in line swatting COVID germs away, and unlike many Americans, I tend not to like drive-through windows. Maybe that's my 60-year-old mindset kicking in: Why sit in a car in a long line when I can walk in and get it faster? (And the people who like drive-through windows could say, "Because, dummy, you won't be exposed to as many germs!") But as with other boomers, long-established routines stubbornly remain.

One morning I saw the need for change. I was in a short line inside my Starbucks store when I noticed a lot of people who had ordered their drinks online were just walking in, getting their order, and walking out. No waiting. "Hmmm," I thought. "Maybe it's time to use that Starbucks app I downloaded onto my phone a while back and never opened?"

Here's my boomer thought process: I asked, "Is this new way going to be a lot better than the old way? Is it worth the time to tap my way through the app to figure out how to use it?" I decided it was worth it: I could still get out of my car, walk in to get my coffee, and not wait in line. Plus, I hoped it was harder for COVID germs to hit a moving target. So I started using the app.

I admit I was frustrated the first time I opened it. I couldn't find where to order my coffee. I scrolled down and saw advertisements for pumpkin spiced lattes, new sandwiches, and all the ways that Starbucks loves the environment and is committed to social change, which is also Starbucks's way of targeting their products for millennials and Gen Zers. As a boomer, I just wanted to see a massive button in the middle of the screen that says, "ORDER COFFEE HERE, BOOMER!" I finally found the order button at the bottom of the screen. I ordered my coffee, drove to the store, walked in, got my coffee, and walked out—checking the name on the printout on the side of the cup four times to make sure I had the right one. It was a big deal, a huge shift for me.

But I did it. And I liked doing it. Now, ordering online is all I do. Actually, I've downloaded other apps for other restaurants, and I order everything before I go to pick it up, and I laugh at myself and think, "Wow, standing in line in the store is *so pre-COVID!*"

I had to see a reason to change, but when I did see the reason, I adapted. That's what boomer teachers and Gen X teachers must do with incorporating more technology into their lessons. They need to recognize the need for change. I've seen boomer teachers do it successfully. I was talking a while back with an elementary teacher who was close to my age, and I had been making periodic visits to her classroom for three years. At first, her students used no technology—she just used a smart board in front of the room—but she pushed herself to grow. By the time the pandemic arrived, she was ready to transition into remote learning. It wasn't easy. She made a confession to me: "At first, I didn't like you," she said, only half-jokingly, "because your ideas scared me. But now I can't wait to try new apps in my classroom. I want to keep growing."

I've trained thousands of educators, and I've *never* heard millennial or Gen Z teachers say they don't want to use technology, that they need to see a need for it. They just use technology because it's always been a part of their lives. They grab every bit of digital advice I can give them—and then they often show me new ways to use the programs. I learn from them.

It starts with a mindset.

Advice for Changing Mindsets

How can 5-Gen leaders help reluctant boomers and Gen Xers change their mindsets about technology usage? Here are four sentences I use to help teachers change their perceptions of what they can do with technology.

1. **"Make ongoing, personal improvement a priority."** Boomers and Gen X teachers need to lower their shields and accept technology

improvement as a viable goal. Sometimes, they don't even consider it as a worthy objective because they feel so far behind.

2. **"Keep short- and long-term goals and keep track of how you've improved."** No step forward is too small, as long as it's headed toward the goal. Administrators should ask, "How will you use this app in the next two weeks?" Then check on the teacher periodically to ask, "How's it going?" Help them—and let them know it's an expectation.

3. **"Take advice from your peers."** Teachers often learn best from their fellow teachers. Staffs usually have a digital all-star teacher or two who can guide these teachers. Or if there's a designated technology specialist assigned to help teachers, make sure that technologist is spending time with the teachers who need it. Sometimes, the digitally deficient teachers don't reach out for help because they are intimidated by technology or don't want to admit they have a weakness. If needed, administrators should reach out for them to get the conversation started.

4. **"Don't be afraid to fail."** One of the greatest fears for teachers is losing control or failing in front of students; however, losing control and failing are two of the prerequisites for teacher growth in the 2020s. Sometimes, teachers will make a mistake or the teacher does everything right—and the internet goes down or the app has some sort of hiccup that day and won't respond. Teachers need to regroup and try again a few days later. Most of the time, they will be successful, but occasional failure is now an acceptable option. Technology snafus are a part of any professional's life in the 2020s. It happens.

The Digital Gap in Administrators

I've talked about the digital generation gap between the boomers/Gen Xers and the millennials/Gen Zers, but it's time to shine a light on another digital generation gap, one that will be especially perplexing for boomer and Gen X school leaders: the gap in technology ability between their most digitally savvy teachers—the ones who know how to seamlessly use the latest apps and devices—and their *administrators*, who are often boomers and Gen Xers. During my visits in schools, I've heard many administrators speak with awe about their finest teachers who can deftly incorporate various apps and platforms into their teaching; yet while these leaders see the worth of technology prowess, they often don't take the time themselves to learn how to use these apps or how they could be incorporated into the PD they lead for their staffs. These administrators are missing a golden chance to model and to lead.

Five-Gen leaders can answer these two questions to see where they stand in the technology component of their development:

1. Can I have a conversation with my three or four most digitally savvy teachers and know enough details about their apps or programs to give them ideas on how to use them?

2. Do I know enough about these apps and programs to work them into the professional development I lead with the staff?

Put another way, the COVID-19 closures showed the importance of teachers being digitally savvy, and this also ushered in a new era of digital accountability for school leaders. School leaders do not have to be the digital trailblazers on their campuses. They don't have to know more than anyone else about how to use various digital tools, but they have to know enough and use enough technology to be able to join the conversation with their best digital teachers, and they should know how and use some of them in their PD to make learning more efficient and engaging for their staffs.

School leaders can lead the way into the digital space by showing teachers the power of technology and by showing another new professional trait: accepting vulnerability. We can control the textbooks, but we can't control the internet. Weird things happen with technology. Sometimes in the middle of the PD, the internet or the tools won't work, and the administrator, like the teachers, will have to quickly adjust. The administrator can feel what the teachers feel, and just as importantly, the teachers will accept their own need to be vulnerable. Figure 6.2 has five goals 5-Gen leaders can adopt to close their own digital gaps.

Great leadership has many components. Being able to help teachers use technology and using it in PD does not guarantee leadership success, but an inability to use

FIGURE 6.2   Five Technology Goals for 5-Gen Leaders

Five Technology Goals for 5-Gen Leaders

1	Know how to use technology when leading PD sessions.
2	Know enough to have academically rich conversations with tech-driven teachers.
3	Make technology improvement a career-long goal.
4	Network with other administrators to learn how they are using technology.
5	District level administrators should commit the time and resources to train campus level administrators.

technology well in the post-COVID world will be considered a leadership weakness. As more millennials and Gen Zers become administrators, this digital challenge will diminish; these generations are already using technology and will more easily adapt it into their leadership roles (more of this will be covered in Chapter 8). But we can't wait. Teachers and students need those administrators leading now.

FIGURE 6.3 Tips for Transitioning to 5-Gen Leadership

Tips for Transitioning to 5-Gen Leadership

33. Understand the COVID-19 pandemic could do more to reset education than all of the reform movements combined.

34. All teachers must now be able to use technology efficiently; the digital generation gap must be closed between the younger teachers and the more experienced teachers.

35. Helping Gen Z and Gen Alpha students deal with the emotional impact of COVID-19 will be an ongoing challenge of the 2020's.

36. Be aware that while teacher experience is still valuable, the need to use digital tools has closed the ability gap between younger teachers and some older teachers; help mesh staffs by tapping into the strengths of all generations.

37. Help the digitally deficient teachers by giving them tips on adjusting their mindsets and by giving them training and resources.

38. Close the digital ability gap between you and your most digitally savvy teachers.

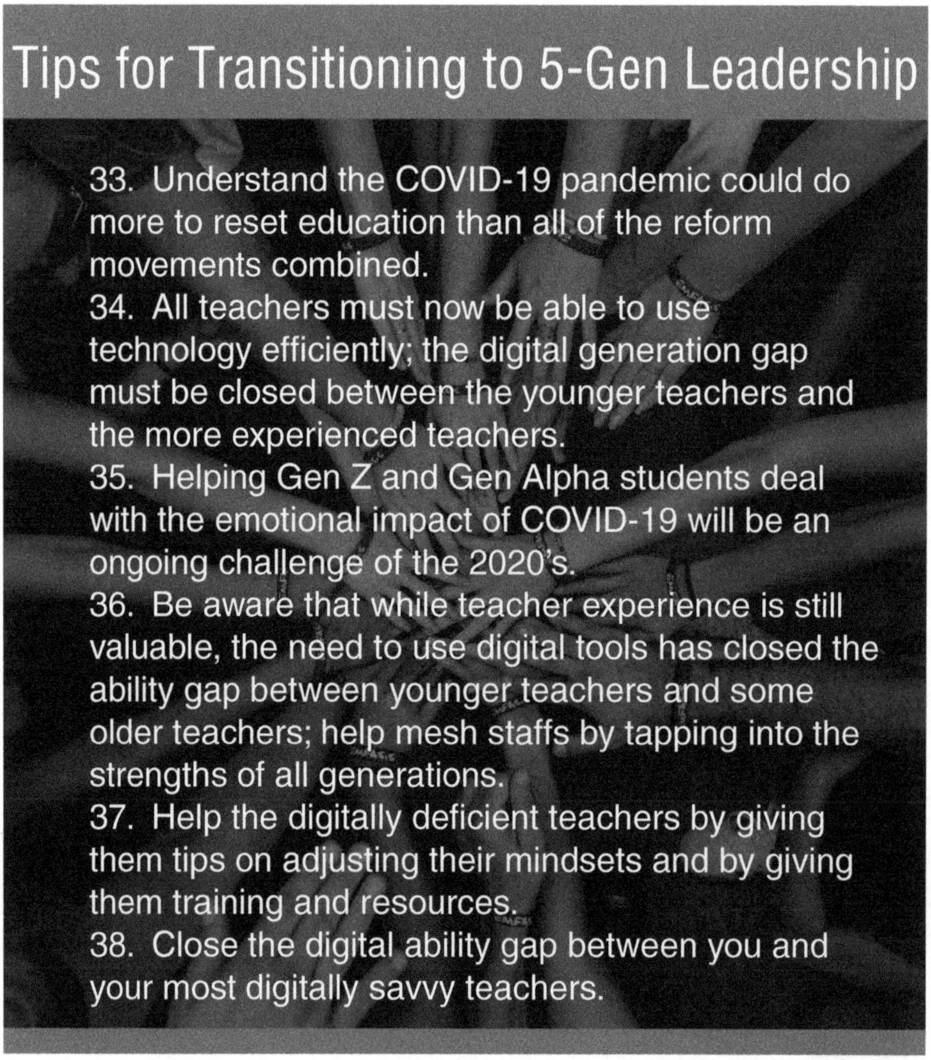

CHAPTER 7

Upagers and Political Activism

Key Points of This Chapter

- Members of Gen Z have become globally famous for their political activism.

- Gen Zers and Gen Alphas are seeing the political work of their peers via the internet and are adapting a more global view of political causes.

- Five-Gen leaders must recognize that today's young people want their views to be heard.

- Five-Gen leaders should be aware of the political causes their students care about and help them find constructive ways to voice their opinions.

One day I was leading a workshop and discussing millennial and Gen Z political activism. I pointed out that today's young people, including our students, tend to be more socially responsive and active than boomers and Gen Xers (Paychex Worx, 2019) because they grew up with the internet connecting them with others and seeing the political stands taken by other young people around the world.

A boomer asked a valid question: "But haven't young people always been the ones to lead protests? In my day, it was the Vietnam War protests." True. As someone who grew up in the 1960s and 1970s, I, too, remember the photos and news video of tear gas floating across university campuses as college students fought back against what they perceived to be an unjust war they were being asked to fight. Those were the days when the generation gap was on full display each night on the national news.

"Yes," I answered, "but those were mainly college students and people in their 20s and 30s. Today, it might be high school teenagers who are leading the way. That's a huge adjustment downward in age. It's one thing for adult college students to protest, but when high school students are walking out of class and organizing protests, that's significant."

Or being named "Person of the Year" by *Time* magazine.

Perhaps the most famous climate activist in the world is Greta Thunberg—and she's a Gen Zer. She was named *Time* magazine's person of the year in 2019 because, within a span of 16 months the 17-year-old had

> addressed heads of state at the U.N., met with the Pope, sparred with the President of the United States and inspired 4 million people to join the global climate strike on September 20, 2019, in what was the largest climate demonstration in human history. Her image has been celebrated in murals and Halloween costumes, and her name has been attached to everything from bike shares to beetles. Margaret Atwood compared her to Joan of Arc. After noticing a hundredfold increase in its usage, lexicographers at Collins Dictionary named Thunberg's pioneering idea, climate strike, the word of the year. (Alter et al., 2019, para. 4)

Thunberg is from Sweden, but she became globally famous through the internet. Gen Zers and Gen Alphas are watching. She has influenced "millions of students around the world" (BBC News, 2020), and one of our most famous members of the Silent Generation, the Pope, has encouraged her to continue her campaign. She's also been noticed by baby boomers—notably, former president Donald Trump, who mocked her by telling her to "work on her anger management problem" (BBC News, 2020). How did the Gen Zer respond? *She mocked him* by briefly changing her Twitter bio to include his words. School leaders had already learned this lesson: A disagreement with a Gen Zer can lead to a pointed rebuke on social media.

Five-Gen leaders need to remember access to the internet has given millennials, Gen Zers, and Gen Alphas a much more global view of the pursuit of social justice and political movements. Their views have shifted from those of earlier generations. I was speaking with a high school principal after the January 6, 2021, riot at the U.S. Capitol, and she was telling me how one of her teachers was indignant that his students didn't seem very upset by the attempt of a mob to stop the peaceful transfer of power to the new president. Part of their nonchalant attitude can be chalked up to just being teenagers who are more interested in other topics, but generational shifts are also a part of their nonresponsiveness. As an American boomer, I was raised by a World War II veteran on a street with houses owned by other World War II veterans. We heard firsthand about their fight to preserve freedom; there was very much an "America: Love it or leave it!" attitude. While all generations can be patriotic, the life-shaping events and fears of World War II have faded into the history books, and today's Gen Zers and Gen Alphas with their global views could be less inclined to quickly wave the American flag before first asking some hard questions about their country that would not have been posed 20 or 30 years ago.

The causes that were untouchable in the past are now embraced by Gen Z. Consider the case of Drew Adams, a transgender student in Florida who was told he couldn't use the men's room in his school. So at the age of 17, he sued the school and spent three years pursuing the case until a federal court ruled in his favor in 2020 (Pandey, 2020). Or Anusha Chinthalapale, a Gen Zer from Maryland who became dissatisfied with the way government was working, so she started the Montgomery County Students for Change, also known as MoCo4Change. She also worked as an organizer in the youth subdivision of the Women's March in 2017 (Chinthalapale, 2021).

Gen Z Survivors Leading the Way on Gun Reform

Gen Zers are taking an active part in fighting one of their greatest fears: shootings in their schools. Think back to the days after the horrific shooting spree at Parkland High School in Florida in 2018. The protests were led by the school's students, not the recent graduates or the parents. Students like David Hogg and Emma Gonzalez became household names.

I saw Gen Z activism firsthand on March 14, 2018, one month after the Parkland shootings that killed 17 students, when one of the biggest student walkouts in American history occurred to protest the lack of gun control and safety in American schools. As described in *The New York Times,*

> The first major coordinated action of the student-led movement for gun control marshaled the same elements that had defined it ever since the Parkland shooting: eloquent young voices, equipped with symbolism and social media savvy, riding a resolve as yet untouched by cynicism. (Yee & Blinder, 2018, para. 4)

In some parts of the country, school leaders punished students who walked out of class—and these principals were thrust into national headlines. Fairly or unfairly, the school leaders were viewed as being out of touch with their students. I've been in tight situations as a principal and superintendent, situations where I felt like I was going to lose any way I turned, but when these situations occur today, I've seen we have to step back and see the big picture and what's really happening—and what's really happening is that social activism is now an essential part of teenage lives. There's no way to stop it. As mentioned in Chapter 2, Gen Alpha (and Gen Z students) are "upagers," which means they are doing things at an earlier age, like taking on school authority en masse. There's no way some of the 20th century discipline philosophies are going to withstand the pressure reshaping Gen Z and Gen Alpha in today's schools.

On the day of the national school walkout, I was consulting in a middle school in the Los Angeles area, and I saw the 13- and 14-year-olds in that school as they participated in the protest. The principal didn't stand in the way; he worked with the students to control the situation as they made their point. He wanted to let his students protest, but he wanted to keep them safe and create a unifying moment in the school culture—without losing a day of instruction. So he had conversations with the student leaders and allotted them some time that day. The students designed a silent protest on the school's blacktop, a square of asphalt on the school grounds used for PE classes. During the 15 minutes of protest, as other students around the country were walking out of class or staging their own demonstrations, these students lined up 17 chairs on the asphalt, and an eighth grader sat silently in each chair, holding a piece of paper in front of his or her chest with the name of a Parkland shooting victim written on it. All of the students in the school were released from class so they could all see the silent protest and be participants. It was powerful. I'll never forget the sixth, seventh, and eighth graders standing in silence as they looked at the 17 chairs and the names of the victims. Seeing it made it real; the students reflected on what they were seeing. They felt the pain. There are so many days of school that students forget, but they'll never forget that day. I won't, either.

This principal, like other principals around the country who supported the students, exhibited 5-Gen leadership skills. He recognized the need in his students to be socially active and assisted them. If he had not worked with the students and instead had challenged them with discipline threats, they probably would have stormed out of the building, and it would have been chaotic and unsafe.

This is not to say we shouldn't have discipline procedures in place today. Students must have safe environments conducive to learning, but school leaders today need to recognize that individual students or groups of students who question authority or take part in protests shouldn't be seen as disrespectful—they should just be seen as Gen Z kids being Gen Z. It's who they have become.

One 11th grader in New York City put it this way: "Adults don't think of children as people. Our view of what happens now is more important than theirs because we are the future" (Reilley & Bubello, 2018). More than ever, administrators must partner with their students; fighting the entire student body is a losing battle, especially in this era of social media. Like our Gen Z teachers, our Gen Z and Gen Alpha students must be coached and not just managed.

We saw in Chapter 1 how Gen Z and millennial teachers are more likely to be more socially conscious and to seek out environments that prioritize social responsibility—that they are seeking more diversity, including diversity of thought (Paychex Worx, 2019). School leaders should tap into their passion when helping their Gen Z and Gen Alpha students tap into their desire to make social statements. When school leaders are confronted with civil rights issues, including issues pertaining to LGBTQIA+ rights and access for individuals with disabilities, they need to include their young teachers (along with teachers of the other generations) in finding solutions. They expect to be included—and they will demand to be included.

This brings up one of the most exciting points about the future of education: As more millennials and Gen Zers fill our profession, we will have more educators who could be even *more purpose driven* than their boomer and Gen X predecessors (who also had a strong commitment—which is why they became teachers). Here's another way of looking at it: When I'm asked, "Why did you become a teacher?" I often answer, "I wanted to make my small part of the world a better place." If we ask that same question to a purpose-driven Gen Z teacher, he or she might answer, "I want to do my part to change the world." We've moved from improving the neighborhood to improving the world. Think of how this deeper commitment could fuel educators as they confront the massive education disruptions of the 2020s, 2030s, and beyond. We should be grateful there's a different sort of fire burning in our young teachers.

Gen Z Leading the Way in the Pursuit of Racial Justice

On May 25, 2020, as many American students and teachers were finishing the end of their first, painful stretch of remote learning, George Floyd was killed while being arrested in Minneapolis, Minnesota. A world already turned upside down was jolted again—and because schools were closed, our students and teachers were home to see the constant news coverage and the horrific, looping video of Floyd on the ground, gasping for air because a police officer was pressing his knee into his neck. School administrators were already prepping for ways to help students deal with new, traumatic topics: fear of the COVID-19 virus, dealing with the death of a family member, understanding why a parent or both parents lost their jobs, not having as much food in the house, and handling the constant stress that comes with an uncertain future. Then the death of George Floyd, the resulting growth of the Black Lives Matter movement, and the sudden American collective soul-searching over racial equality added another layer of complexity to the 5-Gen leadership lens. School leaders had to help guide their communities through the pandemic and the friction that comes when confronting racism and inequities.

As with other issues, the generational gap was evident. In the 20th century, we would have said, "All of this is outside of school. Let's focus on school and academics." Boomers and Gen Xers, after all, represented a more disciplined, loyal, traditional view of the world. There was the real world, but then there was school, and they didn't always overlap. But the world has changed. Students are exposed to so much online media that they can't just turn it off when they walk through our school doors. We saw in the previous example how the middle school principal helped his students deal with school shootings; another real-world opportunity was presented in helping students deal with the trauma of COVID-19 and the pursuit of social justice.

But this could be challenging for a multigenerational staff. I've noticed that some boomers and Gen X teachers, especially at middle school and high school levels, have been transforming their views to be more student-centered than in the past, but others still focus on the curriculum first and the students second. Since millennials and Gen Z teachers bring more of a socially conscious view to their teaching, it could be easier for them to relate to the feelings of students who need to work through traumatic or controversial issues with a nurturing adult. This could be made even more complicated for a staff when views on authority and loyalty come into play: Boomers and Gen Xers will be more inclined to respect authority and be loyal to the administration and to other officials. They tend not to want to do too much to upset the status quo. On the other hand, we've already seen how Gen Alpha, Gen Z, and millennials are more likely to challenge the establishment and ask questions that might make boomers and Gen Xers uncomfortable.

In the summer of 2020, after many of the marches and protests around the world subsided, it was the Gen Zers who often kept the conversations about race going in the families. Teenagers talked with parents and reached out to other relatives through Facebook and then posted about their conversations online. The family secrets were suddenly in the open, and the resulting conversations led to more posts, which led to more conversations, which led to more posts. Some teenagers made Google docs with reading lists and links to videos and shared them with family members. These were not always easy conversations (Morales, 2020).

Carlos Hinojosa, a 17-year-old in Laurel, Maryland, tried unsuccessfully to talk with his mom about the racism they had experienced in their lives. Then he noticed she was watching videos about the Black Lives Matter protests on her favorite social media platform, Facebook, so he and his sister decided to start a conversation with her by sending her videos and messages from their own Facebook accounts. By the time Hinojosa organized a protest in his town, his mom was so engrossed in his efforts that she made signs, handed out water, and distributed yellow volunteer vests. Over 2,000 people attended the rally. "I have been educated by my children," she said (Morales, 2020).

Another Gen Zer, 17-year-old Betsy Schultz from Baltimore, compiled and shared a 37-page Google doc with links to GoFundMe efforts, petitions, and information about books, videos, and other resources. According to historians who study civil rights movements, the protests of 2020 were set apart from previous movements because social media provided platforms to communicate and share resources (Morales, 2020).

Lessons From a University Protest

Gen Z's reluctance to accept the status quo around racial issues is not just a K–12 issue; it's also a university issue. I'm a graduate of the University of Texas at Austin, and I saw my alma mater, steeped in its traditions, rocked to its foundations by the

Black Lives Matter movement. In June of 2020, Black Gen Z athletes banded together and released a list of demands to make the campus more inclusive. Some of the demands dealt with honoring previous black athletes, allocating funding for minority causes, and removing the remaining vestiges of the Confederacy from the campus grounds, which means the university was being asked to rename buildings named after Confederate war heroes and to remove Confederate statues (Barnett, 2020).

In July, the university leadership complied with most of the demands, but it didn't grant one of the group's wishes: that the university discard their school song, "The Eyes of Texas," which is set to a tune that was sung by slaves and was first performed with its current lyrics in a minstrel show over a hundred years ago. The song is deeply ingrained in school's culture, and the acting president, Jay Hartzell, said he hoped the university could "reclaim and redefine what this song stands for by first owning and acknowledging its history in a way that is open and transparent" (Carlton, 2020).

Earlier generations might have accepted the president's words, whether they agreed or not, and moved on. But this is Gen Z. This social consciousness battle was far from over. In August, the drum major of the University of Texas Longhorn Band, Libby Morales, said she would no longer conduct the song because of its racist history. "If the one thing that unites us all is a song, I feel like we're missing the real values of the university and the institution that we love so much," Morales said. "It's about the community that brings us all together. There can be any reason for that, but 'The Eyes of Texas' is no longer synonymous with community" (Briseno, 2020, para. 10).

In my undergraduate days, I was a music major. I spent two years marching in the Longhorn Band. I know its culture. No organization has more school spirit and loyalty to the University of Texas than this group. For its leader and some of its members to come out in opposition to ever again performing "The Eyes of Texas" was stunning. In my years in the band in the 1970s, it would have been unfathomable. But this is a new era. This young Gen Z leader and some of her peers have prioritized the collective good. As Morales said, "It's about the community." Five-Gen leaders need to grasp that for Gen Z it's about inclusivity; the world no longer revolves around tradition—it revolves around people and causes.

Five-Gen leaders need to grasp that for Gen Z it's about inclusivity; the world no longer revolves around tradition—it revolves around people and causes.

Morales added another comment that symbolizes Gen Z: She showed she was willing to directly challenge authority—in this case, the words of the acting university president. "I think President Hartzell made a very—I don't want to say uneducated—but out of all the ways to respond to it, that was not the way to do it,"

Morales said. "Coming from a white man that is the president of this University, it's inappropriate for him to say, 'Let's reclaim this song'" (Briseno, 2020, para. 20).

The band members appeared to be split in their opinions, but Morales had the support of a significant number of members—so many that it would have been impossible to perform the piece at football games in the fall of 2020. (It also would have been a mismatch of instrumentation with half the band refusing to play.) The university responded by using a recorded version of "The Eyes of Texas" at home football games, and the university administrators said the band would be prohibited from performing in any way at the games until the group agreed to play the alma mater. In other words, there would be no marching at halftime or playing other songs.

In previous decades, the administration's dictum probably would have forced the band, which is made up of students who love to march and perform, back into the stadium. They would have acquiesced. But not this generation. It became a high-noon Texas standoff between Gen Z and the president, who's a member of Gen X. In the fall of 2020, the Longhorn Band did not perform at a single football game. In the words of Don McClean's "American Pie," "the marching band refused to yield." The band members said they would rather continue discussions around the topic than compromise their values (CBS Austin, 2020).

As of this writing in the spring of 2021, the debate over "The Eyes of Texas" continues. Like other discussions around race, its origins run deep and personal. Regardless of the outcome of the standoff between the administration and the band, here's the lesson 5-Gen leaders everywhere at all grade levels need to remember: Morales and her fellow band members remind us that Gen Z doesn't blindly line up behind traditional authority figures. Leadership respect has to be earned today more than with previous generations. Gen Z and millennial members are often loyal, but they need to align with causes that match their views.

The Coming of the Minority Majority

The 2020s will be a decade of difficult discussions. Five-Gen leaders recognize that ethnic diversity is growing steadily in America, and inclusivity will be a constant theme for the rest of their careers. The percentage of Americans who are white has dropped steadily. In 1950, over 87 percent of Americans were white. That number dropped to 60 percent in 2017 and will drop below 50 percent by 2050 (Poston & Saenz, 2019). America will be a minority-majority country, one in which no ethnic group is a majority. Another way of viewing it is to say America is moving toward a future in which the majority of citizens are nonwhite, which means whites also will be a minority. This is the future of America, and it's the future of American schools. Today's millennial and Gen Z teachers, along with the Gen Beta teachers of the future, will continue to see student populations becoming more diverse each year. Five-Gen leaders must bring diversity awareness to the front of their priorities. Studies indicate companies with diversity, including generational diversity, in their leadership have higher profit margins (Murray, 2020). The greatest schools will be the ones that embrace diversity of all kinds.

Some districts are already responding by creating positions that oversee diversity, equity, and inclusion (DEI), and sometimes individuals in these positions are titled Diversity, Equity, and Inclusion Officers, or DEI Officers. But creating the position is the first step. It takes commitment and a willingness to have honest, sometimes painful, conversations over a long stretch of time. The challenges of racism, equity, and inclusion aren't solved with assemblies and posters in the hallways. One blogger for ASCD, Erica Buchanan-Rivera (2020), has written,

> This journey of racial equity requires much self-labor and introspection that no one can do for a person. If your ideal image of equity work is managing inequities through diversity celebrations and not dismantling disparities, you may need to reevaluate your commitment to antiracism. This work is not a social event. Hosting an international festival on a Saturday evening is not going to eliminate racism when students return to school on Monday morning. (para. 5)

Buchannan-Rivera also suggests that before schools create a DEI position they should understand their "why" so that the officer can be empowered and all parties can work together. She also recommends that the expectation must be that every person in the district take ownership and be deeply reflective. It takes a strong person to be in this position; the individual must be willing to speak truth to power. And leaders must listen and be strong enough to adjust their own practices and those within the system (Buchanan-Rivera, 2020).

But today, it's more than just what the adults must do; it's also about involving the Gen Z and Gen Alpha students. When I was growing up as a boomer, the teenage heroes were Donnie and Marie Osmond and Michael Jackson—pop music stars who sang about teen love and broken hearts. If they were teenagers today, would they still be singing about the travails of romance? Probably so. Some topics, like teen angst and budding hormones, will remain relevant for each generation. But Donnie, Marie, and Michael would probably have new topics in their repertoire; among them would be lyrics about climate change, racial equity, equal pay for women, equal rights for people who wish to change their gender, and stopping gun violence. For 5-Gen leaders, this means they must keep an open mind and remember the days of silencing political dissent in the student ranks are gone forever.

One outstanding 5-Gen leader who understands this is Dwight Carter, a school leader in Columbus, Ohio. He happens to be my friend and coauthor of my previous two books. He is a Gen Xer, and he explains what needs to be done to bring more equity into America's schools. His words are so powerful that we end the chapter here.

America's browning will continue to challenge our educational system to examine our instructional, assessment, and social structures so that diversity is not merely tolerated but is embraced and normalized.

We are charged with implementing more social-emotional learning strategies, using more formative instructional practices, and examining the resources we use in the classroom to create a culturally relevant and personalized learning environment for all students. To do that, we must consider the kind of professional learning opportunities we make available to our staff. Most, if not all, schools across the country have focused on some form of race, equity, and inclusion training this year. We have to be careful that this work is not simply something to check the box. This work has to be normalized and included in our efforts to create a positive school culture and climate.

Our Generation Z and Generation Alpha students are not satisfied with the status quo. They have witnessed their peers impact change when they use their collective voices in response to injustices. For example, when I was principal at Gahanna Lincoln High School in Ohio, Trayvon Martin was killed. In the days following this tragedy, I met with several students who wanted to take action. They were hurt, angry, and frustrated. They needed to be heard and wanted to take a stand. They proposed that they be allowed to wear hoodies in school in protest, which I thought would have been a nice visual, but I wondered what that would accomplish.

I asked them to think more about their purpose. Afterward, I immediately met with three outstanding educators who had their thumbs on our students' pulse: ELA instructor Dr. Donja Thomas, school psychologist Mrs. Johnel Amerson, and family consumer sciences instructor Mrs. Keah Germany. I told them about my conversation with the students and asked for their advice. Together, we brainstormed some ideas and followed up with the students a few days later. Out of those conversations came a fantastic program called Diaspora: Voices of an Ever-Changing America, where students showcase their thoughts, emotions, and experiences through art, song, dance, spoken word, monologues, and the like. They use this platform to tell their stories and to move others to action. They want to not only share their scars but to celebrate their successes. Nearly 10 years later, the program is still going strong and has received local accolades and state awards.

Fast forward to the spring and summer of 2020 when social justice protests occurred across the globe. Educators ordered many books about anti-racism and researched ways to decolonize the curriculum to provide a more inclusive learning experience. The same thing happened after the death of Trayvon Martin: outrage, protest, and reaction. Will the efforts to create a more equitable educational experience for all students stick this time around? I'm optimistic and believe so because Gen Z and Gen Alpha don't settle, they don't forget what was promised to them, and they know their voice makes things happen. While we, as adults, may settle into a relaxed state, they will continue to ask questions, demand change, and expect us to hear them out and include them in the decision-making process. They are looking to us for guidance, assistance, and support. Our role is to help them overcome hurdles in their way, help them develop the personal skills to navigate through change, and eventually pass the leadership baton onto them. Soon, it will not be an anomaly to have a Black or brown principal or executive leader in a district because we are preparing students to take on these roles in the near future. We can't afford to treat this time as merely a swelling of emotion. We can ride this momentum to create more moments that make social justice for all students. (D. Carter, personal communications, March 16, 2021) ∎

FIGURE 7.1   Tips for Transitioning to 5-Gen Leadership

Tips for Transitioning to 5-Gen Leadership

39. Help staff members understand Gen Z and Gen Alpha have a more global view and are more politically active than their predecessors.

40. Remember that political and civil rights topics that were untouchable 20 years ago could be embraced by Gen Z and Gen Alpha.

41. Some Gen Z students have become global activists through Youtube, social media, and internet; expect your Gen Z students to use Youtube, social media, and the internet to further their causes as they lead locally.

42. Gen Z and Gen Alpha students are much more likely to question authority and reject the status quo; be prepared to work cooperatively with them to find solutions.

43. Consider the steps you can take systemically to further the pursuit of racial justice; it's more than cultural celebrations or social events.

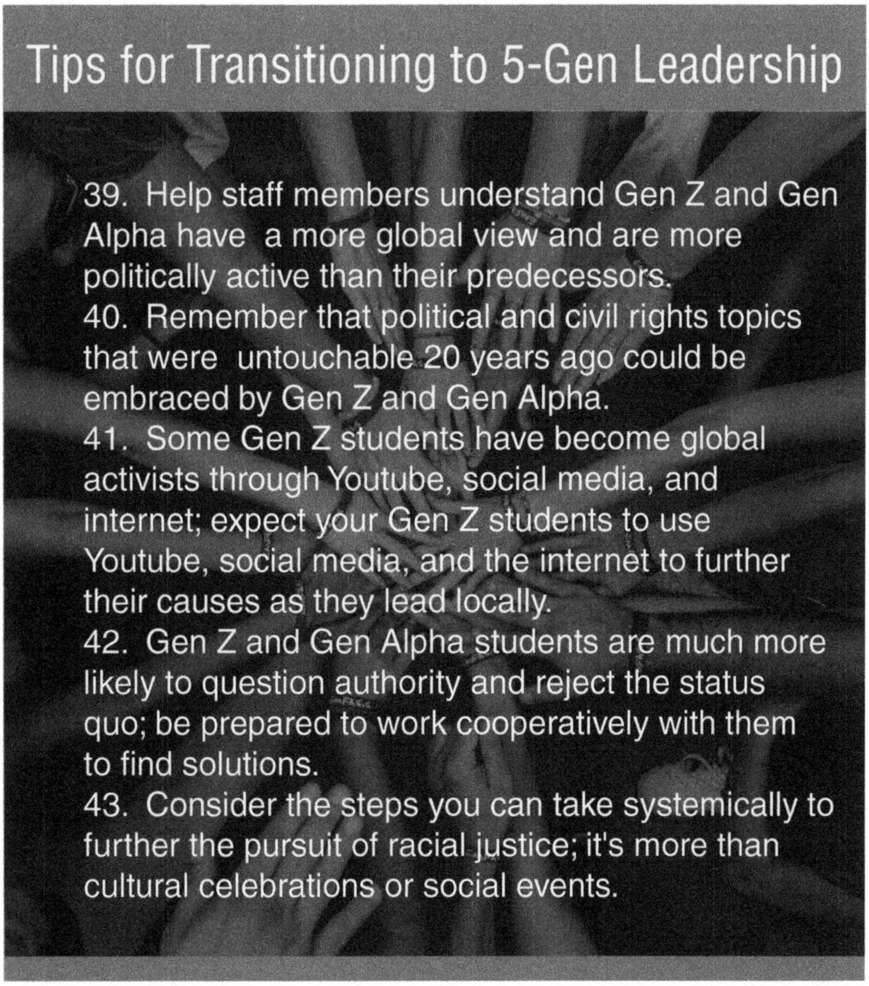

CHAPTER 8

Millennials and Gen Z Ascending in the 2020s

Key Points of This Chapter

- Millennials and Gen Z school leaders will assume more leadership positions by 2030.

- PreK-12 school models will need to be adjusted to fit the needs of Gen Z and Gen Alpha students and their families in a post-COVID world.

- Artificial intelligence will reshape education to the point that it could replace weak and average teachers.

- Schools will have to find ways to help young people connect with other humans and their own humanity as technology plays an increasingly larger role in their lives.

A few months ago, I began the process a lot of other boomer empty nesters have gone through: I began downsizing. I decided I just didn't need as much "stuff." Years ago, my mother had given me and my wife her set of dining room china; it had been given to her as a wedding gift by her father. We wanted to keep the china in the family, so my wife boxed it up and shipped to my millennial son and his wife, who live on the other side of the country. He didn't ask for it. I just did it on my own. Surprise!

Then I came across this latest development: Many millennials and Gen Zers *don't want their parents' possessions* (Crosby, 2019). The china, the hutch, and the quilt sewn by Grandma have been left behind as Amazon Alexa takes over and the generations form their own, new paths. And I thought, "Whoops! Did my son and my daughter-in-law even *want* the family china?" When I spoke with them, they assured me they "loved it" and would use it. Maybe they really did love it, but they're both super nice people—perhaps they were just being nice to their out-of-touch boomer father.

And I wondered: What practices will our millennial and Gen Z education leaders keep in the future as they take more prominent roles in reshaping our schools? Will they keep the best of what we can give them and discard the rest? Or will they choose to keep too many outdated practices that mire them in the past?

First, let's look at the demographics to see the generational makeup of our schools at the end of this decade and the role millennials and Gen Zers will play in leading them. In 2030, we can expect this from our five generations:

- The last of the boomer educators born in 1964 will be 66 years old. Many boomers will have retired from our schools by then, but a few of them will still be teaching and leading schools. To still be relevant, they will have been forced to make dramatic mental and operational adjustments to keep up with the world dominated by AI, new types of students and staffs, and increasingly differentiated education models.

- The Gen Xers will be between the age of 51 and 65. Many of them will still be teacher leaders and in key administrative positions. While generations today tend to work later in life and pension plans are forcing educators into longer careers, a third of the Gen Xers will be over 60 years of age in 2030. A significant number of them could have left the profession, and their exit (along with the departing boomers) will have resulted in a rapid expansion of the number of millennials and Gen Zers in the school leadership ranks.

- Millennials will be between the ages of 35 and 50 by 2030, and more of them will be superintendents and hold district office positions; however, the majority of millennial school leaders could be in the school campuses. Today, millennials make up the largest part of the American teaching force, so by 2030, they could comprise the largest group of school administrators; the impact of their technology/global/altruistic mindsets will be fully impacting elementary, middle, and high school operations.

- The oldest Gen Zers will be 34 years old, and they will have begun to enter the administrative ranks in the lower levels. Consider this shift in collective mindsets: We have many campuses today led by boomers and Gen Xers; within a decade, many campuses will have millennial principals and Gen Z assistant principals. The pre-internet leaders will be succeeded by the post-internet leaders. Any boomer or Gen X teachers (or administrators) on those campuses will be surrounded by millennial and Gen Z teachers; the older teachers will encounter even more pressure to adapt to technology and the learning demands of their Gen Alpha and Gen Beta students. There will be no future in the 2030s for 20th century mindsets.

- The oldest Gen Alphas will be 20 years old, and these young people wishing to be teachers will be in the teacher preparation programs. It used to be we could predict how these programs would function because they've used similar systems built around traditional education courses and various amounts of field experiences, including a capstone student teaching experience. However, the reset of education in the 2020s—with advent of new models and increasingly powerful AI—could reshape the role of teachers, and teacher preparation programs will have to adjust or perish. The use of more AI could result in a need for fewer teachers and even fewer teacher preparation programs. There will still be place for Gen Alphas in the teaching ranks, but they will have to be extremely motivated, talented, and willing to have a career in which they share the stage with increasingly powerful, dominant forms of AI—as will be the case for most professions in the world.

So we can see by 2030 that a few boomers could still be leading, Gen Xers will be leading but eyeing retirement, and millennials and Gen Zers will form the largest block of school administrators as they ascend into the higher levels of administration. If they hold true to their generational trend of rejecting the status quo and questioning the policies and operating procedures bestowed upon them by their boomer and Gen X predecessors, then by 2030 the websites of many schools could have a large banner streaming across the top of the landing page proclaiming, "Under New Management!"

But here's an indicator of how complicated school leadership will become: In 2030, superintendents and principals will be leading these groups:

1. Boomers

2. Gen Xers

3. Millennials

4. Gen Zers

5. Gen Alphas

6. Gen Betas

This means by 2030 the 5-Gen leaders will become new types of leaders: 6-Gen leaders.

Four Key Points and Questions for the 2020s

What are the lessons of the COVID crisis of 2020 and 2021 that can guide school leaders in the 2020s (including boomers and Gen Xers) as this generational transition takes place? In February of 2021, as the first vaccines began to go into arms and people began to see the light at the end of the COVID tunnel, I gave a keynote with Dwight Carter for Ashland University in Ohio for PreK–12 administrators. My crystal ball predicting the future of PreK–12 education was murky, as if it were filled with frozen vaccine, but Figure 8.1 shows us four pandemic points that cut through the fog.

These four points can be the North Star of education transformation in the 2020s: rapid adjustments, expanded technology usage, flexible schooling models, and shift toward new types of accountability measures that are more effective and more accepted by all stakeholders. It's always been said that schools tended to move at glacial speeds, but the pandemic showed how quickly education, like other fields, can cast off the shackles and move into a new model centered on technology usage. It showed how hungry many parents and students are for school systems that can adjust with their unique needs. Educators, students, and parents have all complained about the amount of testing done in public schools and the strict accountability system that drives so many public school agendas; the varied stakeholders saw that schools did not come crashing down because the schools weren't given updated accountability labels in 2020. The pandemic opened the doors to change,

FIGURE 8.1   Lessons From the Pandemic

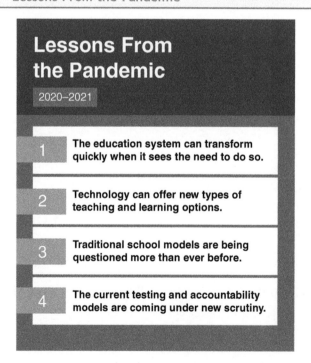

5-GEN LEADERSHIP

and millennial and Gen Z school leaders could be ideally positioned to embrace these points—because their life experiences have prepared them to adjust more quickly than many of their older peers.

In one of my coaching sessions in early 2021, a Gen X teacher said, "Remote learning has forced us all to adjust what we do. It's like we're all first-year teachers again." I agreed. Experienced teachers knew the content, but they had to question and relearn every teaching method they had in their toolkit as they moved their instruction online. Some did better than others. I observed hundreds of online classrooms and noticed a pattern. *Some* of the more experienced teachers adjusted quickly—but *almost all* of the younger, less experienced teachers adjusted swiftly. First, they had the technology acumen to quickly learn to navigate the platforms like Zoom and Google Meets. But here's a second reason I think they were able to more deftly adjust: They have mindsets that are less set by tradition because all they have known is a life dominated by increasingly powerful technology that constantly brings them new apps, new social media, new smartphones, and new types of digital gaming. Remote learning threw teaching and learning into their wheelhouse, so they were more likely to reimagine their methods, including their pacing, their checking for understanding, and how and when to incorporate breakout rooms and other digital tools into their lessons.

This doesn't mean it was always easy for these young teachers or that they were always successful, but I saw a large number of them quickly move from one digital tool to another when they learned which one was best for certain activities. As more Gen Z and millennial teachers enter the teaching force and as more Gen Z and millennial leaders assume more influential positions, they will bring a mindset of more rapid adjustment than we have seen in many of our boomers and Gen X leaders.

This is good news because they'll have to be fast to keep up with the rest of the world.

The University Model Could Affect the PreK–12 Model

We know a significant goal of PreK–12 education has been to prepare students to enter universities; postsecondary practices have always trickled down into the lower levels, especially into our high schools. But we can expect a new type of trickle-down effect from universities—specifically, how Gen Z's new expectations for postsecondary life will help dictate how high schools function.

Most of this decade's university undergraduates will be Gen Zers; the first Gen Alphas will hit the college campuses in 2028. First, let's consider what new demands Gen Zers will make in their university instruction. When campuses closed in March of 2020 and the students went home and stayed home in the fall of 2020, it became very clear they missed being on campus. One survey of over

3,000 college students in April 2020 found that 68 percent found the online instruction worse than what they had in person, and 26 percent of the students questioned if they would continue their studies. Almost half of them said if they had to do online learning they would prefer it to be totally asynchronous, and 36 percent would prefer a blended model of in-person and online learning (Top Hat Staff, 2020). To improve online learning, the students suggested they have more face-to-face interaction with faculty, more learning material, better overall coordination between the deans and administrators and the faculty, and more opportunities for online social experiences with other students. Many of them said they liked the flexibility of online learning.

However, a new lifestyle trend emerged in the fall of 2020 for Gen Z: As universities remained closed, some students banded together to rent houses where they could live as they did their online lessons, and sometimes the houses were far away from the universities—like in other parts of the country. Basically, the Gen Zers said, "We don't want to be at home, but we can't go to back to the campus, so where would we like to live?" They chose cities and regions that fit their Gen Z interests and lifestyles. Students who wanted to live in cities might have chosen New York City, Portland, or Las Vegas. Some students chose the island life of Barbados. Utah was popular because of its many outdoor activities. The students grew up watching YouTube stars and influencers who lived together in large houses, so they already had ideas on how to do it. Like their reality-star heroes, they drew up their own social contracts, including protocols for quarantining. Of course, the contracts were shared online, usually through Google Docs. How did they find their houses to rent? Often though Airbnb (Lorenz, 2020). They used the internet to find living quarters, share their collaborative contracts, and complete their lessons. These students showed us they are resilient, innovative, and viewing college life differently than their predecessors. It was a Gen Z dream come true—one built around the internet.

Gen Alpha and Gen Z students at the PreK–12 level could emulate their older siblings. This idea of remote learning during remote instruction is already taking root in our younger students: In the winter of 2021, an internet ad for the company VRBO, which rents private residences for vacations, showed a Gen Alpha youngster holding up some schoolwork outside a rustic cabin with a child's voice asking, "If school isn't someplace you *have* to be, why not be someplace you *want* to be?"

And they might not want to be in school, especially for five days each week. I heard of a large number of districts around the country that had "asynchronous Fridays" when students learned online, could catch up on what they had missed during the week, took part in targeted interventions, and allowed teachers to plan. Could this be a more regular fixture for all grade levels once school returns to "normal"? Could younger students be given the option of attending school on Fridays or learning from home if they have parental supervision?

I was talking with a high school principal about new types of flexible scheduling, and he told me that, during the pandemic, students had a choice of coming to school or staying home for online instruction. The students in extracurricular activities could learn from home and come to the campus at the end of the day for their activities. A few of them arranged their schedules to get their morning instruction online, but they would attend one or two classes in-person in the afternoon before going to football practice, cheerleader practice, or some other activity. When I asked him what he could see happening in the future for his juniors and seniors, he said, "Why can't some of them do like they'll do in college? They could have a choice. They could take some of the courses online and mix it with in-person instruction for others." Our Gen Z students will be in our high schools until 2028. By then, many 11th- and 12th-grade students—our students who are the most mature, most independent, and most likely to seek out their own learning paths—will probably demand flexible models that allow them not to come to school every day for every period.

In summary, Gen Alphas are called the "upagers" because they are grasping adult concepts earlier in their lives, but we can see Gen Z university students are also doing things other generations didn't do until later in life: organizing a new sort of life in another part of the country as 18- to 22-year-olds. Now is the time for 5-Gen leaders to be ready to quickly adjust to new Gen Z and Gen Alpha demands for more technology-centered instruction with different schedules and calendars.

New Paths to Leadership

When we think of school leadership today, we tend to think of the traditional positions. In the district office, it's the superintendent, assistant superintendent, and various directors; on the campuses, it's often the principal and assistant principal. In Chapter 1, we looked at the need to involve millennial and Gen Z teachers in leadership decisions, to give them a voice on committees and in hiring practices. Research shows millennial and Gen Z employees are seeking paths of advancement (Gayle, 2019), but what does that mean for today's millennial and Gen Z teachers in the 2020s who want to advance? I recently had a conversation with a millennial teacher, and she told me she was beginning her graduate coursework to receive her principal's certification.

"Why do you want to be a principal?" I asked, and she replied she was wary of the stress that comes with being a principal, but she wanted to lead so she could help others. "You're wanting to lead for the right reason," I told her, "but there are more paths for you today and more will be opening up in the near future. You don't have to be a principal to lead in today's schools."

Twenty years ago I wouldn't have said these words. As a boomer, my path to career advancement was the most predictable one: teacher to assistant principal to principal to assistant superintendent to superintendent. I climbed the 20th century ladder to the top. To be clear, we still need great administrators at these levels; without the right people in those key positions, progress in the 2020s will be difficult, if not impossible. Experience gained while moving through various positions still helps leaders have a greater understanding of the system. But the morphing of the world has begun to open up new leadership positions in schools; there are new paths to leadership.

For example, as technology becomes even more prominent in education, education technology specialists will become even more important, and we will need more of them. And what if more of our future principals will come out of these tech-savvy positions and not just the assistant principals' offices? They will step into the principal's role with a deep background in the best education apps, device characteristics, and—just as importantly—deep experience in helping teachers use technology. When superintendents hire principals today, they should be looking for applicants who are proficient in using technology; we can expect this requirement to be more widespread with an even deeper level of knowledge needed by principals in the future. We're seeing other new types of positions implemented at the district and campus levels: diversity coordinators, interventions directors, community outreach coordinators, academic coaches, and extracurricular activity sponsors (American University, 2019).

As 5-Gen leaders mentor the ascending millennial and Gen Z teachers, they should embrace the idea that school leadership no longer has to be confined to the traditional ladder that goes through the assistant principal and principal offices. A new system will call for new types of positions with varied ways of thinking and leading.

The Future: Millennial Teachers, Gen Z Teachers, and AI Teachers?

I recently had an AI epiphany of how AI could be used in the late 2020s and beyond.

It happened when I visited a high school and watched videos of Algebra I teachers teaching online. The first teacher basically just blasted through the assignment. He "taught" students how to solve problems by using a document camera to project problems onto the screen as he solved each step. He didn't bother to check on his students' emotional well-being when students joined his class, and there was no fun banter during the lesson. Most of the students never spoke a word. These socially isolated teens at risk of developing deepened states of depression never got to verbally interact. The rigor was low; the teacher's direct instruction was at the lower end of Bloom's taxonomy. He just explained each step, hoping the students would understand it without asking questions to get the students to think, to encourage them to analyze what was happening in the steps. There was no relevance in the problems. I'll be the first to say a teacher can't make all content relevant, but no efforts were made in this lesson. The Gen Z kids love digital interaction, but these students didn't interact with digital tools; most of them had logged into the lesson via a computer, but they didn't get to show their thinking or level of understanding with a Jamboard or any other interactive program. After 14 minutes of direct instruction with no interaction with the students, he asked, "Everybody understand?" and then he quickly resumed his instruction when no one answered. Of course they didn't answer! I'm sure most of them were intimidated, confused, or weren't listening. Perhaps they were no longer even sitting at the computer. They were part of the multitude of pandemic era students who logged in to get attendance credit, turned off the camera, and then wandered off to play Xbox or scroll through their social media.

This wasn't really school; it was just a time for the students to log in and get the facts of how to solve the problems. If they were one of the handful of students who could learn algebra in this way, then they could succeed. Of course, most students couldn't. Failure rates in the class were high. Students weren't logging on, and many of those who did log on couldn't understand the concepts and weren't submitting their work. The human element was absent in the teacher, buried some place on the other side of the teacher's screen.

Then I watched another math teacher lead an online lesson in the school, and his lesson was pretty much the same. Then I watched another math teacher, and she, too, just plowed through the content. I watched two more math teachers. I wish I could say I found a math superhero, or at least a regular hero, but alas, they, too, were lacking in personality and ability. They all knew their content. They were working hard. They all cared and wanted their students to be successful, but either through fatigue or callousness, they had developed a teaching philosophy of "Here's the content. I'll show you how to solve the problems. Then it's up to you to know how to solve them. Good luck."

I had observed all of these teachers prior to the pandemic when they were doing traditional face-to-face teaching, and they had all been average. What is average teaching? A lack of personality, a lack of interaction, a lack of checking for understanding. These problems in a normal classroom were exacerbated during the COVID crisis. These average teachers had slipped to below average when their students were no longer held captive in their classrooms and were forced to listen to them and learn in this way. These algebra teachers weren't the only teachers who were teaching like this in the pandemic and getting these low results; across America, too many students had logged in but checked out—and so had too many teachers.

I turned to the administrator who had been watching the videos with me, and I said, "AI."

Of course, she looked at me with a puzzled look, so I added, "If this is the way they're going to teach, either online or in person, by 2030 many of them could be replaced by artificial intelligence. I would trust a software program to do better than these teachers. At least the software could build in questioning built around student data, respond to answers, and insert activities that check for understanding." Then I said, "And probably show more personality. My Amazon Alexa at home is more personable than these guys."

It was a tough comment, but tough times call for honest answers.

In this pandemic age, AI is becoming more human while some teachers have become less human. Throw in the race to prepare students for standardized tests and we could say the humans who lack training, initiative, support, or imagination are turning into teaching machines. They rush through the material as quickly as they can so they can make sure the standards are covered. In my coaching, I saw too many other teachers reading slides to students. I saw too many human-designed lessons that were too boring and ineffective for the majority of students to sit through on a daily basis. We need the human touch in teaching, but if the humans aren't human, they should be replaced with software that at least pretends to be. Many teachers have told me a computer can never bring to teaching what a human teacher can bring—but I say that's true only if the teachers choose to bring those human qualities into their jobs.

Artificial intelligence is already helping to teach some students. An article from November of 2020 by Dylan Furness posted on *Digital Trends* details how AI was recently used in a class at the Georgia Institute of Technology. The students in a class had a teaching assistant (TA) named Jill Watson, and this TA would respond to their emails promptly and in a casual tone that helped the answers be understood. At the end of the semester, the students were told Ms. Watson was not a human, but an AI program, also known as a chatbot or a bot. Furness (2020) writes,

> Like computers and the internet, AI will alter both the face and function—the what, why, and how—of education. Many students will be taught by bots instead of teachers. Intelligent systems will advise, tutor, and grade assignments. Meanwhile, courses themselves will fundamentally change, as educators prepare students for a job market in which millions of roles have been automated by machines. (para. 4)

This will not just happen at the college level. Toys for young kids that use AI are already on the market, and they will become increasingly stronger. One AI expert predicts a growing role for them in classrooms and at home. According to Danny Friedman, director of curriculum and experience at Elemental Path,

> I foresee them in every classroom, as a supplemental learning tool that is not only integrated in a teacher's curriculum but connected to a student's personalized data, such as preferred learning methods and areas of interest. I also foresee them in every home, not only to help answer questions, but to help instill pro-social interactions. AI-powered toys

will be as ubiquitous in households as the cell phone. (Furness, 2020, para. 7)

As students progress through the grade levels in the future, AI will be play an increasingly larger role in their education. Pearson, the massive education and assessment service, released a report in 2016 titled *Intelligence Unleashed: An Argument for AI in Education* in which it said all students could one day have an AI "learning companion" that could assist individuals in their personal and academic lives as the companion accompanies them from grade to grade, from class to class, as it connects data, trends, learning requests, and experiences. Furthermore, the report states

> There are no technical barriers to the development of learning companions that can accompany and support individual learners throughout their studies—in and beyond school. These lifelong learning companions could be based in the cloud, accessible via a multiplicity of devices, and be operated offline as needed. (Luckin et al., 2016, p. 38)

So how will this look in future classrooms? Imagine a data bank for each student that has been growing increasingly deeper since the student's preschool days. The teacher might be presenting material with assistance from the AI—or the AI might be presenting the material with assistance from the teacher. Perhaps the student will interface with AI through a keyboard or maybe through an Alexa-like system that can personalize answers, refer to the student by name, tell a few jokes, and is linked to the student data bank and can differentiate instruction for each student.

Great teachers of the future will still bring great lesson plans, strong teaching methods, and caring, entrepreneurial cultures; when those great teachers integrate the AI into their lessons, they will reach the next level of superstar teaching as they continue to provide the human touch through relationships and empathy.

But what about the weaker teachers, like the algebra teachers I observed? The AI could help them be better teachers—or the AI could eliminate the need to retain them as the AI assumes a more powerful, central role in teaching. School leaders in the late 2020s and beyond could be asking, "Are my students in this class better off learning from this average or below-average teacher—or from a software program that brings great lesson design and differentiated methods?" We might not need as many teachers, especially at the secondary level, as AI becomes more of an equal partner.

Which brings us to another challenge millennial and Gen Z school leaders will face later in this decade and into the 2030s and 2040s: how to incorporate stronger AI into teaching and how to decide which teachers to retain, hire, or phase out. Schools of the future might consist almost exclusively of great teachers—those who made the cut when using (or competing with) AI.

When we look at our staffs today, this vision of a having staffs filled with our greatest teachers might seem far-fetched, especially when we consider how hard it is to dismiss weak public school teachers. In states with strong teacher unions, it's almost impossible. Also consider this: If students begin to leave a school system for another one that better serves their needs, the original school system will have to reduce the number of teachers. Most reduction-in-force procedures are done through seniority. The teachers who have been there the shortest amount of time are the ones released. And who will these teachers be? The young teachers who have the most technology skills and the most adaptive mindsets. They could be the ones hired by the charter school down the street trying to break out of the mold. The teachers left behind in the public schools could be the boomers and Gen Xers who struggle to log into their online teaching platforms. Now is the time for school leaders to prepare for a period of incredible staffing disruptions by looking ahead to their see how their staffs might need to look in a decade. It will be difficult.

But wait. There's reason for hope. I found it in conversations with two young educators who were noble representatives of the millennial and Gen Z generations.

I was talking with a high school administrator in the winter of 2021, one of the darkest winters in school history, one in which teachers and students worked in what felt like perpetual isolation. Teachers and students struggled with sagging morale, as I had seen in the online algebra classes. Around 96 percent of this administrator's students had chosen to learn from home; for various reasons, they didn't want to come to school. He and I discussed how his high school might function after the pandemic recedes and then reopens in a fashion we used to know as normal.

"How many students do you think will return?" I asked him.

"I think a lot will want to come back," he answered, "but others will go someplace else if they offer schedules or options we don't have. I keep telling our teachers, 'You need to be your best NOW and we need to adjust NOW because the state funding will follow our students next year. If we have less funding, we'll need fewer teachers.'" He was already concerned about laying teachers off. He was prescient in seeing it; the accelerated reset of education had begun on his watch.

In the winter of 2021, I also had a profound conversation with a Gen Z teacher who was navigating the shoals of remote learning. I was working with a group of high school teachers, and I was stressing the need to build a positive classroom culture to nurture their Gen Z students who were awash in self-doubt. A study released in December of 2020 found that depression and suicide ideation had risen dramatically among youth (Hill et al., 2020). It was truly the winter of school discontent. The teacher made a heartfelt confession: She felt she had spent the first semester caring more about teaching her content than teaching her students. There's a difference, and this second-year teacher had figured it out. "I had lot of material to cover online, and it was hard, so I would just start presenting the content from the first minute of the class on the first day of school," she said. Her career-changing epiphany came at the end of the first semester. "Then I found out one of my students had been battling cancer, and I didn't know it. I'd never given her a chance to tell me. I hadn't tried to get to know her as a person. Now, I make a real effort, even in remote learning, to try to find out what's happening in their lives. I try to get to know them as people."

And that brings us back again to a theme that will prevail in education models of the future: the need to nurture students as we educate them. It's the thread we've seen run through the generations of educators, the thread of being human. Gen Alpha and Gen Beta students in the 2030s and 2040s might interact more with AI, but as developing humans, they will still need relationships with other humans who can understand them, motivate them, and console them.

This millennial administrator and Gen Z teacher were both sharp and passionate about the power of education to transform lives. If they have to compete with AI, these two will make the cut. I imagine their career and the changes they will encounter in 2030, 2040, and 2050. They will still be educating students, but they might not be in public schools, especially the type of schools we see today.

The changes I saw in my career in the 1990s, 2000s, and 2010s, such as the introduction of the internet, digital devices, and software into schools, were minor in comparison. That was just the beginning of the disruptions our school leaders are seeing today. I experienced what can now be described as the sun rising on a new day for education; this millennial administrator and Gen Z teacher, along with their peers, will lead multiple new generations through the morning fog and into the afternoon sunshine. The light of disruption will be intense. They'll need sunscreen.

But it will be amazing.

Being Human in the 2020s

Finally, as we look at the different generations of teachers, our new types of students, and consider the sweeping changes that are coming to education, let's consider the ideas of two master teachers. Both of these teachers work at Gahanna Lincoln High School in Gahanna, Ohio. While they both happen to be performing arts teachers, their voices represent all effective PreK–12 teachers in all subjects who use teaching methods to fit the needs of Gen Z and Gen Alpha. Their words can also be reminders to 5-Gen leaders of what is essential as we move forward.

Cindi Macioce is the school's award-winning drama teacher, and Jeremy Lehman is its acclaimed choir director. Macioce has had troupes represent Ohio in the world-famous Fringe Festival in Edinburgh, Scotland, and Lehman consistently receives the highest adjudication scores for his multiple choirs in local and state competitions. They both have taught students who have made professional careers on Broadway, in Hollywood, and in North American and European opera companies. Both Macioce and Lahman are extremely respected by their students and former students, and their programs are held in high esteem in the community. Macioce is a boomer, and Lahman is a Gen Xer. They have accrued a vast amount of knowledge about today's students and how to teach them; they have successfully adapted through the decades. They both have strong opinions about their roles and the necessity of the arts in helping Gen Z, Gen Alpha, and Gen Beta in the future. Five-Gen leaders can turn to teachers like these for ideas on how to balance technology, AI, and humanity in the 2020s.

First, let's look at some of Macioce's ideas. She acknowledges she has experienced the changes other boomer educators have experienced. In the pandemic school year of 2020–2021, Macioce quickly realized she would need to emphasize one of the most important emotions of humanity: empathy.

Let's start with basic facts. I am old. I am an old teacher. Not "veteran," not "seasoned," just plain old. I began my teacher career right out of college, where I had to learn how to thread a projector. Google was the Dewey Decimal System. I am both embarrassed and proud to say, "Yes, I DID smell the ditto copies that left my nose purple." It was waayyy before the internet and social media.

One of the things I know to be true is that the study of theatre (either as a student or audience member) helps develop a more empathetic person; we are able to see and experience the world through someone else's lens, and hopefully, that will in turn allow us to think and feel in ways we may not have ever considered. I just started Googling words that I felt needed to be explored in this newly developed unit. I hit upon the word "empathy," and our Empathy Project was born.

After the initial explanation of the unit, we discussed WHY empathy is important for people to develop. We then expanded that conversation to include theatre—as in, how does theatre help us develop empathy? I spelled out the very simple requirements: They had to perform three random acts of kindness for three different people and create a flip grid explaining what they did and how the students (and their recipients) reacted and felt. We created an ongoing list of ways we could perform the "random acts of kindness" without using money and, in most cases, how to do it while keeping social distancing in mind. I encouraged the addition of pictures from the experiences. I did this in all my classes. The students did not disappoint.

My theatre appreciation class is a small class and all girls; they asked if we could make it a yearlong assignment and wanted to know if we could do the acts of kindness as a class. Since this pandemic is "the year of the yes," I agreed we could make it an ongoing unit. They chose one BIG act of kindness, which was to give a handwritten letter to anyone who wanted one. (We had to work at narrowing down the filters so they agreed, for this first go-around, to make middle school students their target audience.) They created a website, contacted the middle school counselors and principals to introduce themselves and what they wanted to do, and created a Google form for the counselors so they could send it out to the students, asking them a little bit about themselves and if they wanted to receive a letter. (Sometimes, the guidance counselors and principals actually "requested" that a specific student receive a letter.) The Theatre App students worked on a master calendar and deadlines as a group and agreed that if one person was feeling stressed about writing letters due to their own school work that the group would pick up the letters for that person. . . . I applied for a small grant and had special stationery and envelopes made so that each letter would be uniformed. We discussed what proper encouragement needed to look like . . . and they were off! Our first go-around we had 12 letters; this last round we had 51. Talk about authentic learning in the middle of a pandemic. . . . I am one proud teacher. (C. Macioce, personal communications, March 21, 2021) ∎

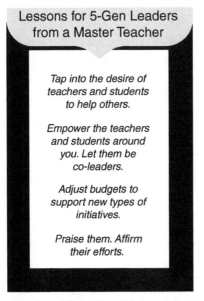

FIGURE 8.2   Lessons for 5-Gen Leaders From a Master Teacher

Lessons for 5-Gen Leaders from a Master Teacher

Tap into the desire of teachers and students to help others.

Empower the teachers and students around you. Let them be co-leaders.

Adjust budgets to support new types of initiatives.

Praise them. Affirm their efforts.

Note how Macioce was able to understand her Gen Z students. She tapped into their desire to help others and empowered them by adjusting her curriculum. She let them be co-leaders and create their own website. They helped each other when they were stressed. She applied for a small grant to help them get their supplies for the project. They felt affirmed when their project went from 12 to 51 letters. They will be stronger performers because of what they learned by empathizing with others. They will draw on their experiences to see the world through the eyes of other people.

Macioce provides a blueprint for 5-Gen leaders: They should do with their staffs and students what she does with her students (see Figure 8.2).

I have been fortunate to have a few supportive administrators who value what the arts are able to do for students, but in the majority of schools, arts classes are the first to get chopped when the budget gets tight.

I fear that now that a huge part of our population has learned how to "work from home," Zoom productions will be expected to be "the new normal" of theatre (and other arts) and not the exception. While I think there is a place for online theatre, we have to remember that the arts are meant to be felt and explored in the moment . . . and certainly not through a square on a screen.

I think that the advancing technology in the arts world is a double-edged sword. We have been able to get theatre and music into people's homes so that it can be seen, but again, we attend a concert or the musical because it is meant to be experienced. I also worry that technology has made us a bit too comfortable. After all, we can watch a streamed Broadway production in our jammies from our couches. The problem is that we don't have any way to connect to others. We aren't sharing moments that are meant to be shared. We aren't learning live-audience etiquette; we aren't able to engage and discuss the piece of music or the show. I fear we might be regressing in this live performance arena. (C. Macioce, personal communications, March 21, 2021) ∎

Artificial intelligence will never be able to do these things:

- Pick up the meaning of a student's eye roll.

- Look a student in the eye and tell them you are proud of them for not forgetting their one line in the show.

- Hold a student's hand when they suffer a panic attack because they don't see an end to their academic workload.

- Hug a student whose mother was murdered by her boyfriend.

- Put a hand on a student's shoulder to help calm them when they think their girlfriend is pregnant.

- Celebrate and applaud a group's success after their opening night.

- Respond when a student texts your phone at midnight, wondering what to do because their best friend talked of taking their own life.

- Give a student some cheese and crackers from your school fridge because they haven't eaten.

- Address truth with love when a student's actions do not live up to expectations.

- Apologize for misreading situations and promise to do better.

- Take the lead in a teachable moment.

- Stay past a long rehearsal to share laughs with students because that is what is needed in the moment.

- Share lunches and dinners with alumni of your program because they want to share what has been happening in their lives.

- Shape student behavior because you model it.

These are just a few reasons why artificial intelligence, no matter how smart it is or becomes, will EVER be able to replace me as a teacher. Maybe AI will be able to regurgitate facts and information about subject matter, but that isn't true teaching and it never will be—there is a reason it is called "artificial."

The secret about teaching is that teaching is not always about content. It's also about understanding and knowing how to nuance every minute you are with your kids so that you can help them develop into decent human beings. (C. Macioce, personal communications, March 21, 2021) ∎

Like other educators, Macioce has questions and concerns about how the education reset in the 2020s will affect education and especially the arts.

Macioce's ideas lead to pertinent questions for 5-Gen leaders. As technology becomes stronger in the Zoom world, how will they preserve human interaction in education? In the 2020s, how will they preserve the arts? In the opening of this chapter, I wondered which practices school leaders would hold on to and which ones they would discard. Macioce brings up the idea of regression. For 5-Gen leaders, where is the line between progressing and regressing?

When asked if she could ever see a day when AI could replace her, Macioce responded with these points.

Many of Macicoe's points, from hugging a distraught student to giving some cheese and crackers to a hungry student, affirm the humanity that will always be needed by all PreK–12 teachers when teaching young people. Artificial intelligence, as Macioce says, will always be artificial.

But just as importantly, note another one of her key points: "Address truth with love when a student's actions do not live up to expectations." Macicoe's troupes have achieved spectacular success, and some of her students have ascended to the highest levels of their profession—this shows her expectations for her students are high in both her behavioral expectations and academic expectations. She holds her Gen Z students accountable. She expects them to work. She provides rigorous instruction in that she constantly asks them to analyze, evaluate, and create, which are the rigor levels at the upper end of Bloom's taxonomy. These actions create the skills students must possess to live productive lives in the 21st century and into the 22nd century. These are the skills 5-Gen leaders should be encouraging teachers to use in all classes.

Now let's look at another great teacher, Jeremy Lahman, and see how his ideas parallel Macioce's, especially with the need for students to be human. There are lessons here for 5-Gen leaders.

In my 22 years as an educator, I think the biggest shift I've seen in young people is their ability to communicate—more specifically, how they communicate. With the emergence of screens as a form of communication, I've seen the breakdown of students' ability to express themselves face-to-face—to each other and to adults.

I started teaching in 1999. There were no cell phones and no Chromebooks. Interaction and engagement were at 100 percent. It was the original Face-Time. Students communicated and learned differently during that time. Over the course of two decades, that human connection has waned, but I find that students seek out the arts because there is a strong yearning for human connection and shared experience.

The arts are what often keep kids coming back to school. It's because of the connection they have with their peers and their instructor. It's not limited to kids who struggle academically or emotionally. It's often high achievers that say the arts are what keep them coming to school. The data shows that despite their use of social media to connect with each other students are lonelier than ever and suicide ideation is up 25 percent. Students are longing for real connection, not virtual connection. I've had students tell me that my class saved their life. (J. Lahman, personal communications, April 3, 2021)

While Lahman stresses the need for the arts in the lives of today's students, notice how many of his points about Gen Z could apply to all educators.

Despite their excessive use of social media, students are lonelier than ever. They know that social media is largely fake, seen through a filter, but they continue to engage in it. The constant comparison of themselves to what appears to be a perfect life or person has been harmful to young people. They are longing for real human connection, which participating in the performing arts gives them. It fills a certain void in the human soul that cannot be replaced with anything else.

The goal of a rehearsal is to practice for a performance. Performance allows students to show what they have learned in a positive way to others. When it's over, they receive validation and recognition, along with a huge sense of accomplishment for their work. This shared experience is not something that can be done with, or on, a computer. It's good old-fashioned human connection. And they love it.

What I find interesting is that when my students are engaged in a rehearsal they aren't sneaking looks at their phones. They don't even try. They go into their phones for stimulation and entertainment. When they are engaged in singing, that need is being met at all times.

Research shows that one of the largest factors of school success is a student's sense of belonging to the school community. In our high school, we have seven bands, four orchestras, and five choirs. If you include theater, nearly half of the school of 2,400 students is involved in the performing arts. In 2021, that speaks volumes about what young people are yearning for—that human connection, shared experience, sense of belonging, and feeling of accomplishment. (J. Lahman, personal communications, April 3, 2021) ▪

Let's look at the significance of the numbers. According to Lahman, half of the Gen Z students in his school are involved in the arts. Like most large high schools, a significant number of students are probably involved in athletics. Then there are students in various clubs. This shows us that while Gen Z is tethered to the internet, the majority of the students in the school still value what we could call "old-school" activities. This, like Lahman tells us, is where they get the human interaction. As 5-Gen leaders determine which initiatives to retain and which ones to discard, they should collect data and look closely at their Gen Z and Gen Alpha students' preferences. The arts and extracurricular activities are perhaps more essential than ever in our increasingly digital society.

Here's another sobering reality: Think of what was lost by Macioce's and Lahman's students during the COVID school closures. Researchers have tried to measure the academic losses of the pandemic in math and reading, but it's not possible to measure the extracurricular losses. The connections, the friendships, and student growth were stymied when the activities shut down. When students of all ages participate in school plays, musicals, concerts, art shows, and athletics, they gain confidence, resilience, and creative skills that propel them through the rest of their lives. Five-Gen leaders will need to address the COVID-19 academic regression in the 2020s, but they must also seek ways to recoup some of the personal growth lost in the nonacademic fields.

As mentioned, Lahman's choirs consistently receive high marks at state-adjudicated events. This happens because his students are constantly analyzing the nuances of their singing, evaluating its quality, and creating ways to be better. He, like Macioce, operates at the upper levels of Bloom's taxonomy. Like other teachers during the pandemic year, he did his best to be highly rigorous; yet he knew his students needed more than rigor as they learned from home in a world turned upside down—they needed kindness.

No significant learning happens without a significant relationship. This year I have prioritized connection over content. I start each class with "Tell Me Something Good," which is a time for students to share positive experiences or stories. At the beginning of the year, it was somewhat forced because the relationships weren't forged yet. But with time, it has blossomed into an amazing experience for students and for me. I've learned to listen in a different way. I've gotten to know students in a way that I never have before. What has come out of it is a classroom community that is supportive, nurturing, and more connected than ever. It also has given a lot to me as their instructor and guide. Students have routinely said, "This is the only class that I talk in." Incidentally, my retention rate for next year is the highest it's been in my career—in a year without performances! Students feel seen, heard, and validated. A digital tool or automated chat box simply cannot do that.

During my tenure, I've had about a dozen student teachers. At some point in our process, I tell them that there are four essential elements to being an effective teacher: content knowledge, pedagogical acumen, classroom management, and the special sauce. They always get their pencils out to take notes in their journal and get on the edge of their seat with wide eyes and say, "This is great! What's the special sauce?" I look at them with the eyes of a sage and say, "The special sauce is YOU! It's what you bring to the classroom that cannot be replaced by someone else or a computer. It's the magic that you bring to the room every day."

Every human civilization that has been unearthed has some commonalities. What endures from cultures is often art, music, dance, and writing—all ways to express the human condition and reflect the human experience. If we continue to take the teacher out of the classroom, what sort of enduring legacy are we going to leave behind as it relates to teaching, learning, and the importance of quality education practices for our most beloved resource—our children? (J. Lahman, personal communications, April 3, 2021) ∎

FIGURE 8.3   Special Sauce

Lahman, like Macioce, also points out the limitations of AI and reminds us that teachers bring "the special sauce" to learning. Of course, it's not just the teachers of the arts who bring the special sauce (see Figure 8.3) into teaching and learning; teachers of all subjects and grade levels who form strong, rigorous cultures also "bring the magic."

Five-Gen leaders can view Macioce and Lahman as examples of a boomer teacher and a Gen X teacher who successfully transitioned their teaching from the 20th to the 21st century. Through the decades, they constantly reassessed the emotional needs of their students as they provided highly rigorous instruction. They, and teachers from all generations who bring their humanity to teaching while providing high rigor in learning, cannot be replaced by AI or teacherbots.

But what about the algebra teachers I mentioned earlier, the ones who were deficient in these areas? After I observed their online teaching, I met with them and asked if they considered humanity and rigor to be essential traits in their teaching. Of course, they said they did. All teachers want to be humane and rigorous. These teachers didn't want to be viewed as callous or ineffective. But great teaching is an art, and sometimes there's a gap between what teachers *think they are doing* and what they are *actually doing*. In the Digital Age, where the demands on schools will be greater than ever before, it will be the 5-Gen leader's job to help struggling teachers find their special sauce—or replace them, perhaps by a new form of AI.

Ultimately, 5-Gen leaders must remember Macioce's and Lahman's most important lesson: Regardless of where our technology takes us in the years ahead, we will still be leading and teaching humans who need other humans. As boomers, Gen Xers, millennials, Gen Zers, Gen Alphas (and eventually Gen Betas) bring their disparate generational experiences and views into our schools, it is the job of the 5-Gen leader to understand them and unite them with the eternal thread of humanity.

This will be the special sauce of leadership in the 2020s.

FIGURE 8.4   Tips for Transitioning to 5-Gen Leadership

Tips for Transitioning to 5-Gen Leadership

44. Question everything. Keep what is worth keeping and discard the rest.

45. Study what is happening at the university level the practices will trickle down into PreK-12 systems.

46. New requirements in school systems are leading to new types of administrative positions; embrace them.

47. Know that student learning data will be more abundant and will be used to drive instruction.

48. Prepare for the day when AI can replace some teachers.

49. As technology makes the world less human, the arts will be needed more than ever.

50. Five-Gen Leaders must never lose their own humanity.

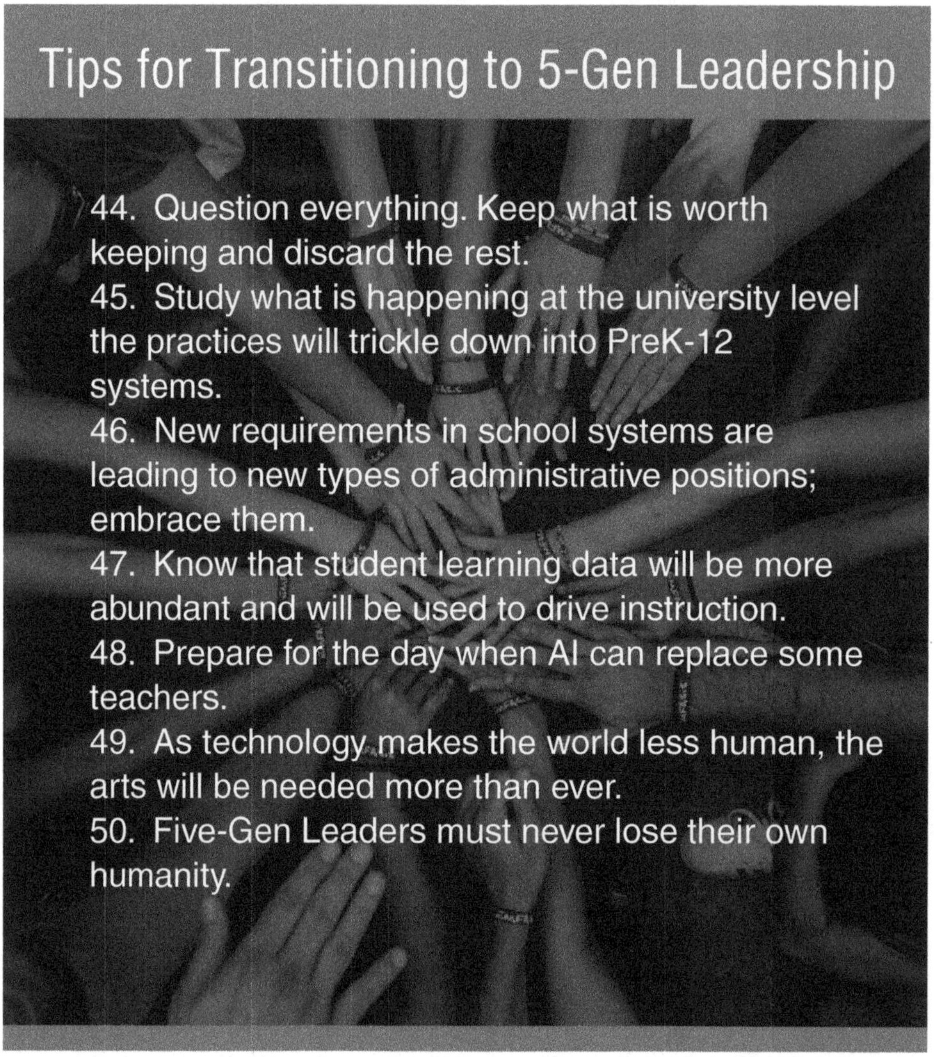

50 Tips for Transitioning to 5-Gen Leadership

Chapter 1

1. Know four distinct generations are in our teaching staffs, including Gen Z.

2. Understand the differences in the four teaching generations.

3. Recognize the digital generation gaps between each generation.

4. Realize the biggest digital generation gap is the one between the boomers/Gen Xers and the millennials/Gen Zers.

5. Know millennials are leaving the profession in record numbers and fewer Gen Zers are joining the teaching profession.

6. Study the characteristics millennials and Gen Zers are looking for in a workplace and adjust practices.

7. Adjust recruiting strategies to find the best Gen Z teaching candidates.

8. Study the district's recruiting and retention data, brainstorm solutions, create a loose format, and then create a written Teacher Recruiting and Retention Plan (TRRP).

Chapter 2

9. Honor and build upon the work of previous generations of educators.

10. Recognize the themes that link the generations of school leaders: the love of working with students, the power of teachers, and the need to mentor the next generation of leaders.

11. Continue the work done before us to equalize opportunities for all ethnicities, genders, and lifestyles.

12. Understand the speed with which technology is reshaping our lives and education.

13. Know the characteristics of Gen Alpha and consider how to adjust teaching and learning to fit its needs.

14. Examine school culture to ensure it has the pillars needed to support Gen Alpha.

Chapter 3

15. Be a coach, not a manager.

16. Understand how new parenting models require more attention to be given to millennial and Gen Z teachers.

17. Remember how stressed younger teachers get over their evaluations.

18. When doing evaluations, give faster feedback, create dialogue, and be specific and clear of what is expected.

19. Stress professionalism to all generations.

20. Help staffs work through communication issues that are caused by generation gaps.

Chapter 4

21. Remember that all generations of teachers are more distracted than in the past, which makes them harder to train.

22. Know our Gen Z and Gen Alpha students are more distracted than in the past, which makes them harder to teach.

23. Recognize the constant interaction with technology is changing brains and how people want to be taught.

24. Know the four generations of teachers have different views and needs, but the four generations share new similarities because of their digital lifestyles.

25. Look to different fields outside of education for tips on how to connect with Teacher Z.

Chapter 5

26. Examine the effectiveness of the PD.

27. Know that companies in all fields are searching for effective ways to train professionals.

28. Create effective PD initiatives by ensuring they are ongoing, that coaching and support are provided to teachers, and by providing relevant content.

29. Understand the eight types of PD and their relevance for the different generations.

30. Know which teachers are in which generation.

31. Plan PD through a multigenerational lens.

32. Differentiate PD by generation.

Chapter 6

33. Understand the COVID-19 pandemic could do more to reset education than all of the reform movements combined.

34. The digital generation gap must be closed between the younger teachers and the more experienced teachers.

35. Helping Gen Z and Gen Alpha students deal with the emotional impact of COVID-19 will be an ongoing challenge of the 2020s.

36. Be aware that while teacher experience is still valuable, the need to use digital tools has closed the ability gap between younger teachers and some older teachers; help mesh staffs by tapping into the strengths of all generations.

37. Help the digitally deficient teachers by giving them tips on adjusting their mindsets and by giving them training and resources.

38. Close the digital ability gap between you and your most digitally savvy teachers.

Chapter 7

39. Help staff members understand Gen Z and Gen Alpha have a more global view and are more politically active than their predecessors.

40. Remember that political and civil rights topics that were untouchable 20 years ago could be embraced by Gen Z and Gen Alpha.

41. Some Gen Z students have become global activists through YouTube, social media, and the internet; expect your Gen Z students to use these resources to further their causes as they lead locally.

42. Gen Z and Gen Alpha students are much more likely to question authority and reject the status quo, so be prepared to work cooperatively with them to find solutions.

43. Consider the steps you can take systemically to further the pursuit of racial justice; it's more than cultural celebrations or social events.

Chapter 8

44. Question everything. Keep what is worth keeping and discard the rest.

45. Study what is happening at the university level because the practices will trickle down into PreK–12 systems.

46. New requirements in school systems are leading to new types of administrative positions; embrace them.

47. Know that student learning data will be more abundant and will be used to drive instruction.

48. Prepare for the day when AI can replace some teachers.

49. As technology makes the world less human, the arts will be needed more than ever.

50. Five-Gen leaders must never lose their own humanity.

References

Ackerman, C. E. (2020). What is neuroplasticity? A psychologist explains [+14 exercises]. *PositivePsychology.com.* www.positivepsychology.com/neuroplasticity/

Akhtar, A. (2019). The number of Americans training to become teachers has dropped by a third since 2010, and it's creating a critical educator shortage that will affect every state. *Business Insider.* www.businessinsider.com/one-third-fewer-people-are-training-to-become-teachers

Alter, C., Haynes, S., & Worland, J. (2019). Greta Thunberg: TIME's person of the year 2019. *Time.* www.time.com/person-of-the-year-2019-greta-thunberg/

American University School of Education. (2018). *What makes professional development for teachers effective?* https://soeonline.american.edu/blog/what-makes-professional-development-for-teachers-effective

American University School of Education. (2019). *Teacher leadership roles inside and outside of the classroom.* soeonline.american.edu/blog/teacher-leadership-roles.

Anrig, G. (2015). How we know collaboration works. *ASCD.* www.ascd.org/publications/educational-leadership/feb15/vol72/num05/How-We-Know-Collaboration-Works.aspx

Apple. (2020). *Jobs at Apple.* www.apple.com/jobs/us/retail.html

APQC. (2021). Home page. *APQC.* www.apqc.org/

Asurion. (2019). Americans check their phones 96 times a day. *PR Newswire.* www.prnewswire.com/news-releases/americans-check-their-phones-96-times-a-day-300962643.html

Barnett, Z. (2020). Texas athletes release list of demands for campus changes. *FootballScoop.* footballscoop.com/news/texas-athletes-release-list-of-demands-for-campus-changes/

Bayern, M. (2019). Some millennials fail to dress professionally enough for work. *TechRepublic.* www.techrepublic.com/article/some-millennials-fail-to-dress-professionally-enough-for-work/

BBC News. (2020). *Greta Thunberg: Who is she and what does she want?* www.bbc
.com/news/world-europe-49918719

Blum, D., & Miller, F. (2020). What parents need to know about learning pods.
The New York Times. www.nytimes.com/article/learning-pods-coronavirus
.html

Bologna, C. (2019). *What's the deal with Generation Alpha?* HuffPost. https://
www.huffpost.com/entry/generation-alpha-after-gen-z_l_5d420ef4e
4b0aca341181574

Boyce, P. (2019). The teacher shortage is real and about to get much worse.
Here's why. *FEE.* https://fee.org/articles/the-teacher-shortage-is-real-and-
about-to-get-much-worse-heres-why/

Briseno, A. (2020). UT drum major says she won't lead "The Eyes of Texas"
when football returns. *The Dallas Morning News.* www.dallasnews.com/news/
education/2020/08/16/ut-drum-major-says-she-won't-lead-the-eyes-
of-texas-when-football-returns/

Britten, J. (2019). Innovating for Generation Alpha in our schools. *Medium.*
https://jodybritten.medium.com/innovating-for-generation-alpha-in-
our-schools-12a8006516b8

Buchanan-Rivera, E. (2020). So, you want to hire a DEI officer? Here's what to
know first. *ASCD Inservice.* https://inservice.ascd.org/want-to-hire-a-diversity-
equity-inclusion-officer-heres-what-to-know-first/

Campbell, L. (2019). Is your teen getting enough sleep? 73% don't. Here's why.
Healthline. www.healthline.com/health-news/73-of-high-school-
students-dont-get-enough-sleep

Carlton, C. (2020). UT to keep "The Eyes of Texas," but make other changes sup-
porting Black athletes. *The Dallas Morning News.* www.dallasnews.com/
sports/texas-longhorns/2020/07/13/texas-longhorns-to-keep-the-eyes-
of-texas-fight-song-despite-athlete-demands/

Carr, N. G. (2011). *The shallows: What the internet is doing to our brains.*
W. W. Norton.

Carter, D., & White, M. (2018/2021). *Leading schools in disruptive times: How to
survive hyper-change.* Corwin.

Carver-Thomas, D., & Darling-Hammond, L. (2017). Teacher turnover: Why it
matters and what we can do about it. *Learning Policy Institute.* https://learn-
ingpolicyinstitute.org/sites/default/files/product-files/Teacher_Turnover_
REPORT.pdf

CBS Austin. (2020). Longhorn band will not perform at final UT football games
over "Eyes of Texas" controversy. *KEYE.* cbsaustin.com/news/local/

longhorn-band-will-not-perform-at-final-ut-football-games-over-eyes-of-
texas-controversy

Chae, R. (2019). Overprotective parents and a new generation of American children. *Berkeley Political Review*. www.bpr.berkeley.edu/2019/04/16/
overprotective-parents-and-a-new-generation-of-american-children/

Chinthalapale, A. (2021). *LinkedIn profile*.

Cianci, L. (2018). Family location apps: Yes or no for college kids? *Orlando Senti-
nel*. www.orlandosentinel.com/features/family/os-phone-tracking-apps-
college-kids-20180620-story.html

Clark, B. (2020). People are skipping Zoom meetings by looping videos of themselves paying attention. *The Next Web*. www.thenextweb.com/corona/2020/03/
23/adapt-evolve-overcome/

Costello, E. J., Copeland, W., & Angold, A. (2016). The great Smoky Mountains
study: Developmental epidemiology in the southeastern United States. *Social
Psychiatry and Psychiatric Epidemiology, 51*(5), 639–646. www.ncbi.nlm.nih
.gov/pmc/articles/PMC4846561/

Crosby, D. (2019). As millennials reject family treasures, baby boomers start to ask,
"What do we do with all this stuff?" *Chicagotribune.com*. www.chicagotribune
.com/suburbs/aurora-beacon-news/opinion/ct-abn-crosby-treasures-junk-
st-0512-story.html

Cuban, L. (2011). The open classroom. *Education Next*. www.educationnext.org/
theopenclassroom/

Davis, M. L. (2008). The effect of the middle school concept on student achievement in coastal Mississippi middle level schools. The University of Southern
Mississippi: *The Aquila Digital Community*. aquila.usm.edu/cgi/viewcontent
.cg?article=2205&contenet=dissertations

DeGeurin, M. (2019). With school shootings an increasingly common fear, some
students and teachers have started writing their own wills. *Insider*. www
.insider.com/school-shootings-are-causing-teachers-and-students-
to-write-wills-2019-8

Digital Media Solutions. (2019). Boomers and Gen Xers are embracing technology at a faster rate than millennials. *DMS Insights*. https://insights.digitalme-
diasolutions.com/articles/technology-adoption-older-generations

Dorn, E., Hancock, B., Sarakatsannis, J., & Viruleg, E. (2020). COVID-19 and
student learning in the United States: The hurt could last a lifetime.
McKinsey & Company. www.mckinsey.com/industries/public-and-social-
sector/our-insights/covid-19-and-student-learning-in-the-united-states-the-
hurt-could-last-a-lifetime

Doss, R. (2017). What skills are new graduates missing when they start their first jobs? *Transforming Education*. www.transformingeducation.org/2016427what-skills-are-new-graduates-missing-when-they-start-their-first-jobs/

Duckworth, A. (2016). *Why millennials struggle for success*. CNN. www.cnn.com/2016/05/03/opinions/grit-is-a-gift-of-age-duckworth/index.html

Dua, A., Cheng, W. L., Lund, S., De Smet, A., Robinson, O., & Sanghvi, S. (2020). What 800 executives envision for the postpandemic workforce. *McKinsey & Company*. www.mckinsey.com/featured-insights/future-of-work/what-800-executives-envision-for-the-postpandemic-workforce

Duncan, G., & Le Menestrel, S. (Eds.). (2019). *A Roadmap to Reducing Child Poverty*. The National Academies Press. www.nap.edu/catalog/25246/a-roadmap-to-reducing-child-poverty.

The Economist Staff. (2019, February 27). *Generation Z is stressed, depressed and exam-obsessed*. www.economist.com/graphic-detail/2019/02/27/generation-z-is-stressed-depressed-and-exam-obsessed

The Editors of *Encyclopaedia Britannica*. (2019). *Lost generation*. https://www.britannica.com/topic/Lost-Generation

Encyclopedia.com. (2020). *The 1970s education: Overview*. www.encyclopedia.com/social- soeonline.american.edu/blog/teacher-leadership-roles sciences/culture-magazines/1970s-education-overview.

Encyclopedia.com. (2021). Minority groups and the Great Depression. *Great Depression and the New Deal Reference Library*. https://www.encyclopedia.com/economics/encyclopedias-almanacs-transcripts-and-maps/minority-groups-and-great-depression

Entrepreneur Staff. (2019). *41 percent of Gen Z-ers plan to become entrepreneurs* [Infographic]. www.entrepreneur.com/article/326354

Friedman, Z. (2020). Student loan debt statistics in 2020: A record $1.6 trillion. *Forbes*. www.forbes.com/sites/zackfriedman/2020/02/03/student-loan-debt-statistics/#6e189b08281f

Fry, R. (2020). Millennials are largest generation in the U.S. labor force. *Pew Research Center*. www.pewresearch.org/fact-tank/2018/04/11/millennials-largest-generation-us-labor-force/

Fry, R., & Parker, K. (2020). Post-millennial generation on track to be most diverse, best-educated. *Pew Research Center's Social & Demographic Trends Project*. www.pewresearch.org/social-trends/2018/11/15/early-benchmarks-show-post-millennials-on-track-to-be-most-diverse-best-educated-generation-yet/

Fuller, R. B. (1981). *Critical path*. St. Martin's Press.

Fulwood, S. (2018). Teachers quit their jobs in record numbers during 2018. *Think-Progress.* https://archive.thinkprogress.org/teachers-quit-their-jobs-in-record-numbers-during-2018-497f2162b3a6/.

Furness, D. (2020). How AI will completely transform education. *Digital Trends.* www.digitaltrends.com/computing/how-ai-is-changing-education/

Fuscaldo, D. (2020). How boomers and millennials can work together. *Investopedia.* www.investopedia.com/articles/professionals/093015/how-get-boomers-millennials-working-together.asp

Gauthier, M. (2019). Travel trends: Gen Alpha having huge impact on family trips. *WEX Inc.* www.wexinc.com/insights/blog/wex-travel/consumer/gen-alpha-littlest-travelers-have-big-impact-on-family-trips/

Gayle, L. (2019). How Generation Z is transforming the workplace. *FEI.* www.financialexecutives.org/FEI-Daily/August-2019/How-Generation-Z-Is-Transforming-the-Workplace.aspx

Gould, E. (2019). Back-to-school jobs report shows a continued shortfall in public education jobs. *Economic Policy Institute.* www.epi.org/publication/back-to-school-jobs-report-shows-a-continued-shortfall-in-public-education-jobs/

Greenthall, S. (2021). Is tracking college kids on their smartphones a good idea? *College Ave.* www.collegeavestudentloans.com/blog/is-tracking-college-kids-on-their-smartphones-a-good-idea/

Harris, D. N. (2020). How will COVID-19 change our schools in the long run? *Brookings.* www.brookings.edu/blog/brown-center-chalkboard/2020/04/24/how-will-covid-19-change-our-schools-in-the-long-run/

Helterbran, V. R., & Rieg, S. A. (2004). Women as school principals: What is the challenge? *Journal of Women in Educational Leadership,* p. 12.

Hemingway, E. (1952). *The old man and the sea.* Charles Scribner & Sons.

Hill, R. M., Rufino, K., Kurian, S., Saxena, J., Saxena, K., & Williams, L. (2020). Suicide ideation and attempts in a pediatric emergency department before and during COVID-19. *Pediatrics.* https://doi.org/10.1542/peds.2020-029280

Hodges, T. (2020). Managing millennial teachers: Major challenge for schools. *Gallup.* www.gallup.com/education/231749/managing-millennial-teachers-major-challenge-schools.aspx

Horvath, A. (2015). How does technology affect our brains? *Faculty of Medicine, Dentistry and Health Sciences.* mdhs.unimelb.edu.au/news-and-events/news-archive/how-does-technology-affect-our-brains

Howe, N. (2014). The silent generation, "The lucky few" (part 3 of 7). *Forbes.* www.forbes.com/sites/neilhowe/2014/08/13/the-silent-generation-the-lucky-few-part-3-of-7/#5805926b2c63

Inman, R. (2020). Three major millennial communication mistakes and what to do about them. *UrbanBlog*. www.urbanbound.com/blog/three-major-millennial-communication-mistakes-and-what-to-do-about-them

Intel. (n.d.). *Over 50 years of Moore's law*. https://www.intel.com/content/www/us/en/silicon-innovations/moores-law-technology.html?wapkw=50%20years%20of%20moore%27s%20law

Irons, P. (2004). Jim Crow's schools. *American Federation of Teachers*. www.aft.org/periodical/american-educator/summer-2004/jim-crows-schools.

Jacobo, J. (2019). *Teens spend more than 7 hours on screens for entertainment a day: Report*. ABC News. www.abcnews.go.com/US/teens-spend-hours-screens-entertainment-day-report/story? id=66607555

Jayaram, K., Moffit, A., & Scott, D. (2012). Breaking the habit of ineffective professional development for teachers. *McKinsey & Company*. www.mckinsey.com/industries/public-and-social-sector/our-insights/breaking-the-habit-of-ineffective-professional-development-for-teachers

Jenco, M. (2020). Study: 73% of high school students not getting enough sleep. *American Academy of Pediatrics*. www.aappublications.org/news/2018/01/25/Sleep012518

Jenkins, J. (2019, January 24). Leading the four generations at work. American Management Association. www.amanet.org/articles/leading-the-four-generations-at-work/

Johnson, S. (2017). Finding common ground: How to effectively train different generations." *Knowledge Anywhere*. www.knowledgeanywhere.com/resources/article-detail/how-to-effectively-train-different-generations

Kamenetz, A. (2017). Young children are spending much more time in front of small screens. *NPR*. www.npr.org/sections/ed/2017/10/19/558178851/young-children-are-spending-much-more-time-in-front-of-small-screens

Kane, S. (2019). Common workplace characteristics of the silent generation. *The Balance Careers*. www.thebalancecareers.com/workplace-characteristics-silent-generation-2164692

Kasasa. (2019). *Boomers, Gen X, Gen Y, and Gen Z explained*. www.kasasa.com/articles/generations/gen-x-gen-y-gen-z

Keating, L. (2020). Survey finds most people check their smartphones before getting out of bed in the morning. *Tech Times*. www.techtimes.com/articles/199967/20170302/survey-finds-people-check-smartphones-before-getting-out-bed.htm

Kelly, M. L. (2020). The long-term effects of months-long school closures on U.S. children. *NPR*. www.npr.org/2020/04/24/844562989/the-long-term-effects-of-months-long-school-closures-on-u-s-children

Koning, L. (2015). Education in the 1930s. *Medium.* https://medium.com/the-thirties/education-in-the-1930-s-bc0e4b94fb2d

The Learning Network. (2020). What students are saying about remote learning. *The New York Times.* www.nytimes.com/2020/04/09/learning/what-students-are-saying-about-remote-learning.html? searchResultPosition=6

Lockley, S. K. (2017). Generation Z in the workplace: 5 ways to be a better employer. *Staffbase.* https://staffbase.com/blog/generation-z-in-the-workplace-5-ways-to-be-a-better-employer/

Lorenz, T. (2020). College is everywhere now. *The New York Times.* www.nytimes.com/2020/08/28/style/dormpods-college-collab-houses-coronavirus.html?action=click&module=Features&pgtype=Homepage

Lowrey, A. (2020). Millennials don't stand a chance. *The Atlantic.* www.theatlantic.com/ideas/archive/2020/04/millennials-are-new-lost-generation/609832/

Luckin, R., Holmes, W., Griffiths, M., & Forcier, L. B. (2016). *Intelligence Unleashed: An Argument for AI in Education.* Pearson. www.pearson.com/content/dam/corporate/global/pearson-dot-com/files/innovation/Intelligence-Unleashed-Publication.pdf

MacGillis, A. (2020). The students left behind by remote learning. *ProPublica.* www.propublica.org/article/the-students-left-behind-by-remote-learning

Malito, A. (2019). Good news and bad news: Kids born today will probably live to be older than 100—and they'll need to pay for it. *MarketWatch.* www.marketwatch.com/story/good-news-and-bad-news-kids-born-today-will-probably-live-to-be-older-than-100-and-theyll-need-to-pay-for-it-2019-06-14

Manjoo, F. (2020). How do you know a human wrote this? *The New York Times.* www.nytimes.com/2020/07/29/opinion/gpt-3-ai-automation.html?searchResultPosition=1

McBirney, J. (2018). What millennial parents think about schools and their children's education. *The Thomas B. Fordham Institute.* www.fordhaminstitute.org/national/commentary/what-millennial-parents-think-about-schools-and-their-childrens-education

McCrindle Staff. (n.d.a). *Generation next: Meet Gen Z and the Alphas.* mccrindle.com.au/insights/blog/generation-next-meet-gen-z-alphas/

McCrindle Staff. (n.d.b). *Understanding Generation Alpha.* https://mccrindle.com.au/insights/blog/gen-alpha-defined/

McCrindle Staff. (n.d.c). *Gen Z and Gen Alpha infographic update.* https://mccrindle.com.au/insights/blogarchive/gen-z-and-gen-alpha-infographic-update/

McLaren, S. (2019). 6 Gen Z traits you need to know to attract, hire, and retain them. *LinkedIn*. https://business.linkedin.com/talent-solutions/blog/hiring-generation-z/2019/how-to-hire-and-retain-generation-z

McLean, D. (1971). "American Pie." United Artists.

McSpadden, K. (2015). Science: You now have a shorter attention span than a goldfish. *Time*. www.time.com/3858309/attention-spans-goldfish/

Middle Schools. (2021). *Education Encyclopedia–State University.com*. https://education.stateuniversity.com/pages/2229/Middle-Schools.html

Mintz, V. (2020). Why I'm learning more with distance learning than I do in school. *The New York Times*. www.nytimes.com/2020/05/05/opinion/coronavirus-pandemic-distance-learning.html? searchResultPosition=8

Molla, R. (2020). Tech companies tried to help us spend less time on our phones. It didn't work. *Vox*. www.vox.com/recode/2020/1/6/21048116/tech-companies-time-well-spent-mobile-phone-usage-data

Morales, C. (2020). How teenage activists are talking to family about racial injustice. *The New York Times*. www.nytimes.com/2020/08/22/us/black-lives-matter-parents.html? action=click&module=News&pgtype=Homepage

Morgan, J. (2015). *What do "American Pie's" lyrics mean?* BBC News. www.bbc.com/news/magazine-32196117

Mulvahill, E. (2019). Why teachers quit. *WeAreTeachers*. www.weareteachers.com/why-teachers-quit/

Murray, S. (2020). The other 5G: Learning to lead the five-generation workforce. *Financial Times*. www.ft.com/content/8e849486-8173-11ea-b6e9-a94cffd1d9bf

New Zealand Parliament. (2019*). "OK, boomer: Millennial MP responds to heckler in New Zealand parliament.* The Guardian. https://www.theguardian.com/world/video/2019/nov/06/ok-boomer-millennial-mp-responds-to-heckler-in-new-zealand-parliament-video

Noonoo, S. (2018). This neuroscientist explains why today's kids have different brains.*EdSurge*.www.edsurge.com/news/2018-06-26-this-neuroscientist-explains-why-today-s-kids-have-different-brains

O'Dea, S. (2020). US smartphone ownership, 2011–2019. *Statista*. www.statista.com/statistics/219865/percentage-of-us-adults-who-own-a-smartphone/

Pandey, M. (2020). *US trans rights: The teen who sued his school, and won, over bathroom use.* BBC News. www.bbc.com/news/newsbeat-53834065

Partelow, L. (2019). What to make of declining enrollment in teacher preparation programs. *Center for American Progress*. www.americanprogress.org/issues/

education-k-12/reports/2019/12/03/477311/make-declining-enrollment-teacher-preparation-programs/

Pasquarelli, A., & Schultz, E. J. (2019). Move over Gen Z, Generation Alpha is the one to watch. *Ad Age*. www.adage.com/article/cmo-strategy/move-gen-z-generation-alpha-watch/316314

Paychex Worx. (2019). *How to manage the 5 generations in the workplace*. www.paychex.com/articles/human-resources/how-to-manage-multiple-generations-in-the-workplace.

Perucci, D. (2020). Everything you need to make a winning employee retention plan. *BambooHR*. www.bamboohr.com/blog/make-an-employee-retention-plan/

Pew Research Center. (2015). *Why aren't more women in . . .* www.pewresearch.org/social-trends/2015/01/14/women-and-leadership/st_2015-01-14_women-leadership-3-01/

Poston, D., & Saenz, R. (2019). The US white majority will soon disappear forever. *Chicago Reporter*. chicagoreporter.com/the-us-white-majority-will-soon-disappear-forever/

Preville, P. (2019). How to teach Generation Z in the classroom. *Top Hat*. www.tophat.com/blog/generation-z-teach-classroom/

Purdue Global. (2021). *Generational differences in the workplace* [Infographic]. www.purdueglobal.edu/education-partnerships/generational-workforce-differences-infographic/

Quast, L., & Hedges, K. (2011). Reverse mentoring: What it is and why it is beneficial. *Forbes*. www.forbes.com/sites/work-in-progress/2011/01/03/reverse-mentoring-what-is-it-and-why-is-it-beneficial/

Ramaswamy, S. V. V. (2020). School superintendents are overwhelmingly male. What's holding women back from the top job? *USA Today*. www.usatoday.com/story/news/education/2020/02/20/female-school-district-superintendents-westchester-rockland/4798754002/

Reagan, C. (2019). *Bulletproof backpacks have become another back-to-school staple*. CNBC. www.cnbc.com/2019/08/06/bullet-resistant-backpacks-have-become-another-back-to-school-staple.html

Recchiuti, J. L. (n.d.). America moves to the city. *Khan Academy*. www.khanacademy.org/humanities/us-history/the-gilded-age/gilded-age/a/america-moves-to-the-city

Reilly, K., & Bubello, K. (2018). See photos from the national school walkout led by students protesting gun violence. *Time*. www.time.com/national-school-walkout-gun-control-photos/

Rideout, V., & Robb, M. B. (2019). *The Common Sense census: Media use by tweens and teens.* Common Sense Media. www.commonsensemedia.org/sites/default/files/uploads/research/2019-census-8-to-18-full-report-updated.pdf

Rivers, T. B. (2019). 8 tips to improve communication between generations in the workplace. *Facility Management Software Designed for the Digital Workplace.* www.iofficecorp.com/blog/communication-between-generations-in-the-workplace-4-different-generations-in-the-workplace

RMI. (2015). *Five common dress code violations and how to address them.* rmi-solutions.com/5-common-dress-code-violations-and-how-to-address-them/

Robert Walters/Totaljobs. (2019). *Driving diversity & inclusion in the workforce: An ageing workforce.* www.robertwaltersgroup.com/content/dam/robert-walters/corporate/news-and-pr/files/whitepapers/rw-uk-en-driving-diversity-and-inclusion-ageing-workforce.pdf

Romero, S. (2018). Speech-to-text apps: Typing faster is possible. *NEWS BBVA.* www.bbva.com/en/speech-text-apps-typing-faster-possible/

Roose, K. (2019). Do not disturb: How I ditched my phone and unbroke my brain. *The New York Times.* www.nytimes.com/2019/02/23/business/cell-phone-addiction.html

Rosenberg, M. (2017). Marc my words: The coming knowledge tsunami. *Learning Solutions Magazine.* www.learningsolutionsmag.com/articles/2468/marc-my-words-the-coming-knowledge-tsunami

Scheve, T. (2011). 10 modern technologies baby boomers are using. *HowStuffWorks.* health.howstuffworks.com/wellness/aging/baby-boomers/10-modern-technologies-baby-boomers-are-using.htm

Scott, C. E. (n.d). The history of the radio in the United States to 1940. *EHNet.* ehnet/encyclopedia/the-history-of-the-radio-in-the-United-States-to-1940/

Snyder, B. (2010). Nicholas Carr: The internet is hurting our brains. *Computerworld.* www.computerworld.com/article/2518413/nicholas-carr--the-internet-is-hurting-our-brains.html

Suglia, C. (2017). How millennial parents are disciplining their kids. *Romper.* www.romper.com/p/studies-prove-millennial-parents-are-disciplining-their-kids-less-than-their-parents-43769

Testa, J. (2020). The Girl Scout uniform, updated for Gen Z. *The New York Times.* www.nytimes.com/2020/08/25/fashion/new-girl-scout-uniform.html?searchResultPosition=1

Thebault, R. (2019, November 5). "OK, boomer": 25-year-old lawmaker shuts down heckler during climate change speech. *The Washington Post.* www.washingtonpost.com/climate-environment/2019/11/05/ok-boomer-year-old-lawmaker-shuts-down-heckler-during-climate-change-speech/

TNTP. (2015). *The mirage.* tntp.org/publications/view/the-mirage-confronting-the-truth-about-our-quest-for-teacher-development

Top Hat Staff. (2020). Adrift in a pandemic: Survey of 3,089 students finds uncertainty about returning to college [Infographic]. *Top Hat Blog.* tophat.com/blog/adrift-in-a-pandemic-survey-infographic/

TriNet. (2015). *Survey: Performance reviews drive one in four millennials to search for a new job or call in sick* [Press release]. www.trinet.com/about-us/news-press/press-releases/survey-performance-reviews-drive-one-in-four-millennials-to-search-for-a-new-job-or-call-in-sick

USA Facts. (2020). *More than 9 million children lack internet access at home for online learning.* www.usafacts.org/articles/internet-access-students-at-home/

Varathan, P. (2018). The US is having a hard time keeping teachers in their jobs. *Quartz.* https://qz.com/1284903/american-teachers-leave-their-jobs-at-higher-rates-than-other-countries-with-top-ranked-school-systems/

Vogels, E. A. (2020). Millennials stand out for their technology use, but older generations also embrace digital life. *Pew Research Center.* www.pewresearch.org/fact-tank/2019/09/09/us-generations-technology-use/

Vonnegut, K. (2012). Dear future generations: Please accept our apologies. We were rolling drunk on petroleum. *Twitter.* twitter.com/kurt_vonnegut/status/245644153097158658? lang=en

Wade, R. (2019). Almost half of teachers work a second job: Survey. *Yahoo! Finance.* https://finance.yahoo.com/news/half-of-teachers-work-second-job-fishbowl-survey-191713515.html

The Washington Post. (2015, September 14). *Millennials—coming of age.* www.washingtonpost.com/sf/brand-connect/millennials/

Westminster College. (n.d.). *About us: Churchill's iron curtain speech.* www.wcmo.edu/about/history/iron-curtain-speech.html

Wiggins, G. (2012). Seven keys to effective feedback. *ASCD.* www.ascd.org/publications/educational-leadership/sept12/vol70/num01/Seven-Keys-to-Effective-Feedback.aspx

Wiggins, P. D. (2018). Metric of the month: Learning days per employee. *CFO.* www.cfo.com/training/2018/09/metric-month-learning-days-per-employee/

Will, M. (2018). 5 things to know about today's teaching force. *Education Week.* https://blogs.edweek.org/edweek/teacherbeat/2018/10/today_teaching_force_richard_ingersoll.html

Yee, V., & Blinder, A. (2018). National school walkout: Thousands protest against gun violence across the U.S. *The New York Times.* www.nytimes.com/2018/03/14/us/school-walkout.html

Youn, S. (2019). *Women are less aggressive than men when applying for jobs, despite getting hired more frequently: LinkedIn.* ABC News. https://abcnews.go.com/Business/women-aggressive-men-applying-jobs-hired-frequently-linkedin/story?id=61531741

Zachos, E. (2019). Technology is changing the millennial brain: News for a better Pittsburgh. *PublicSource.* www.publicsource.org/technology-is-changing-the-millennial-brain/

Zarrow, J. (2020). 5 strategies for better teacher professional development. *TeachThought.* www.teachthought.com/pedagogy/5-strategies-better-teacher-professional-development/

Zdonek, P. (2016). Why don't we differentiate professional development? *Edutopia.* www.edutopia.org/blog/why-dont-we-differentiate-pd-pauline-zdonek

Index

5-Gen leaders, 35–37, 41–42, 48–49, 52, 56–58, 65–66, 75–76, 80, 88, 94–99, 103, 107, 117, 135, 137–39, 141
  lesson, 116
5-GEN LEADERSHIP, 2, 4, 6–8, 10, 12, 14–16, 20–21, 23–24, 38–39, 58, 70, 90–91, 108, 118–19, 142–46
5-Gen Leadership Tips, 51
12th-grade students, 127

ability, 13, 28, 38, 54, 60, 93, 98, 102, 129, 138
  applicant's, 103
abstract generational information, 85
accelerant, 94
access, 6, 13, 85, 93, 98–99, 110, 112
access to technology, 98
AC schools, 69
activities, 61, 75, 81, 83, 86–88, 90, 125, 127, 130, 139
  old-school, 139
administrator in Dublin City Schools, 55
administrator in Dublin City Schools in Dublin, 55
administrators, 12–14, 17–18, 21, 30, 37–38, 44, 51, 54–55, 72, 94, 99, 106–8, 122, 124, 126
  female, 29
administrators and teachers, 47, 99
administrator's students, 132
administrator to change districts, 30
advancement, 10, 14, 19, 127
affirmation, 55, 85
African American students, 29
agenda, 83, 90
ages, 4–6, 10, 28, 31–32, 35, 58, 61, 66, 102, 105, 109, 111, 122
algebra, 128–29
altruistic, 38
American boomer, 110
American education, 10, 27, 94, 96
Americans, 25, 27, 65, 104, 116
  adult, 65
American schools, 24, 28–29, 94, 111, 116
American school students, 98

American school values, 33
American students and teachers, 113
American teachers, 10
American teachers work, 11
American teaching force, 6, 43, 122
American University School of Education, 75
American workforce, 6, 43
America's schools, 117
answers, 5, 16, 29–30, 45, 62, 74, 84, 107, 113, 129–30
AoI, 86
apologies, 103
appeal, 18–19, 43, 71, 74–75, 88–89
appeal to teachers, 89
Apple, 41–43
applicant's ability to use technology, 103
apps, 3, 6–7, 26, 31–33, 44, 47, 77, 83, 102, 104–7
  tracking, 47–48
apps and programs, 107
apps and programs to work, 107
apps teachers, 79
APQC, 75
artificial intelligence, 6, 33–36, 38, 121, 130, 136–37
arts, 118, 134, 136–42, 146
  performing, 138–39
asphalt, 112
assistance, 84, 119, 131
assistant, 53–55, 127–28
assistant superintendent, 28, 37, 44, 127
athletics, 139
atmosphere, 43
attention, 34, 51, 55, 58, 61–62, 65–68, 82–83, 98–99, 144
audience, 1, 59, 65–66, 69, 76, 82–84, 88
authority, 33, 114–15
authority figures, 46
average score, 13

baby boomer candidates, 19
baby boomers, 1–3, 5, 7, 13, 66, 80, 110
  fellow, 4
band, 115–16, 139

batteries, 26
BBC News, 110
BC schools and AC schools, 69
blend, 74–75
Bologna, 30, 32–33
boomer administrators, 42
boomer educators, 122, 134
boomer heart, 2
boomer peers, 104
boomers, 1–9, 11–15, 17, 19, 21, 28–29, 41–49,
     51–54, 69, 79–81, 83–88, 100–106, 109,
     113–14, 121–25
   experienced, 88
   older, 99
boomers and Gen Xers change, 105
boomers and Gen Xers to use technology, 102
boomers and Xers, 3, 46, 52, 79–80, 84
boomer set, 72
boomers/Gen, 9
Boomers to Alphas, 3, 5, 7, 9, 11, 13, 15, 17, 19, 21
boomer teacher rolling drunk, 103
boomer teachers, 9, 61, 77, 84, 86, 103–5, 141
   baby, 100
   young, 54
boomer thought process, 104
boomer women, 29
boss, 15, 29, 44
bots, 130
brains, 9, 43, 59–61, 65, 68–69
   changing, 70, 144
breaking news, 68
breakout rooms, 77, 125
Briseno, 115–16
budgets, 9, 135–36
business world, 51, 57, 98
bygone technology, 86
campus, 53, 115, 125–27
campuses, 107, 122, 125, 127
candidates, 17–19
   interviewing teacher, 11
capstone student teaching experience, 123
careers, 27, 29, 37, 52, 58, 71, 77–79, 116,
     122–23, 133, 140
Carver-Thomas & Darling-Hammond, 10–12
century, 8, 14, 27, 32–33, 35–36, 38, 42–44, 79,
     88, 138, 141
century leadership model, 45
century school leadership, 4
century teacher, 59
century teaching, 52, 78
Chae, 47
chairs, 44, 112
challenges, 9, 24, 29, 52, 74, 117
chances, 14, 42, 104, 133
change, 5, 7–9, 29, 31, 33, 83–86, 88–89, 94, 96,
     104–5, 111, 113, 117, 119, 133–34

climate, 1, 7, 117
   peers impact, 118
   societal, 14, 21
Change's staff, 86
change teachers, 76
Chapter, 3, 15, 27–29, 37, 45, 51–53, 57, 77, 81,
     89, 101–3, 107–9, 111–13, 127, 143–46
characteristics, generational, 4, 80, 82–83
characteristics millennials, 21, 143
characteristics of Gen Alpha, 39, 144
charge, 20
cheese, 136–37
child, 26–27, 47–48
   average Gen Alpha, 34
children, 29, 38, 45–47, 112, 114, 140
china, 96, 121
choices, 10, 62, 65, 69, 85, 127
cities, 25, 81, 126
class, 43, 47, 53, 61, 69, 100, 110–12, 128–31,
     133–35, 138, 140
classrooms, 10–11, 34–36, 46–47, 52, 54–55,
     60–61, 76, 78, 80, 88–89, 94, 100, 102–5,
     129–31, 140
closures, 96–97
clues, 66
CNN, 67
coach, 15, 41–42, 54–55, 57–58, 89, 144
coaching, 15, 18, 41, 43, 45, 47–49, 51–53, 55,
     57, 91, 102
coffee, 83, 89, 104–5
co-leaders, 135
collaborative teams, 42–43
college students, 48, 109, 126
   adult, 109
colors, 10, 30, 67–68, 89, 97–98
commitment, 51–52, 117
committee of teachers, 51
committees, 12, 14, 51–52, 88, 127
Common Sense Media, 31–32
Communicating, 57
communication, 13, 37, 48–49, 51–52, 55–57,
     87, 138
   constant, 48–49
community, 29, 32, 44, 79, 113, 115, 134, 141
companies, 12, 15, 30, 36, 75, 82, 91, 98, 102–3,
     117, 145
computers, 41, 60, 65, 69, 104, 129–30, 139–40
conflicts, 28, 43–44, 52, 83
   experienced intergenerational, 102
constant interaction, 13, 17, 69–70, 144
content, 53, 65, 68, 72–73, 75–76, 80, 85,
     88–90, 125, 129, 132–33, 137, 140
contracts, teacher union, 51
control, 12, 42, 107, 112
   gun, 111
   losing, 106

conversations, 13, 15, 17, 19, 50, 52–54, 56, 106–7, 112, 114, 117–18, 132, 134
cost, 11, 31, 33
country, 10, 64, 110–12, 118, 121, 126–27
COVID-19, 93–95, 97–99, 101, 103, 105, 107, 113, 139
COVID-19 school closures, 93
COVID-19 school dominoes, 94
COVID school closures, 99, 139
crack, 9
crackers, 136–37
cravings to use technology, 69
Creating Multigenerational PD, 73, 75, 77, 79, 81, 83, 85, 87, 89, 91
crux, 7, 43
culture, 23, 42–43, 115, 140
   school's, 115
curriculum, teacher's, 130
Daggett, 94
data
   retention, 11, 19–21, 143
   school's, 78
   student learning, 142, 146
days, 32, 38, 51–53, 55–57, 61, 65–67, 73, 75–77, 79, 83, 94–96, 103, 106, 109, 111–12, 117–18, 126–27
death, 113, 118
debt, 6, 12, 14
decade, 3, 8, 21, 29, 32, 34, 36, 61, 65, 116, 122, 131–32
demands, 13, 36–37, 94–95, 115, 141
demands on schools, 141
design, 73–74, 77, 81
detractors, 44
devices, 6, 13–14, 18, 31–36, 61, 65, 78, 80, 106, 131
devices and screen time, 34
dialogue, 47, 49–52, 58, 83, 144
   generational, 86
   multigenerational, 81, 83
differences, 11, 19, 21, 42, 57–58, 86–87, 132, 143
differences in generations, 58
Digital Ability, 101
digital generation gaps, 8–9, 21, 106, 108, 143, 145
digital tools, 13–14, 96, 107–8, 125, 129, 140, 145
Diley, Jim, 37
direct instruction, 85, 97, 128–29
disadvantaged students, 98
discipline students, 28
disobeying, 46
disparate generational, 8, 50
disparate generational experiences, 141
disruptions, 53, 62, 96, 133
   unprecedented school, 95
Disruptive Times, 8, 31, 95–96
dissatisfactions, 10

Distracted Students, Distracted Teachers, 61
Distracted Word Cloud, 62–64
districts, 10–12, 14, 28, 30, 36, 43, 72, 74–76, 78, 117, 119, 126, 128
diversity, 112, 117–18
Donnie, 117
dramatic teaching, 32
dress, 50–51
Dublin City Schools, 55

economy, 98, 103
educating students, 133
education, 5, 21, 23, 32–33, 37–39, 69–70, 94, 97, 103, 123–25, 128, 130–33, 137, 144–45
   traditional, 33
education apps, 37, 80, 84
education leaders, 122
education model for Gen Alpha and Gen, 34
education models, 34, 94, 133
education system, 94, 124
education technology, 14, 36
education technology specialists, 128
education technology usage, 18
educators, 28, 30, 37–39, 49, 51, 56–57, 60, 78, 81, 95–96, 102, 118, 122, 124, 137–38
educators and parents, 95
elementary school playground, 26
email, 6, 53, 55–57, 69
emotions, 118–19, 134
empathy, 131, 134
employees, 12–13, 42, 51, 74–75, 102, 127
engagement, 13–14, 86, 138
English learners, 63
Entrepreneurship, 35
equity, 25, 117–18
   racial, 117
evaluations, 41, 49–50, 52–53, 58, 80, 144
evaluation scores, 49–50, 54
evaluators, 49, 53–55
Examples of bygone technology, 86
exercise, 2, 6, 62–65, 81–83, 85
expectations, 5, 45, 55, 106, 117, 136–37
experienced new generational problems in schools, 16
experience in helping teachers use technology, 128
experiences, 8, 10, 12, 27, 29, 33–34, 52, 54, 57, 74, 76, 79–80, 128, 130–31, 134–35
exterior information, 77, 79

Facebook, 66, 114
FaceTime, 26, 138
FaceTime conversations, 27
faculty, 126
families, 11, 32, 37–38, 46, 95–98, 114, 121
farmers, 26, 38
father, out-of-touch boomer, 121

feedback, 13–14, 48, 52–55, 58, 74, 144
  clear, 49
  constructive, 55
  honest, 42–43
fellow boomers, 5, 45
females, 29–30
fewer Gen Zers, 1, 15, 19, 21, 143
Figure, 3–4, 7–9, 14–15, 17–18, 20–21, 25, 31,
    34–35, 49–51, 56–58, 62–64, 67–68, 86–87,
    89–91, 101, 107–8, 124, 135, 141–42
figure it out, 3
findings, 3, 48, 80, 84, 98
fitness, 41–42
fit school leadership, 43
Five-Gen leaders, 79–80, 87–89, 93, 99, 107,
    109–10, 115–17, 134, 139, 141–42, 146
Five Steps, 35
Five Steps to Lead Gen Alpha, 35
Five Technology Goals, 107
Flexible School Hours, 35
Florida, 104, 111
Floyd, George, 113
focus, 17, 28, 44–45, 49, 67, 71, 95, 113–14
food, 26, 83, 89, 113
forgot, 65–66
formative assessments, 16, 72, 100
Franke, 32
fulfillment, 38
Furness, 130–31

Gahanna Lincoln High School, 118, 133
games, 4, 26, 41–42, 116
gap, 8–9, 69, 80–83, 86–88, 93, 97, 106, 141
  generational, 113
gap in technology ability, 106
gaps for low-income students, 97
Gen, 2–3, 5–17, 19–21, 30–37, 41–43, 45–55,
    57–60, 69–70, 78–81, 84–86, 93–106, 109,
    111–19, 121–23, 125–29, 131–33, 135,
    137–39, 143–44, 146
  fewer, 16
  school administrators recruiting, 17
Gen Alpha, 3, 21, 23, 25–39, 45–46, 95, 97–98,
    100, 109–11, 118–19, 123, 126–27,
    133–34, 144, 146
  first, 125
  name, 30
  support, 39, 144
Gen Alpha and Gen Beta students, 123, 133
Gen Alpha and Gen Z, 32–35, 78, 94, 126
Gen Alpha demands, 127
Gen Alpha's constant exposure, 34
Gen Alpha's efforts, 96
Gen Alpha's efforts to use technology, 96
Gen Alpha's Impact, 33
Gen Alpha's Impact on Education, 33

Gen Alpha's life, 35
Gen Alpha spending, 32
Gen Alpha students, 46–47, 59–60, 62, 81,
    84–85, 93, 97–100, 102, 108, 117, 119,
    121, 144–46
Gen Alpha students tap, 112
Gen Alpha students visions, 97
Gen Beta students, 123, 133
generational, 54, 87
Generational Challenges, 8
generational conflicts, 75
generational differences, 7–8, 56, 81–83, 90
generational differences and conflicts, 83
generational disparity, 3
generational diversity, 117
generational issues, addressing, 82
generational lens, 74
Generational Lessons, 93, 95, 97, 99, 101, 103,
    105, 107
generational perspectives, 57
Generation Alpha, 33
Generation Alpha students, 34, 118
generational problem-solving, 80
generational shifts, 110
generational stereotyping, 4
generational teaching ranks, 15, 99
generational transition, 124
generational trend, 123
generational viewpoint, 12
generation commonalities, 58
generation gaps, 1, 4, 8–9, 12, 45, 57–59,
    81–82, 102, 109, 144
Generation Glass, 32, 45
generations, 2–5, 8–10, 15, 19, 21, 23–25,
    29–35, 37–39, 49, 51–52, 54–62, 68–71,
    74–75, 79–80, 82–89, 91, 102–3, 115–18,
    132–33, 143–45
  advanced, 23
  boomer, 44
  distinct, 1, 21, 143
  experienced teaching, 80
  figure-it-out, 3
  first, 6, 16, 35, 79
  fit, 45
  highest-educated, 7
  lost, 6, 97
  most tested, 16
  multiple, 12, 19
  newest, 3
  older, 2, 8, 11, 13, 43, 49, 74, 84
  pre-internet, 5
  previous, 2–3, 5–8, 11–14, 31, 39, 46, 52, 83,
    116, 143
  teacher's, 80
  tech-savvy, 32
  wealthiest, 24

generations form, 121
generation's reliance, 103
generations ride, 93
generations share, 70, 144
Gen Xers, 2–3, 5–6, 12–13, 41–45, 47–48, 69, 72, 74, 79–81, 83–88, 102, 104, 106, 113–14, 122–24
Gen Xers change, 105
Gen Xers to use technology, 102
Gen Zers, 1–3, 5–9, 15–17, 19–21, 43–45, 47–49, 51–52, 79–80, 83, 85, 87–88, 110–11, 113–14, 121–23, 125–26
Gen Zers and Gen Alphas, 109–10
Gen Z Teachers, 50
Global Leadership Question, 74
goals, 2, 16, 20, 33, 50, 54, 106, 125, 138
    school's, 18
    teachers set, 54
Google, 17, 62, 85, 134
grades, 16, 27, 73, 100, 131
graduates, 34, 111, 114
grandparents, 26, 55
grant, small, 135
great teachers and leaders, 45
grit, 48–49, 102
group of millennial teachers, 10
groups, 2–3, 7, 10, 51–52, 64, 66, 74, 77, 79–81, 83–85, 87, 112, 115–16, 132, 135
    generational, 80–81
    largest, 6, 122
    next, 37
guiding staff to change, 29

helping, 7, 14, 21, 37, 42, 48, 87, 99, 102, 112, 130
helping students, 38, 88
Help Millennial, 50
Help staff members, 119, 146
Help staffs work, 58, 144
high school classes, 99
high school department head, 7
high school graduates, 16
high school levels, 114
high school operations, 122
high school science, 27
high schools, large, 139
high schools function, 125
high school students, 7, 13, 16, 28, 61, 63, 110
high school teenagers, 109
hiring, 20
history, 4, 8, 11, 23–24, 30, 60, 69, 115
history of generational leadership in schools, 24
home, 27–28, 32, 34, 36, 41, 65–66, 69, 95, 99–100, 103, 125–27, 130, 132
home health care technology, 104
hoodies, wear, 118
Hope School, named, 83

hours, 1, 6, 31–32, 34, 42, 53, 61, 68, 73, 75–76
hours of sleep, 61
hours online, 61
houses, 6, 26, 101, 110, 113, 126
Houston, 63–64
human connection, 138–39
humanity, 121, 134, 137, 141–42, 146
humans, 121, 130, 133, 141
hungry student, 137
hyper-change, 8, 78, 94

if you got a paddling at school, 28
immigrant students, 29
impact, 21, 23–25, 27–29, 31, 33, 35, 37, 39, 78–80, 94, 97
Impact of Digital Ability on Teacher Seniority, 101
impact of family income, 97
impact of family income on student, 97
impact of Ted's generation, 24
impact of Ted's generation on American schools, 24
impact on schools, 21
impact on teachers, 80
inclusion, 117
inclusivity, 115–16
individuals, 4, 11, 28, 57, 82, 112, 117, 131
Inexperienced Teacher, 101
information, 16–17, 20, 31, 49, 56, 60, 62, 67, 69, 76–80, 85, 90
    relevant, 78–79
input, 11, 14, 49, 51, 53, 83
instruction, technology- centered, 127
interaction, 46, 60, 62, 129, 138
interests, 33, 79, 90, 126, 130
International Center for Leadership in Education, 94
internet, 5–7, 9, 61, 66, 69, 71, 99, 102, 106–7, 109–10, 119, 126, 130, 133–34
internet and social media, 66, 134
internet gap, 9
iPads, 26, 32–33, 61, 104
issues, 7, 11–12, 14, 19, 21, 51–52, 112–14
i use more technology, 84

Jim Crow's Schools, 25
job description, 42–43
job fairs, 11, 17
jobs, 7, 10–11, 15, 17–18, 24, 29–30, 38, 47–48, 53, 66, 102
Johnson, 74
journalists, 67–68
jump, 30, 36, 55–56
junior, 27, 36, 127
Junior high, 27

Kasasa, 4, 6
Kelly, 97
KEY QUESTIONS, 20
kids, 2, 28, 30, 32, 45–47, 60–61, 94, 96, 98–99, 112, 137–38
kindness, 37, 134–35, 140
Know, 21, 31, 39, 70, 91, 107, 142–46
knowledge, 8, 31, 74, 98, 100, 102, 128, 134
    generational, 12
Know millennials, 21, 143
Koning, 25

lack, 1, 10–11, 13, 47, 49, 77, 98, 102, 111, 129
lack of gun control and safety in American schools, 111
lack of technology prowess, 102
lack technology skills, 103
Lahman, 134, 138–41
Lahman's students, 139
language, 43
laptops, school-issued, 69
leaders, 5, 7, 12–15, 17, 19–20, 24–25, 27, 37, 39, 42–45, 51, 80, 82–85, 115, 117
    5-Gen school, 19
    boomer school, 44
    business, 3, 102
    collaborative school, 42
    discipline challenges school, 28
    guide school, 124
    high-profile school, 44
    informal, 5, 52
    millennial school, 122
    post-internet, 122
    practices school, 137
    pre-internet, 122
    stress school, 12
    time government, 28
    well-meaning school, 71
leaders and peers, 57
leadership, 3, 8, 14, 21, 43–44, 52, 54–55, 73, 79, 86, 116–17, 127–28
    educational, 73
    generational, 3, 24
leadership days, 29
leadership doors, 29
leadership philosophies, 19, 43
leadership positions, 13, 29–30, 121
leadership roles, 30, 108
leadership skills, 13, 44
leadership training, 13
Lead Gen Alpha, 35
leading schools, 7–8, 14, 31, 95–96, 122
leading teachers, 3
    started, 7
learners, 2–3, 84, 90, 131

learning, 27, 29, 32–37, 39, 46–47, 55, 57, 72, 74–75, 88–89, 100–101, 125–26, 140–41, 144
    remote, 76, 95, 97–100, 102, 105, 113, 125–26, 132–33
learning companions, 131
Learning Network, 94
learning preferences of Gen Alpha and Gen, 35
learning time, 36
lenses
    multigenerational, 42, 81–82, 145
    multigenerations, 91
Leo, 29–30, 38
lessons, 54, 56, 78, 86, 90, 105, 110, 114, 124–26, 128–29, 131, 138, 141
lessons for 5-Gen leaders, 56, 135
letters, 36, 135
life, 13, 15, 19, 32, 36, 38, 41, 87–88, 122, 125, 127, 136, 138
life experiences, 3, 8, 49, 86, 125
life of Gen Alpha, 32
lifestyles, digital, 69–70, 80, 144
lifetime of Gen Alpha, 32
limb, 96
Lockley, 12–13
log, 56, 69, 100, 129, 132
lonelier, 138
longing, 138
Los Angeles, 9, 62–63
love, 6, 34, 39, 41, 110, 115–16, 121, 136–37, 139, 143
low-income students, 97
loyal, 4, 57, 113–14, 116

Macioce, 133–37, 139–41
magic thread, 38
Making Generational Adjustments, 12
manager, 41–42, 50, 58, 144
marching, 115–16
Master Teacher, 133, 135
material, 90, 130–32
matter, 4, 42, 57, 80, 137
McCrindle Staff, 31–32, 34–35
member of Gen Alpha, 23, 26, 38
members, 1, 7, 23–25, 27, 31, 45, 66, 83–84, 115–16
    band, 116
mentoring, 18–19, 103
mentoring and reverse mentoring, 103
mentors, 8, 14, 37, 39, 88, 143
middle school concept, 27–28
middle school counselors, 135
middle school educators, 27
middle schools, 7, 27–28, 30, 46, 61, 99, 111, 113–14
    male, 29
middle school students, 135

millennial administrator, 133
millennial assistant superintendent, 44
millennial candidates, 19
millennial employee, 42
millennial evaluations, 49
millennial leaders, 45, 100, 125
millennial managers, 6, 17
millennial members, 116
millennial parents, 46
millennial principals, 122
millennial professionals, 48–50
millennials, 1–3, 5–10, 12–17, 19–21, 37, 41–54,
     57–58, 66, 79–81, 83–88, 104–5, 108–10,
     113–14, 121–23, 125, 127, 131–33, 141
  ascending, 128
  benefit, 85
  coach, 49
  fit, 55
  leading, 3
  role, 122
millennials and older teachers, 16
millennials/Gen, 9
millennial siblings, 21
  older, 3
millennial son, 121
Millennials' Shifts, 15
Millennials' Shifts in Priorities, 15
millennial teachers, 1, 9–11, 17, 20, 48, 112,
     125, 127–28
millennial workers, 13
Mind, 62, 81–83, 86–88, 134
mindsets, 6, 45, 55, 87, 104–5, 108, 125, 145
minutes, 32, 53, 66, 77, 85, 87, 112, 129
mix, 8, 34, 67–68, 75, 85, 127
model, flexible schooling, 124
model technology, 93
model technology in PD, 93
mom, 114
money, 11–12, 24, 97–98, 134
moniker, 30
Montgomery County Students for Change, 111
Moore's Law, 8, 31
Morales, 114–16
movement, student-led, 111
Ms, 83–86, 88–89, 130
MTV generation, 5
multigenerational, 86
multigenerational awareness, 83
multigenerational issues, 84
Multigenerational PD, 71–72
multigenerational techniques, 83
Multigenerational Workforce, 57
Mulvahill, 11
Murray, 56–57, 102–3, 117
music, 42, 61, 65, 68–69, 115, 136, 140
national school walkout, 111

nation's teacher shortages, 11
new and unprecedented school disruptions, 95
newest generation of student, 3
New generations, 3, 30, 35
  multiple, 133
new hybrid school/learning models, 97
new leadership positions, 128
new leadership positions in schools, 128
new paths, 35, 121, 127–28
new pillars, 35
New Pillars for Gen Alpha, 35
news, 13, 56, 66–68, 73, 87, 97, 102, 125
new school models, 97
new school year, 95
new teacher/mentor relationship, traditional, 88
new type of audience, 59
new types, 2–3, 33, 37, 48, 84, 122–25, 127,
     133, 135, 142, 146
new types of devices, 6, 35, 80
new types of devices and education apps, 80
new types of leaders, 123
new types of positions, 128
new types of schools for Gen Alpha, 33
new way to use technology, 104
New York, 64, 100
New York City, 64, 95, 112, 126
New York Times, 95, 111
New Zealand Parliament, 1–2
next generation of leaders, 39, 143
next group of leaders, 37
nurture students, 133

observation, 53–54
officer, 117
offline students, 98
Ohio, 25, 28, 55, 117–18, 124, 133
Ohio school leader, 102
older teachers, 8–9, 16, 28, 55, 57, 79–80, 88,
     99–100, 102–4, 108, 122
older teachers to rip, 103
ongoing, 49, 76, 91, 105, 108, 145
online, 16, 18, 32, 61, 100–101, 126,
     129, 132
  teachers teaching, 128
online in school, 32
online learning, 94, 99, 126
order, 104–5
organizational, 79
organizations, 13, 78–79, 82–83, 115
pace, 13, 77, 85, 90
pandemic, 95–98, 102, 104–5, 113, 124, 127,
     129, 135, 139
pandemic era students, 129
pandemic school year, 134
paradigm, 101–2
parenting, overprotective, 47

parents, 24, 26, 28–29, 32, 34, 38, 43, 45–48, 56–57, 94–96, 98–99, 111, 113–14, 121, 124
parents and students, 124
Parkland High School, 7, 111
Parkland shootings, 111
part, 14, 18, 23, 26, 33, 35, 38, 47–48, 53–55, 83–85, 105–6, 110, 112–13, 126–27, 129
participants, 63, 90, 112
passions, 32, 34, 41–43, 112
past, 9–13, 15, 45–46, 49, 52, 69–70, 77, 111, 114, 137, 144
paths, 97, 127
patient, 9
PD (professional development), 2–3, 21, 59, 69, 71–77, 79, 86, 88–91, 93, 106–7, 145
PD by generation, 91, 145
PD days, 73, 75–76, 83
PD designers, 73–74
PD leaders, 71
PD Problem, 71–72
PD sessions, 3, 65, 69, 73, 76–77, 80, 83, 88
PD sessions and generations, 79
PD Topics, 71, 79
PD to teachers, 72
peers, 3, 7, 49, 52, 57, 62–63, 81, 84, 100, 102, 106, 109, 133
  experienced, 2, 8, 55
peers and school issues, 81
performance, 54, 75, 138, 140
person, 20, 43, 53–54, 87, 117, 126, 129, 133, 135, 138
personal communications, 23, 25, 29, 38, 55, 102, 119, 135–40
personality, 54, 129–30
personal technology, 3, 65
Person in charge of gathering, 20
perspectives, 18, 57
pertinent questions for 5-Gen leaders, 137
phones, 17, 26, 36, 41, 65–66, 72, 84, 93, 104, 136, 139
  college student's, 47
phrase, 1, 54, 97
place, 1, 3, 14–16, 25, 49, 66, 89, 112, 123–24, 129, 136
place for Gen Alphas, 123
plan, 7, 19, 72, 126
political activism, 109, 111, 113, 115, 117, 119
poll, 11, 66–67
Pope, 110
positions, 12–14, 117, 125, 128
  principal, 30
posts, 114
poverty, 97–98
power of technology to reshape parenting, 47
praise, 37, 46, 53, 57, 85, 135
precocious boomers, 45

pre-internet generation of leaders, 5
PreK, 64, 121, 124–26, 137, 146
preparation programs, fewer teacher, 123
preparing students, 24, 119
Presentation Methods for Teacher Z, 88
president, 27, 44, 67, 97, 110, 115–16
principals, 5, 8, 18, 24–25, 29, 38, 103, 111–12, 123, 128, 135
  female school, 29
priorities, 15, 117
private sector, 48, 75, 89, 102
problems, 10, 12, 15, 37, 43–44, 46–47, 66, 80, 82, 128–29, 136
  experienced new generational, 16
profession, 1, 5, 9–10, 12, 16, 21, 86, 88, 122–23, 137, 143
professional development. See PD
professional dress, 50–51
programs, 12, 14–15, 18, 25, 100, 105, 107, 118, 123, 130, 134, 137
project, 135
protests, 109–12, 114, 118
  silent, 112
punished students, 111
Purdue Global, 4–7
purpose, 15, 19, 38, 113, 118
pursuit, 110, 113, 119, 146

qualifications, 30
questions, pertinent, 137

racism, 113–14, 117
Ramaswamy, 29–30
rate of change, 8–9, 31
Recruiting Gen Z Teachers, 16
Redesign school days, 35
Red Rover, 26
regressing, 136–37
rehearsal, 138–39
reinventing, 42
relationships, 37, 42–43, 45, 57, 85, 131, 133, 140
relevancy, 62, 75–77, 79, 86
Relevancy in teaching and learning, 79
remind, 18, 37–38, 52, 57, 88, 141
reminders, 37, 52, 133
remind teachers, 82, 88
Remote learning and new hybrid school/ learning models, 97
rents, 126
research, 4, 33, 69, 75–76, 85, 87, 127, 139
reshaping, 8, 39, 94, 122, 144
resources, 14, 50, 107–8, 114, 118, 140, 145–46
Retaining Millennial Teachers, 14
retreat, 44
reverse mentoring, 57, 71, 88, 103
revolves, 115

risks, 47, 52, 71, 128
role of teachers, 123
room, 3, 12, 18, 33, 83–85, 89, 93, 105, 111, 140
Rosenberg, 31
Rutgers Business School, 102

safety, 16, 33, 80, 111
salaries, 12, 14, 25
sales rep, 41
savvy teachers, 106–8, 145
schedules, 14, 34, 36, 127, 132
school administrators, 12, 25, 37, 42–43, 50, 77,
    113, 122–23
  burdened, 53
  high, 132
  retired, 23
school agendas, public, 124
school apocalypse, 94
school authority, 111
school building, 80
school campuses, 122
school closings, 97
school closures, 32, 56, 93, 102
  prolonged, 97
school colors, 51
school communication, 56
school community, 139
school culture, 14, 33, 39, 112, 144
  positive, 118
school days, 34, 61, 75
school development, 53
school discontent, 132
school district personnel, 20
school districts, 20, 37–38, 76, 94
school doors, 113
school environments, 13, 16
school fridge, 136
school history, 8–9, 132
schooling, 27
school in protest, 118
school issues, 81
school leaders, 1, 3–4, 12–16, 18–19, 24–25, 27,
    29, 37–39, 42–44, 48, 51–52, 94–96,
    106–7, 110–13, 131–33
school leaders give stress, 14
school leadership, 3, 12, 29, 127–28
  complicated, 123
school leadership positions, 95
school leadership ranks, 122
school leaders recognize, 14
school leaders work, 16
school logos, 51
school machine, 43
school models, 121
school online, 32
school parking, 10

school PD, 72
school principal, 42
school psychologist, 118
school reform movements, 28
schools, 3–5, 10–21, 23–28, 32–34, 36–38,
    46–49, 51–53, 59–63, 72, 77–79, 88–89,
    93–101, 111–13, 117–18, 121–24, 126–29,
    131–33, 138–39, 141
  5-Gen, 76
  charter, 132
  country, 28
  elementary, 9, 26–27, 64
  fictional, 83
  force, 36
  greatest, 117
  high, 26–28, 30, 34, 36–37, 53, 59, 62–63,
    103, 110, 125, 127–28, 132, 139
  intermediary, 27
  large, 57
  missionary, 25
  nation's, 93
  new, 36
  old, 103
  public, 16, 28, 79, 124, 132–33
  reconfigure, 35
  regular, 95
  reshape, 18, 97
  small, 26, 33
school safety, 95
school's blacktop, 112
schools for Gen Alpha, 33
school shooter, active, 78
school shootings, 11, 16, 24, 78, 113
school's mission, 88
school song, 115
school's students, 111
school staffs, 6, 81–82
school staff stew, 3
school success, 139
school systems, 12, 24, 42, 46, 124, 132, 142, 146
  local, 78
  next, 93
school websites, 43
school work, 135
schoolwork, 126
school year, 38, 63, 75
scores, 18, 53
screens, 34, 45, 62, 67–69, 84, 89, 100, 105, 128,
    136, 138
  teacher's, 129
Secondary schools, 27
Secondary School Studies, 27
seconds, 61, 67
sentence, 1, 59, 105
sessions, 2, 29, 76–77, 84, 90
shared experience, 138–39

shift, 3, 15, 27–28, 43, 55, 69, 97, 102, 105, 122, 124
shortage, national teacher, 10
shot, 67–68
showcasing student, 18
Showexamples of teacher and student work, 18
Silent Generation, 4, 7, 23–27, 29, 33–35, 37, 45, 66, 110
Silent Generation and boomer administrators, 42
Silent Generation form, 33
sin, 73
sin in educational leadership, 73
skills, 11, 34–35, 38, 42–43, 46, 103
skills students, 138
sleep, 61
slide rules, 36
slides, 41, 68, 85, 90, 130
smartphones, 44, 57, 61, 65–66, 69
Smith, 23, 25
social media, 6, 9, 14, 16, 19, 24, 44, 89–90, 110, 112, 114, 119, 138
software, 130, 133
software updates, 60
someplace, 126, 132
song, 115–16, 118
specialists, 41
special sauce, 140–41
speeds, processing, 8, 31
staff and parents, 29
staff and parents and community, 29
staff meetings, 18, 75, 77
staff members, 52, 56, 83, 87
staffs, 3–5, 15–18, 36–37, 52, 55–56, 59, 74–75, 80–84, 87–88, 100, 102–3, 106–7, 132, 135
  guiding, 29
  mesh, 108, 145
  multigenerational, 114
staff workroom, 56
standardized tests, 16, 28, 130
Starbucks, 6, 49, 89, 104–5
state, 5, 11–12, 15, 24, 72, 78, 110, 132–33
station, 67–68
steps, 7, 19, 25, 35, 37, 49–50, 81, 86, 90, 106, 111, 128
Steps to Help Millennial and Gen, 50
stories, personal, 83
stress, 14, 18, 50, 57, 60, 64, 86, 88, 127
stress levels, 13, 80
stress school leaders and teachers, 12
student behavior, 137
student body, 112
student data, 130
student data bank, 131
student growth, 139
student in America, 99
student leaders, 112

student logs, 100
student populations, 21, 116
student ranks, 117
students, 2–3, 7–9, 14–16, 18, 23–24, 27–29, 32–39, 45–46, 54–55, 57–65, 69, 77–79, 84–86, 88, 94–103, 105–6, 108–14, 118–19, 124–41, 146
student's actions, 136–37
students and parents, 34, 57, 96
student's eye roll, 136
students of color, 10, 97–98
students plug, 100
student's preschool days, 131
students protest, 112
student's sense, 139
student's shoulder, 136
students showcase, 118
students stick, 118
students to share, 140
students use technology, 99
student texts, 136
student unrest, 28
student walkouts, 111
student work, 18
styles, 43, 45
subject matter, 78–80, 137
subject matter and teaching method information, 80
subjects, 78–80, 100, 133, 141
subway, 81
superintendents, 5, 8, 12, 24, 29–30, 51, 74, 111, 122–23, 127–28
support, 33, 44, 50, 54, 75–77, 91, 116, 119, 130–31, 135, 145
Swarbrick, 1–2
systemized, 14
systems, 14, 16, 27–28, 34, 72, 79, 94–96, 117, 123, 128, 131
  district teacher evaluation, 78

TABLE, 79–80
tactics, 4, 14–15, 19, 21, 71
Tactics for Creating Multigenerational PD, 73, 75, 77, 79, 81, 83, 85, 87, 89, 91
taste, first, 59–60
taught students, 128
teacher and student work, 18
teacherbots, 141
teacher bravely, 2
teacher career, 134
teacher data, 20
teacher dress, 52
teacher dress code issues, 51
teacher dress code issues in schools, 51
teacher dress codes, 52
teacher evaluation information, 78

teacher evaluations, 54
teacher experience, 108, 145
teacher force, 51, 68, 89
teacher growth, 106
teacher leaders, 14, 122
teacher learn, 14
teacher lecture, 100
teacher mailboxes, 56
teacher pipeline, 15
teacher preparation programs, 15, 28, 123
teacher ranks, 101
teacher ratings, 78
Teacher Recruiting, 20
  written, 21, 143
Teacher Recruiting and Retention Plan
  (TRRP), 20–21, 143
teachers, 1–21, 26, 28, 34–39, 41–59, 61–62,
  65–66, 68–91, 93–95, 97–108, 112–14,
  122–23, 125–35, 137–38, 140–46
  algebra, 129, 131, 141
  average, 121, 129
  award-winning drama, 133
  below-average, 131
  best digital, 107
  better, 53, 58, 131
  black, 25
  breakable, 48
  coach, 53
  coaching, 55
  computer science, 59
  contracted, 95
  days, 75
  deficient, 106, 108, 145
  digital all-star, 106
  distracted, 88
  effective, 140
  elementary, 2, 26, 105
  emailed, 52
  experienced, 13, 52, 61, 65, 79, 101–2, 108,
    125, 145
  fellow, 106
  fewer, 15, 123, 132
  finest, 93, 106
  first, 128
  great, 45, 131, 138
  greatest, 132
  high school, 45, 65, 132
  hired, 81
  history, 27
  human, 130
  impacting, 77
  math, 129
  middle-aged, 66
  new, 11, 55
  old, 134
  performing arts, 133
  proficient, 101
  proud, 135
  removing weak, 103
  secondary, 65
  senior, 55
  stressed younger, 58, 144
  student, 140
  substitute, 53
  technology-deficient, 103
  tech-savvy, 79
  trained, 3
  training, 84
  watched, 9
  weaker, 131
  weak public school, 132
  white, 25
teacher's age, 80
teacher salaries, 12
  low, 12
teachers and administrators, 51, 99
teachers approach, 49
teachers chances, 14
teachers chances to model, 14
teachers change, 105
teachers complain, 72
teacher's courage, 54
teachers energy, 83
Teacher Seniority, 101
teachers in leadership decisions, 127
teachers laugh, 84
teachers of color, 10
teachers of older generations, 11
teachers on Ms, 86
teachers quit, 10
teachers start, 21, 75
teachers support, 75
teachers tend, 14
teachers tend to smile, 72
teachers tend to use, 14
teachers tend to value stability, 88
teachers to answer, 84
teachers use, 62, 96, 104
teachers use technology, 107
teacher's webpage, 100
teachers work, 18, 133
teacher to assistant, 127
teacher training, 66
teacher unions, strong, 132
teacher vacancies, 11
Teacher Z, 88
Teacher Z PD Checklist, 90
teaching, 5–7, 26–27, 34–37, 39, 45–46, 51–53,
  59–60, 74–77, 79–80, 85–86, 88–89,
  124–25, 129–32, 137, 140–41
  better, 75, 78
teaching box, 11

teaching candidates, 11, 17, 21, 143
Teaching Distracted Generations, 61, 63, 65, 67, 69
teaching force, 6, 21, 46, 82, 125
teaching generations, 21, 143
teaching information, 78–79
teaching jobs, 26, 100
teaching/learning process, 29
teaching method information, 80
teaching methods, 82, 125
teaching profession, 9, 11, 21, 35, 143
teaching ranks, 37, 123
teaching staffs, 1–2, 5, 8, 12, 18, 21, 61, 143
team, 17–18, 26, 33, 41–42, 57, 82–83
    internal questions leadership, 81
team leaders, 8, 41–42, 44
tech ninja millennial, 41
technological advancements, 33
technologist, 106
technology, 7–9, 13–14, 31–32, 35–36, 38–39,
        59–60, 65–66, 69–70, 76–77, 82–84,
        86–88, 93–94, 96–98, 100–102, 104–8,
        121–22, 128, 136–37, 141–42, 144
    automation, 98
    balance, 134
    digital, 65
    incorporating, 102
    latest, 13, 19
    new, 6, 35, 42, 83, 104
    old, 36
    powerful, 32, 125
    shunned, 100
    value, 14, 18
technology ability, 76, 106
technology accelerations, 23, 31
technology acumen, 125
technology advancements, 8
technology availability, 60
technology challenges, 84
technology component, 79, 107
    strong, 34
technology deficiency, 102
technology element, strong, 69
technology fantasy, 60
technology generation, 32
technology generation gaps, 71
technology improvement a, 107
technology iterations, 86
technology proficiency, 101
technology prowess, 102, 106
technology savvy, 57, 93
technology skills, 103, 132
    basic, 103
technology snafus, 106
technology specialists, 56, 99
    designated, 106
    district's, 72

technology Theo, 27
technology to reshape parenting, 47
technology training, 14
technology transition, 26
technology usage, 53, 105, 124
    5-Gen leaders model, 88
    expanded, 124
Ted, 23, 25–28, 33, 37–38
Ted's childhood, 26
Ted's generation, 24, 29
teenagers, 7, 32–33, 61, 110, 114, 117
teens, 96
testing, 10, 12, 16, 124
tests, 5, 16, 28, 79
test scores, 18, 78–79, 95
Texas, 29, 63, 114–16
texting, 52, 57, 65
theatre, 134, 136
Theatre App students, 135
Thebault, 1
Theo, 23, 26–27, 31, 33–35, 38
Theodore, 23
thread, 133–34
time, 11–13, 17–18, 24–25, 27–29, 45, 60–61,
        64–67, 73, 75, 78–79, 86–90, 103–7, 110,
        117–19, 132, 140
    first, 55, 72, 105
    long, 60, 71
    screen, 34, 61, 65
    teacher's, 73
time for 5-Gen leaders, 127
time for students to share, 140
tips, 17–18, 56–57, 70, 76, 95, 108, 145
Tips for Transitioning to 5-Gen
        Leadership, 21, 39, 58, 70, 91,
        108, 119, 142–43
tips to school leaders, 95
tips to school leaders for surviving, 95
titles, 42, 103
topics, 28, 62, 79, 83–84, 110, 116–17
    generational, 89
towns, small, 25, 27
toys, 26
trade, 102
tradition, 103, 114–15, 125
Traditional school models, 124
train, 65, 70, 74–75, 107, 144
trainers, 69, 72–74, 77
Training boomer and Gen, 104
training for teachers, 14
training methods, 74–75
trainings, 2, 14, 35, 62–64, 68–69, 71–72,
        74–75, 77, 100, 104, 108
traits of Gen Alpha, 34
transform, 28, 33, 96, 124, 133
transformative days, 94

transformative days for education, 94
transgender student, 111
Transitioning, 21, 39, 43, 58, 70, 91, 108, 119,
    142–43, 145
transitioning to 5-Gen leadership, 21
Transitioning to 5-Gen Leadership, 21, 39, 58,
    70, 91, 108, 119, 142
Trayvon Martin, 118
tree, 96
tricks, 47, 102
TriNet, 48
TRRP. *See* Teacher Recruiting and Retention
    Plan
truth, 117, 136–37
tweens, 61
Twitter, 56

underserved students, 98
understanding, 4, 15, 51, 78, 86, 113, 125,
    128–30, 137
  better, 82, 86
unit, 78, 134
universities, 47–48, 102, 115–16, 125–26
university lifestyle boomers, 48
university students, 127
use, 6, 14, 17–20, 35–36, 41–44, 49, 56–57, 65,
    76–82, 84, 89, 100–101, 104–8, 118, 138,
    145–46
use education apps, 76, 100, 104
use methods, 88–89
Use SOCIAL MEDIA for showcasing student
    and teacher work, 18
use technology, 17, 69, 72, 84–85, 93, 96, 99,
    102–5, 107–8
  helping teachers, 128
use technology and platforms, 102

Varathan, 10–11
Venne, 55, 102, 104
videos, 18, 41–42, 54, 85, 87, 89–90, 96,
    114, 129
videos of teachers, 18
videos of teachers and students, 18
voices, 5, 34, 109, 118, 127, 133

Walter Cronkite, 66–67
waste, 36, 73
water, 83, 89, 114
way, 10–11, 19, 29–30, 34, 37, 47–48, 52,
    55–56, 60, 81–84, 107, 111–13, 115–16,
    129, 140
way boomers, 49
way millennial, 52

Wayne, John, 44, 47
weaknesses, 15, 106
wear hoodies in school in protest, 118
websites, 3, 41–42, 123, 135
welcome, 43
windows, 104
wind-up, 26
winter, 126, 132
women, 26, 29–30, 117
word cloud, 62–64
words, 3–4, 36, 42, 44, 46, 52, 62–63, 67–69, 71,
    110, 115–17, 127–28, 133–34
work, 4–8, 17–19, 39, 41–42, 47, 49, 72–74,
    85–86, 107, 117–19, 135, 137, 139,
    143–44, 146
  hard, 24, 33
work environment, 12, 18
workers, 13, 17, 56, 74, 102
workforce, 6, 10, 12, 16–17, 89
  changing, 42
work groups, establishing, 57
work multigenerational PD techniques, 81
workplace, 12, 21, 49, 51–52, 55, 57, 85, 143
worksheets, 98, 100
workshop participants, 45, 62
workshops, 45, 93, 98, 109
world war II, 4, 7, 24, 26, 29, 110

Xers, 3, 5, 8, 46, 52, 79–80, 84
  boomers/Gen, 21, 106, 143

year of teaching, 2, 53
young, 14
young adolescents, 27
younger educators work, 7
younger generations, 3, 8–9, 33, 38, 57, 74, 88
younger staff members, 49, 84, 102
younger students, 27, 126
younger teachers, 2–3, 8–9, 13, 53–55, 57, 75,
    79–80, 84, 100, 102, 104, 108, 145
younger teachers to use, 84
younger teaching generations, 100
young teachers, 1–2, 8–9, 11–15, 17–20, 47, 49,
    52, 54, 65, 71, 112–13, 125, 132
young teachers approach, 49
young teachers of previous generations, 8
young teachers to share, 71
YouTube videos, 26–27

Zdonek, 73
Zers, 3, 46
  millennials/Gen, 21, 106, 143
Zoom sessions, 94, 100

Leadership That Makes an Impact

PETER M. DeWITT

This step-by-step how-to guide presents the six driving forces of instructional leadership within a multistage model for implementation, delivering lasting improvement through small collaborative changes.

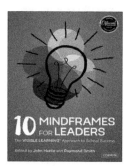

JOHN HATTIE & RAYMOND L. SMITH

Based on the most current Visible Learning® research with contributions from education thought leaders around the world, this book includes practical ideas for leaders to implement high-impact strategies to strengthen entire school cultures and advocate for all students.

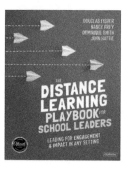

DOUGLAS FISHER, NANCY FREY, DOMINIQUE SMITH, & JOHN HATTIE

This essential hands-on resource offers guidance on leading school and school systems from a distance and delivering on the promise of equitable, quality learning experiences for students.

STEVEN M. CONSTANTINO

Explore the how-to's of establishing family empowerment through building trust, and reflect on implicit bias, equitable learning outcomes, and the role family engagement plays.

MICHAEL FULLAN, JOANNE QUINN, & JOANNE MCEACHEN

The comprehensive strategy of deep learning incorporates practical tools and processes to engage educational stakeholders in new partnerships, mobilize whole-system change, and transform learning for all students.

JOANNE QUINN, JOANNE MCEACHEN, MICHAEL FULLAN, MAG GARDNER, & MAX DRUMMY

Dive into deep learning with this hands-on guide to creating learning experiences that give purpose, unleash student potential, and transform not only learning, but life itself.

DAVIS CAMPBELL & MICHAEL FULLAN

The model outlined in this book develops a systems approach to governing local schools collaboratively to become exemplars of highly effective decision making, leadership, and action.

DAVIS CAMPBELL, MICHAEL FULLAN, BABS KAVANAUGH, & ELEANOR ADAM

As a supplement to the best-selling *The Governance Core*, this guide will help trustees and superintendents adopt a governance mindset and cohesive partnership.

To order your copies, visit **corwin.com/leadership**

**SIMON BREAKSPEAR &
BRONWYN RYRIE JONES**

Realistic in demand and
innovative in approach,
this practical and powerful
improvement process is
designed to help all teachers
get going, and keep going,
with incremental professional
improvement in schools.

**JAMES BAILEY &
RANDY WEINER**

The thought-provoking
daily reflections in this
guided journal are
designed to strengthen
the social and emotional
skills of leaders and create
a strong social-emotional
environment for leaders,
teachers, and students.

**MARK WHITE &
DWIGHT L. CARTER**

Through understanding
the past and envisioning
the future, the authors
use practical exercises
and real-life examples
to draw the blueprint for
adapting schools to the
age of hyper-change.

**ALLAN G. OSBORNE, JR.
& CHARLES J. RUSSO**

With its user-friendly
format, this resource will
help educators understand
the law so they can focus
on providing exemplary
education to students.

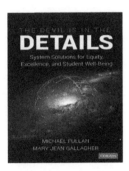

**MICHAEL FULLAN &
MARY JEAN GALLAGHER**

With the goal of
transforming the culture
of learning to develop
greater equity, excellence,
and student well-being,
this book will help you
liberate the system and
maintain focus.

**TOM VANDER ARK
& EMILY LIEBTAG**

Diverse case studies
and a framework based
on timely issues help
educators focus students'
talents and interests
on developing an
entrepreneurial mindset
and leadership skills.

THOMAS HATCH

By highlighting what works
and demonstrating what
can be accomplished if
we redefine conventional
schools, we can have more
efficient, more effective, and
more equitable schools and
create powerful opportunities
to support all aspects of
students' development.

LYN SHARRATT

Explore 14 essential
parameters to guide
system and school
leaders toward building
powerful collaborative
learning cultures.

CORWIN

A SAGE Publishing Company

Helping educators make the greatest impact

CORWIN HAS ONE MISSION: to enhance education through intentional professional learning.

We build long-term relationships with our authors, educators, clients, and associations who partner with us to develop and continuously improve the best evidence-based practices that establish and support lifelong learning.